New directions in telecollaborative research and practice: selected papers from the second conference on telecollaboration in higher education

Edited by Sake Jager, Malgorzata Kurek, and Breffni O'Rourke

Published by Research-publishing.net, not-for-profit association
Dublin, Ireland; Voillans, France, info@research-publishing.net

© 2016 by Editors (collective work)
© 2016 by Authors (individual work)

New directions in telecollaborative research and practice: selected papers from the second conference on telecollaboration in higher education
Edited by Sake Jager, Malgorzata Kurek, and Breffni O'Rourke

Rights: All articles in this collection are published under the Attribution-NonCommercial -NoDerivatives 4.0 International (CC BY-NC-ND 4.0) licence. Under this licence, the contents are freely available online as PDF files (https://doi.org/10.14705/rpnet.2016.telecollab2016.9781908416414) for anybody to read, download, copy, and redistribute provided that the author(s), editorial team, and publisher are properly cited. Commercial use and derivative works are, however, not permitted.

Disclaimer: Research-publishing.net does not take any responsibility for the content of the pages written by the authors of this book. The authors have recognised that the work described was not published before, or that it was not under consideration for publication elsewhere. While the information in this book are believed to be true and accurate on the date of its going to press, neither the editorial team, nor the publisher can accept any legal responsibility for any errors or omissions that may be made. The publisher makes no warranty, expressed or implied, with respect to the material contained herein. While Research-publishing.net is committed to publishing works of integrity, the words are the authors' alone.

Trademark notice: product or corporate names may be trademarks or registered trademarks, and are used only for identification and explanation without intent to infringe.

Copyrighted material: every effort has been made by the editorial team to trace copyright holders and to obtain their permission for the use of copyrighted material in this book. In the event of errors or omissions, please notify the publisher of any corrections that will need to be incorporated in future editions of this book.

Typeset by Research-publishing.net
Cover design and cover photos by © Raphaël Savina (raphael@savina.net)
UNICollab logo – Harriett Cornish, Graphic Designer, KMi, The Open University

ISBN13: 978-1-908416-40-7 (Paperback - Print on demand, black and white)
Print on demand technology is a high-quality, innovative and ecological printing method; with which the book is never 'out of stock' or 'out of print'.

ISBN13: 978-1-908416-41-4 (Ebook, PDF, colour)
ISBN13: 978-1-908416-42-1 (Ebook, EPUB, colour)

Legal deposit, Ireland: The National Library of Ireland, The Library of Trinity College, The Library of the University of Limerick, The Library of Dublin City University, The Library of NUI Cork, The Library of NUI Maynooth, The Library of University College Dublin, The Library of NUI Galway.
Legal deposit, United Kingdom: The British Library.
British Library Cataloguing-in-Publication Data.
A cataloguing record for this book is available from the British Library.
Legal deposit, France: Bibliothèque Nationale de France - Dépôt légal: novembre 2016.

Table of contents

viii   Notes on contributors

xxiv   Scientific committee

xxv   Preface
Breffni O'Rourke

1   New directions in telecollaborative research and practice: introduction
Sake Jager, Malgorzata Kurek, and Breffni O'Rourke

Section 1. Keynote papers

19   Telecollaboration and student mobility for language learning
Celeste Kinginger

31   A task is a task is a task is a task… or is it?
Researching telecollaborative teacher competence development –
the need for more qualitative research
Andreas Müller-Hartmann

45   Learner autonomy and telecollaborative language learning
David Little

Section 2. Telecollaboration in support of culture and language-oriented education

59   Developing intercultural communicative competence
across the Americas
Diane Ceo-DiFrancesco, Oscar Mora, and Andrea Serna Collazos

69   CHILCAN: a Chilean-Canadian intercultural telecollaborative
language exchange
Constanza Rojas-Primus

Table of contents

77   Multifaceted dimensions of telecollaboration through English as a Lingua Franca (ELF): Paris-Valladolid intercultural telecollaboration project
     Paloma Castro and Martine Derivry-Plard

83   Student perspectives on intercultural learning from an online teacher education partnership
     Shannon Sauro

89   Blogging as a tool for intercultural learning in a telecollaborative study
     Se Jeong Yang

97   Intergenerational telecollaboration: what risks for what rewards?
     Erica Johnson

105 Telecollaboration, challenges and oppportunities
     Emmanuel Abruquah, Ildiko Dosa, and Grażyna Duda

113 Exploring telecollaboration through the lens of university students: a Spanish-Cypriot telecollaborative exchange
     Anna Nicolaou and Ana Sevilla-Pavón

121 A comparison of telecollaborative classes between Japan and Asian-Pacific countries – Asian-Pacific Exchange Collaboration (APEC) project
     Yoshihiko Shimizu, Dwayne Pack, Mikio Kano, Hiroyuki Okazaki, and Hiroto Yamamura

Section 3. Training teachers through telecollaboration

131 Incorporating cross-cultural videoconferencing to enhance Content and Language Integrated Learning (CLIL) at the tertiary level
     Barbara Loranc-Paszylk

139 Multimodal strategies allowing corrective feedback to be softened during webconferencing-supported interactions
Ciara R. Wigham and Julie Vidal

147 Problem-solving interaction in GFL videoconferencing
Makiko Hoshii and Nicole Schumacher

155 Interactional dimension of online asynchronous exchange in an asymmetric telecollaboration
Dora Loizidou and François Mangenot

163 Telecollaboration in secondary EFL: a blended teacher education course
Shona Whyte and Linda Gijsen

171 It takes two to tango: online teacher tandems for teaching in English
Jennifer Valcke and Elena Romero Alfaro

179 Getting their feet wet: trainee EFL teachers in Germany and Israel collaborate online to promote their telecollaboration competence through experiential learning
Tina Waldman, Efrat Harel, and Götz Schwab

185 Teacher competences for telecollaboration: the role of coaching
Sabela Melchor-Couto and Kristi Jauregi

Section 4. Telecollaboration in service of mobility

195 Preparing student mobility through telecollaboration
Marta Giralt and Catherine Jeanneau

201 What are the perceived effects of telecollaboration compared to other communication-scenarios with peers?
Elke Nissen

211 The "Bologna-München" Tandem – experiencing interculturality
Sandro De Martino

Table of contents

217 Comparing the development of transversal skills between virtual and physical exchanges
Bart van der Velden, Sophie Millner, and Casper van der Heijden

225 Making virtual exchange/telecollaboration mainstream – large scale exchanges
Eric Hagley

Section 5. Telecollaboration for other disciplines and skills

233 Searching for telecollaboration in secondary geography education in Germany
Jelena Deutscher

239 Communication strategies in a telecollaboration project with a focus on Latin American history
Susana S. Fernández

245 Students' perspective on Web 2.0-enhanced telecollaboration as added value in translator education
Mariusz Marczak

253 Intercultural communication for professional development: creative approaches in higher education
Linda Joy Mesh

261 Illustrating challenges and practicing competencies for global technology-assisted collaboration: lessons from a real-time north-south teaching collaboration
Stephen Capobianco, Nadia Rubaii, and Sebastian Líppez-De Castro

267 Telecollaboration as a tool for building intercultural and interreligious understanding: the Sousse-Villanova programme
Jonathan Mason

Section 6. Analysing interaction in telecollaborative exchanges

277 Vicious cycles of turn negotiation in video-mediated telecollaboration: interactional sociolinguistics perspective
Yuka Akiyama

283 A corpus-based study of the use of pronouns in the asynchronous discussion forums in the online intercultural exchange MexCo
Marina Orsini-Jones, Zoe Gazeley-Eke, and Hannah Leinster

291 Cooperative autonomy in online lingua franca exchanges: a case study on foreign language education in secondary schools
Petra Hoffstaedter and Kurt Kohn

297 Emerging affordances in telecollaborative multimodal interactions
Aparajita Dey-Plissonneau and Françoise Blin

305 Telecollaboration in online communities for L2 learning
Maria Luisa Malerba and Christine Appel

313 Fostering students' engagement with topical issues through different modes of online exchange
Marie-Thérèse Batardière and Francesca Helm

321 A conversation analysis approach to researching eTandems – the challenges of data collection
Julia Renner

327 DOTI: Databank of Oral Teletandem Interactions
Solange Aranha and Paola Leone

333 Author index

Notes on contributors

Editors

Sake Jager is Assistant Professor in Applied Linguistics, specialising in Computer-Assisted Language Learning, and Head/Project Manager in the department of ICT in Education, University of Groningen, The Netherlands. His research focus is on the integration of CALL in institutional environments. He is also one of the board members of UNICollaboration (www.unicollaboration.org).

Malgorzata Kurek is Assistant Professor in Applied Linguistics at Jan Dlugosz University, Czestochowa, Poland. She teaches teacher training courses (TEFL). She has been long involved in academic-level intercultural online exchanges. Her principal research area in this field addresses the issue of task design and computer-mediated collaborative learning, especially in teacher training contexts. She is a member of the UNICollaboration board.

Breffni O'Rourke is Assistant Professor of Applied Linguistics and Manager of Language Learning Technologies and Resources in Trinity College Dublin. His research interests centre around cognition, language, and discourse in telecollaborative NS/NNS settings. He is a member of the board of UNICollaboration (www.unicollaboration.org) and is incoming Editor-in-Chief of *Language Learning in Higher Education* (de Gruyter). He was local organiser of the Trinity conference and Chair of the Scientific Committee.

Reviewers

Melinda Dooly holds a Serra Húnter Fellowship as researcher and Senior Lecturer at the Education Faculty of the Universitat Autònoma de Barcelona (Spain). She teaches English as a Foreign Language Methodology and research methods courses, focusing on telecollaboration in education at both undergraduate and graduate levels. Her principal research addresses technology enhanced project-based language learning in teacher education. She has published widely in international journals and authored chapters and books in this area of study. She is co-editor of the book series Telecollaboration in Education (Peter Lang), with Dr.

Robert O'Dowd. Her current research interest is in project-based telecollaborative language learning and very young learners.

Mirjam Hauck is a Senior Lecturer in the Faculty of Education and Language Studies at the Open University, UK. Her scholarly work focuses on the use of technologies for the learning and teaching of languages and cultures covering aspects such as task design, tutor role and training, and digital literacy skills. Apart from regular presentations at conferences, seminars and workshops in Europe and the USA, she has served on the CALICO executive board and is a member of the EUROCALL executive committee. She is the Associate Editor of the *CALL Journal* and a member of the editorial board of *ReCALL*.

Sarah Guth is an EFL teacher at the University of Padova, Italy where she implements and does research on telecollaboration. She worked at the SUNY COIL Center as the Coordinator for Programs and Professional Development from 2013 to 2014 and continues to collaborate as a consultant. Her research interests lie in the use of technology in language learning, intercultural communication, telecollaboration and the normalisation of virtual exchange across the curriculum.

Francesca Helm is an English language teacher and researcher at the Department of Political Science, Law and International Studies of the University of Padova in Italy. Her research interests lie in computer-mediated communication and collaboration, virtual exchange, intercultural dialogue, critical approaches to technology and learning, as well as 'internationalisation' in higher education.

Teresa MacKinnon is a Principal Teaching Fellow at the School of Modern Languages and Cultures at the University of Warwick, UK. She is an award winning language teacher and Certified Member of the Association for Learning Technology. She is Chair of the EUROCALL Computer-mediated communication SIG and Co-Chair of the ALT Open Education SIG. As an open practitioner, she curates professional development resources online for language teachers. Teresa's website: https://sites.google.com/site/lamodification/home; Teresa's blog: http://teresa-nextsteps.blogspot.ie/; Teresa's social networks: https://about.me/teresamackinnon.

Notes on contributors

Andreas Müller-Hartmann is a Professor of TEFL and American Studies at the University of Education in Heidelberg, Germany. He has done research and published in the areas of task-supported language learning (TSLL), the development of intercultural communicative competence, the use of technology in the EFL classroom, teacher education, and American Studies.

Elke Nissen is Associate Professor at University Grenoble Alpes (France). Her research interests focus on online and blended learning, specifically regarding course design, online communication, telecollaboration and tuition within CALL.

Robert O'Dowd is Associate Professor for English as a Foreign Language and Applied Linguistics at the University of León, Spain. He has taught English at universities in Ireland, Germany and Spain and has published widely on the application of collaborative online learning in university education. His most recent publication is the co-edited volume *Online Intercultural Exchange Policy, Pedagogy, Practice* for Routledge. He recently coordinated INTENT – an award-winning project financed by the European Commission aimed at promoting online intercultural exchange in European Higher Education and is currently president of the UNICollaboration academic organization for telecollaboration and virtual exchange (www.unicollaboration.org).

Shannon Sauro is Associate Professor in the Department of Culture, Languages and Media at Malmö University, Sweden. Her areas of research include computer-mediated second language acquisition, task-based language teaching in online environments, and the intersection of online media fandoms and language learning. She is the 2016-2017 president of the Computer-Assisted Language Instruction Consortium (CALICO).

Authors

Emmanuel Abruquah is a lecturer of Business Communication at TAMK. He has been actively involved in developing intercultural communication skills of

TAMK's engineering students through Telecollaborative projects. Constant development in online teaching plays an essential role in his professional life.

Yuka Akiyama is a Ph.D. candidate in Applied Linguistics at Georgetown University and an instructor of Japanese and English. Her research interests include the development of comprehensibility and interactional competence, the role of corrective feedback, and task-based language teaching, and discourse analysis in the context of video-based telecollaboration/eTandem.

Christine Appel is the Senior Lecturer in the Centre for Modern Languages at the Universitat Oberta de Catalunya (UOC) in Barcelona, Spain. She has coordinated several European projects, amongst them the LLP project SpeakApps. She holds a PhD in Applied Linguistics from the University of Dublin, Trinity College. Her current research interests include Computer-mediated Communication, Distance education, Task-based Learning, and Computer-supported collaborative learning in the L2.

Solange Aranha has a PhD in Linguistics and Portuguese and teaches English for undergraduate students in Language and Literature and Translation programmes. She has been working at Sao Paolo State University since 2001, where she also advises Masters and Doctorate students in the Applied Linguistics programme. Her current research includes telecollaborative learning, EAP teaching and genres. She is the vice coordinator of the research group Teletandem and Multiculturality.

Marie-Thérèse Batardière is a lecturer in French at the University of Limerick, Ireland. She is a strong advocate of an interdisciplinary and multicultural approach to teaching and learning. Her main research interest lies in the area of CALL and more specifically on the use of Computer Mediated Communication tools (CMC) to promote intercultural collaboration and authentic dialogue.

Françoise Blin is Associate Professor and the Head of the School of Applied Language and Intercultural Studies (SALIS) at Dublin City University. She is President of the European Association for Computer Assisted Language Learning (EUROCALL) and editor of ReCALL (published by CUP). She has been a lecturer

Notes on contributors

of French as a foreign language and an active researcher in CALL for the last 30 years. Her research interests includes ecological CALL and the use and application of Activity Theory in CALL research and design.

Stephen Capobianco is an education abroad advisor at Cornell University and a Ph.D. student in Community and Public Affairs at Binghamton University. His research interests engage the field of international education, intercultural competence, and structural inequalities for the LGBT community. He received his Master of Public Administration and Bachelor of Arts in Spanish Language and Literature from Binghamton University.

Paloma Castro is Assistant Professor of Valladolid University. She is currently interested in the intercultural dimension in foreign language teacher education and the implementation of internationalisation in Higher Education through Telecollaboration. She has experience in internationalisation as vice-dean and coordinator of Erasmus and mobility programmes at the University of Valladolid.

Diane Ceo-DiFrancesco, PhD, is Associate Professor of Spanish and Director of the Center for Teaching Excellence at Xavier University, Cincinnati, Ohio. She has published articles in such journals as *Hispania*, *Language Educator*, *Central States Reports* and *The NAMTA Journal*. Her research interests include strategy training, target language use, telecollaboration, intercultural communicative competence, immersion and study abroad.

Martine Derivry-Plard is a Professor in Applied Linguistics in the School of Education at the University of Bordeaux and is a member of the research group LACES EA 7437 (Cultures, Education, Societies). Her research interest is in languages education in linguistically and culturally hyper diverse societies in an era of globalisation. Find out more on her current projects with the following links: http://www.ecola.eu and http://transitlingua.org/.

Jelena Deutscher is a doctoral student researching on telecollaboration in bilingual geography education and a former member of teaching staff for geography didactics at the Ruhr-Universität Bochum, Germany. She completed a

Notes on contributors

M.Ed.-programme in the subjects English and geography at the Ruhr-University in 2010 and the M.A.-programme 'Literature, Culture and Media' at Lunds universitet, Sweden, in 2011.

Aparajita Dey-Plissonneau is a PhD student in Dublin City University. Her research interests are specifically in the domain of designed and emerging affordances in videoconferencing for language learning and more generally in the fields of computer-assisted language learning and online teaching and learning. She has ten years' teaching experience as a foreign language teacher in the secondary and tertiary levels in France and Ireland respectively.

Sandro De Martino works as a German language teacher at the Dipartimento di Lingue, Letterature e Culture Moderne at the University of Bologna. His interests are intercultural communication and shared lessons of foreign language learners and native speakers. For this reason, he has been carrying out a tandem project in collaboration with the Ludwig-Maximilians-University of Munich since 2011.

Ildiko Dosa, PhD, teaches Business English and Communication subjects at the Budapest Business School College of Finance and Accounting in Hungary. Her special field of interest is teaching communication and intercultural competences through telecollaboration and teamwork.

Grażyna Duda is a senior lecturer at the Silesian University of Technology in Gliwice, Poland. She is an experienced teacher and trainer. She has designed and carried out courses and teacher training workshops for students and academic staff. Her interests include the practical ways to engage students in active learning with the use of telecollaboration, multimedia and new technologies.

Susana S. Fernández is an associate professor at Aarhus University. She is the coordinator of Spanish and Latin American Studies and head of the foreign language group at the Pedagogical Education for upper secondary high school teachers in Denmark. Her research areas include Spanish grammar and foreign language pedagogy, with particular focus on pedagogical applications of Cognitive Linguistics.

Notes on contributors

Zoe Gazeley-Eke is a lecturer in English for Academic Purposes in the School of Humanities at Coventry University (UK) and also teaches English for Business on the MA programme. Her research interests include intercultural communication in language learning and teaching along with the development of digital literacies in language learning. She has published work on telecollaboration and EAP.

Linda Gijsen is a teacher educator at the English department of Fontys University of Applied Sciences, Tilburg, the Netherlands. She teaches general and applied linguistics subjects and foreign language pedagogy. Her research interests include teacher education and the use of technology in the foreign language classroom. She is currently studying for her PhD at the University of Antwerp, Belgium.

Marta Giralt is a Lecturer in Applied Linguistics and Spanish at the University of Limerick. Her research interests are in applied linguistics, in particular, second language acquisition and oral language, ICT and language learning and intercultural communication. In 2007 she was awarded with first prize in the *II Premio Cristobal de Villalón* for Pedagogic Innovation by Universidad de Valladolid, Spain. A list of recent publications: https://www.researchgate.net/profile/Marta_Giralt2/publications

Eric Hagley teaches at Muroran Institute of Technology. His research interests are in virtual exchange, telecollaboration and extensive reading. He is the chair of the Asia Pacific Virtual Exchange Association (APVEA) and head of the quiz quality assurance project for MoodleReader and mReader.

Efrat Harel, PhD, is a researcher in the domain of language acquisition among bilingual children, and she is involved in an international project whose aim is to create a diagnostic tool designed for the bilingual population. In addition, she is a lecturer in the EAP department in Kibbutzim College and trains student teachers to deal with issues of multilingualism and multiculturalism in Israel.

Casper van der Heijden is the co-founder and Programme Manager at the Sharing Perspectives Foundation. Van der Heijden holds an MSc in Political Science, focused on Conflict Resolution. Prior to co-founding the Sharing Perspectives Foundation, he was a lecturer at the University of Amsterdam.

Francesca Helm is an English language teacher and researcher at the Department of Political Science, Law and International Studies of the University of Padova in Italy. Her research interests lie in computer-mediated communication and collaboration, virtual exchange, intercultural dialogue, critical approaches to technology and learning, as well as 'internationalisation' in higher education.

Petra Hoffstaedter (Dr. phil.) is co-director of the Steinbeis Transfer Center Language Learning Media. Working in the field of computer assisted language learning, her more recent activities focus on video-based pedagogical interview corpora, interpreter training in virtual reality, telecollaboration exchanges for intercultural communication and foreign language learning, and language teacher education and coaching.

Makiko Hoshii, PhD, is a Professor of German and Linguistics at Waseda University, Tokyo, Japan. Her research interests include SLA, GFL, learner language analysis, and interaction analysis.

Kristi Jauregi is Lecturer-researcher at Utrecht University (The Netherlands). Her main area of research is on CALL, particularly on Telecollaboration carried out with synchronous applications, virtual worlds, and recently in combination with serious games. She has initiated and coordinated different innovative European projects (NIFLAR, TILA & TeCoLa) all funded by the European Commission. She is Co-Chair of the EUROCALL SIG group Virtual Worlds & Serious Games and a member of the Dutch Expertise Team of Foreign Language Pedagogy.

Catherine Jeanneau is the Coordinator of the Language Learning Hub at the University of Limerick. Her research interests include second language acquisition, technology and language learning, particularly social media and online communication as well as learner autonomy. She has published articles and book chapters in the integration of new technologies in the teaching and learning of languages (see: https://www.researchgate.net/profile/Catherine_Jeanneau).

Notes on contributors

Erica Johnson has been teaching English in France since 2003. She currently holds the position of Director of the Language Center at Université Lumière Lyon 2 (Lyon, France) in addition to her teaching responsibilities. Erica enjoys combining her passion for teaching with her love of technology by establishing videoconferencing tandem partnerships between her students and American students learning French. She has been researching videoconferencing exchanges between her French students and American senior citizens since 2014.

Mikio Kano is a Professor at Department of Education, Gifu Shotokugakuen University. He graduated from Hiroshima University. He has experience as a curriculum specialist at Ministry of Education and as an English teacher in Japanese high schools. His research interests include English education methodology.

Celeste Kinginger is a Professor of Applied Linguistics at the Pennsylvania State University (USA). She is affiliated with the Center for Language Acquisition in the University's College of Liberal Arts. Her research has examined telecollaborative, intercultural language learning, second language pragmatics, cross-cultural life writing, teacher education, and study abroad.

Kurt Kohn (Dr. phil.) is professor emeritus of Applied English Linguistics at the University of Tübingen. Adopting a social constructivist perspective, his more recent research interests focus on intercultural telecollaboration, English as a lingua franca, lingua franca pedagogy, and foreign language teacher education.

Hannah Leinster is a graduate of the Coventry University English Language Teaching MA programme and also worked alongside Marina Orsini-Jones and Zoe Gazeley-Eke teaching Intercultural Communication and Telecollaboration at Coventry University in 2015. Hannah was involved in the project described in the article as part of her MA dissertation.

Paola Leone is a tenure track professor at University of Salento and teaches second language acquisition and foreign language teaching courses at graduate level. She is a member of the Teletandem Network. She is conducting research on implementing learning scenarios based on oral synchronous telecollaboration and in the field of computer mediated communication and language learning. She has published papers in national and international journals.

Sebastian Líppez-De Castro is an assistant professor of Political Science at Pontificia Universidad Javeriana in Bogotá, Colombia, and a PhD student of Community and Public Affairs at Binghamton University, SUNY. He earned his Master in Public Administration from Binghamton University, and received his BA in Political Science, and his specialisation in Municipal Government, from Pontificia Universidad Javeriana, Bogotá, Colombia.

David Little retired in 2008 as Associate Professor of Applied Linguistics at Trinity College Dublin. His principal research interests are the theory and practice of learner autonomy in language education, the exploitation of linguistic diversity in schools and classrooms, and the application of the *Common European Framework of Reference for Languages* to the design of L2 curricula, teaching and assessment.

Dora Loizidou teaches at the Department of French and European Languages of the University of Cyprus. She is a PhD candidate in Applied Linguistics at Grenoble Alpes University in France (research unit *Linguistique et Didactique des Langues Étrangères et Maternelles,* Lidilem). Her PhD thesis examines exchanges between students and their tutors in an asymmetric telecollaboration project.

Barbara Loranc-Paszylk works as Assistant Professor in the Department of English Studies, University of Bielsko-Biała, Poland. Her research interests focus on various aspects of Content and Language Integrated Learning and also include innovative uses of new technologies and e-learning resources in teaching foreign languages.

Maria Luisa Malerba is an assistant researcher in the eLearn Centre at the Open University of Catalonia (UOC) in Barcelona, Spain. She is collaborating in the SpeakApps project and has finished her PhD thesis about informal second language learning in online communities under the supervision of Christine Appel. Her current research interests include social media, online communities, informal learning, distance education and CALL (Computer Assisted Language Learning).

Notes on contributors

François Mangenot is full professor of Applied Linguistics at Université Grenoble Alpes (France). He has been researching in CALL for 25 years, and has been involved in telecollaboration for 14 years. He now coordinates the branch "Foreign Language Education and Technology" of the research unit *Linguistique et Didactique des Langues Étrangères et Maternelles* (Lidilem). He is the initiator of the EPAL Conference, which takes place in Grenoble every second year (http://epal.u-grenoble3.fr).

Mariusz Marczak, PhD, is Assistant Professor at the Chair for Translation Studies and Intercultural Communication at the Jagiellonian University of Cracow, Poland. His research interests include computer-aided translator education and the development of intercultural competence. He is also Editor-in-Chief of the *Journal for Translator Education and Translation Studies* and Secretary of the Consortium for Translation Education Research (CTER).

Jonathan Mason has been teaching in Tunisia for the past 21 years, and is currently an assistant professor in Cultural Studies at the Faculty of Arts and Humanities, University of Sousse. He is a member of the International Association for Languages and Intercultural Communication (IALIC) and is particularly interested in the study of contemporary culture, the development of critical interculturality and East-West intercultural dialogue.

Sabela Melchor-Couto, PhD, is a Senior Lecturer in Spanish at University of Roehampton (London). Her research interests include the use of virtual worlds for telecollaboration and affective variables in language learning. Since 2013, Sabela's main research activity has been strongly linked to EU projects on the use of telecollaboration for language learning, namely TeCoLa (Pedagogical differentiation through telecollaboration and gaming for intercultural and content-integrated language teaching) and the TILA project.

Linda Joy Mesh, MAODE, is the coordinator for Blended Learning at the Siena University Language Centre, Italy, and has taught English as a Second Language, Business and Medical English in higher education for many years. Her research interests include innovative methods for collaborative language learning, rethinking pedagogies for more student-centred approaches and the effects of sociocultural and psychological factors on online, collaborative second language discourse.

Sophie Millner is the Curriculum Officer at the Sharing Perspectives Foundation. Sophie holds a PhD from the Peace Studies Department of the University of Bradford in the U.K. Her thesis highlighted the exclusionary nature of citizenship theory. Sophie also graduated from the Development School, University of East Anglia, UK with a MA Hons Politics & International Development.

Oscar Mora holds a M.Ed. in Higher Education from Pontificia Universidad Javeriana Cali and a BA in Modern Languages from Universidad del Valle. He is currently an assistant professor of English as a foreign language and has taught Spanish as a second language at Pontificia Universidad Javeriana Cali. His research interests include English for academic purposes, telecollaboration and intercultural communicative competence.

Andreas Müller-Hartmann is a Professor of TEFL and American Studies at the University of Education in Heidelberg, Germany. He has done research and published in the areas of Task-Supported Language Learning (TSLL), the development of intercultural communicative competence, the use of technology in the EFL classroom, teacher education, and American Studies.

Anna Nicolaou is an English language instructor at the Language Centre of the Cyprus University of Technology. She is a PhD Candidate at the School of Linguistic, Speech and Communication Sciences at Trinity College Dublin. She holds an MA in English Language Studies and Methods from the University of Warwick. Her research interests include intercultural education, telecollaborative learning, multilingualism and CALL.

Elke Nissen is Associate Professor at University Grenoble Alpes (France). Her research interests focus on online and blended learning, specifically regarding course design, online communication, telecollaboration and tuition within CALL.

Notes on contributors

Hiroyuki Okazaki is Professor and Dean in the Graduate School of Teacher Training Development at the University of Toyama. He has been involved in pre-service and in-service English teacher education since 2007. He also has experience as an English teacher in Japanese high schools. His research interests include teacher development and English language teacher education.

Marina Orsini-Jones is Associate Head of School (International) and Course Director for the MA in English Language Teaching and Applied Linguistics in the School of Humanities at Coventry University (UK). She is a Principal Fellow and NTF of the HEA. She has contributed to over 100 conferences on e-learning and has published work on CALL, action-research-led curricular innovation, threshold concepts in languages and linguistics, MOOCs and digital literacies.

Dwayne Pack is the Director of Computing for the School of Humanities at UC Irvine, where he has worked since 1997. His primary responsibilities are helping faculty with their research in all areas of computing, including telecollaboration, multimedia design, data collection, and analysis.

Julia Renner holds a BA in Communication Studies and a BA/MA in Chinese Studies from the University of Vienna. She has been granted a PhD scholarship (Austrian Academy of Sciences) and is currently pursuing her studies in the field of language teaching and learning research, focusing on interaction in Chinese – German eTandems.

Constanza Rojas-Primus, PhD, teaches Spanish and Intercultural Studies in the department of Language and Cultures at Kwantlen Polytechnic University in Canada. Her current research focuses on the integration of intercultural communicative competence into her Spanish classroom. She is the co-editor of the book *Promoting Intercultural Communication Competencies in Higher Education* to be released by IGI Global in fall 2016.

Elena Romero Alfaro teaches French and Didactics of French as a Foreign Language at the Faculty of Education (University of Cádiz), where she currently holds the position of Vice-Dean for Internationalisation. She coordinates the

Plurilingual Project at the Faculty of Education and is a member of the University Commission for Linguistic Policies representing CLIL issues.

Nadia Rubaii is Associate Professor of Public Administration at Binghamton University, State University of New York. Her research examines issues of quality assurance in higher education institutions and public affairs programmes, effective pedagogies for teaching public affairs, and strategies for more effectively managing diversity within local communities. She was a Fulbright Scholar in Colombia and Fulbright Specialist in Venezuela.

Shannon Sauro is Associate Professor in the Department of Culture, Languages and Media at Malmö University, Sweden. Her areas of research include computer-mediated second language acquisition, task-based language teaching in online environments, and the intersection of online media fandoms and language learning. She is the 2016-2017 president of the Computer-Assisted Language Instruction Consortium (CALICO).

Nicole Schumacher, PhD, is a lecturer for SLA (Second Language Acquisition) and GFL (German as a Foreign Language) teacher training at Humboldt-Universität zu Berlin, Germany. Her professional interests include SLA, second language teaching, GFL, learner language analysis, and interaction analysis.

Götz Schwab is Professor of Applied Linguistics at the Department of English, Karlsruhe University of Education, Germany. As former teacher and Managing Director of the *Forschungsverbund Hauptschule*, he has a wide range of research interests. This includes low achievers and students-at-risk, especially at secondary schools, ELT/FLT methodology in primary and secondary schools, Content and Language Integrated Learning (CLIL), Conversation Analysis for Second Language Acquisition (CA-for-SLA), telecollaboration, and syntax.

Andrea Serna Collazos is pedagogical coordinator of the Office for Fostering the Integration of Technology and Learning at the Pontificia Universidad Javeriana Cali. Specializing in the design of learning environments and the implementation of technology processes in teaching and learning, she holds an MS in psychology.

Notes on contributors

Her research interests include information and communication technologies in educational settings and digital literacy.

Ana Sevilla-Pavón (PhD in Applied Linguistics, Universitat Politècnica de València) is Assistant Professor at the Universitat de València and researcher at IULMA, SILVA and TALIS. Her research interests revolve around computer-assisted language learning and testing, intercultural communication through telecollaboration, and English for Specific Purposes. She has participated in numerous international projects and conferences, and published journal articles, books and book chapters (Springer, De Gruyter, Equinox and Cambridge Scholars).

Yoshihiko Shimizu is Associate Professor of Faculty of Engineering at Toyama Prefectural University. During 2009-2015 he was a professor at the National Institute of Technology, Toyama College. His research interests include the development of students' awareness toward cultural differences and their communicative competence. Much of his work has been on telecollaboration in the Asia Pacific region.

Jennifer Valcke is a senior lecturer and education developer at Karolinska Institutet. Her role includes teaching, training and advising on issues related to international education, intercultural education, EMI and CLIL, and providing support to individual teachers, programme directors and educational leaders.

Bart van der Velden is the Research Officer at the Sharing Perspectives Foundation. He holds an MSc in Political Science, with a focus on protest and repression. He is also interested in psychology and its history, and has previously published on the discourse of the DSM.

Julie Vidal is currently doing a PhD in second language acquisition and applied linguistics at Lyon 2 University, France. She is interested in investigating the effects of corrective feedback on learners' language development and competencies, and studies teachers' and learners' activities in online interactions, which are based on synchronous and/or asynchronous tools for distant language tutoring. She also studies the effects of a combination of multimodalities on L2 learners. Additionally, she teaches French as a Foreign Language at an engineering school, the Applied Sciences National Institute (INSA) of Lyon.

Tina Waldman, PhD, is a teacher and researcher in English as a Foreign Language education (EFL). She heads the unit of academic English in Kibbutzim College of Education in Tel Aviv, Israel, where she also teaches a variety of courses in EFL theory and pedagogy to pre-service English teachers.

Shona Whyte is associate professor in UMR7320 Bases, Corpus, Langage, with research interests in L2 interaction in technologically mediated contexts and CALL teacher education. Publications include *Implementing and Researching Technological Innovation in Language Teaching* (Palgrave, 2015) and a co-edited volume on IWB-supported language education, *Teaching languages with technology* (Bloomsbury, 2014).

Ciara R. Wigham is a Senior Lecturer in English and applied linguistics at *Université Blaise Pascal*, France. Her research interests are multimodal pedagogical communication in online language learning and methodologies for the description of online learning situations. She is a member of the *Laboratoire de Recherche sur le Langage* research unit.

Hiroto Yamamura is an assistant professor at National Institute of Technology, Toyama college. He has been teaching English to learners of various levels and needs in Japan since 2006. His research interests include reflective practice and professional development for teachers.

Se Jeong Yang is a PhD candidate in the Department of Teaching and Learning at the Ohio State University. Her research interests lie in the areas of CALL, intercultural competence, and learner identity. Her work on eTandem learning aspires to promote the development of L2 skills and intercultural knowledge.

Scientific committee

Lorna Carson, *Trinity College Dublin, Ireland*

Melinda Dooly, *Universitat Autònoma de Barcelona, Spain*

Mirjam Hauck, *The Open University, UK*

Francesca Helm, *Università degli Studi di Padova, Italy*

Sarah Guth, *Università degli Studi di Padova, Italy*

Sake Jager, *Rijksuniversiteit Groningen, Netherlands*

Małgorzata Kurek, *Jan Długosz University, Częstochowa, Poland*

Tim Lewis, *The Open University, UK*

Andreas Müller-Hartmann, *Pädagogische Hochschule Heidelberg, Germany*

Elke Nissen, *Université Stendhal, Grenoble, France*

Robert O'Dowd, *Universidad de León, Spain*

Breffni O'Rourke, *Trinity College Dublin, Ireland*

Bernd Rüschoff, *Universität Duisburg-Essen, Germany*

Steve Thorne, *Portland State University, USA; Rijksuniversiteit Groningen, Netherlands*

Mario Tomé, *Universidad de León, Spain*

Preface

Breffni O'Rourke[1]

The first International Conference on Telecollaboration in University Foreign Language Education (University of León, 2014) was a landmark event in the academic recognition of telecollaboration. The conference, one of the outcomes of the INTENT project (Integrating Telecollaborative Networks into Foreign Language Higher Education), funded by the European Union's Lifelong Learning Programme, boasted a packed programme and a vibrant, collegial atmosphere. The project team took this as evidence that there is a growing community of teachers and researchers who have embraced telecollaboration as a pedagogical model whose time has come.

To foster this community and maintain the momentum, it was decided to make the conference a regular event, and Trinity College Dublin was proud to host, in April 2016, the Second International Conference on Telecollaboration in Higher Education, with the theme "New Directions in Telecollaborative Research and Practice". The event was officially opened by the university's Senior Lecturer Professor Gillian Martin and by Professor Martine Smith, Head of the School of Linguistic, Speech, and Communication Sciences. It seemed especially fitting that we welcomed colleagues from 25 countries to discuss international educational collaboration just as Ireland was marking the 100th anniversary of the Easter Rising – an event which, in all its political and moral complexity, set the country on a course to independence, and a new relationship with its nearest neighbours and with the rest of the world.

Over two and a half days, 150 participants offered 95 research presentations, posters, and "problem shared" sessions. The thought-provoking keynotes of Professors Celeste Kinginger, Andreas Müller-Hartmann, and David Little

---

1. Trinity College Dublin, Dublin, Ireland; orourkeb@tcd.ie

How to cite: O'Rourke, B. (2016). Preface. In S. Jager, M. Kurek & B. O'Rourke (Eds), *New directions in telecollaborative research and practice: selected papers from the second conference on telecollaboration in higher education* (pp. xxv-xxviii). Research-publishing.net. https://doi.org/10.14705/rpnet.2016.telecollab2016.485

were warmly received. It was extremely gratifying to find oneself immersed in a positive attitude of warm collegiality and palpable shared excitement at the possibilities that have opened up for educators.

It is clear that telecollaboration in education is no longer the exotic niche practice it was twenty years ago. It hardly could be, in a context where working online with distant colleagues is entirely routine in many professions; where online platforms have become the chief medium for the construction, dissemination and interpretation of news and knowledge within and across societies; where social media are central to many people's lives. What could be more natural than bringing students together with international peers online, in a structured, disciplined environment, using the technologies that are second nature to them? But precisely because of that context, veteran telecollaborators might well be surprised that it is not yet a widely established approach to collaborative learning in higher education.

Surprised, but not discouraged: the conference included a highly varied range of reports and theoretical contributions, and there were many vigorous informal discussions in sessions and in the margins, not least on the question of how telecollaboration can best be promoted and ultimately find its place in the curricular offering of universities worldwide. One particular development at the conference promises to play an important role: a centrepiece plenary event in our busy schedule was the launch of a new academic organisation, *UniCollaboration* (www.unicollaboration.org). Its remit will be to support and promote telecollaboration through research activities, training and publication; it will also be the patron of future conferences in the series[2]. The warmth of the welcome given by conference participants to this initiative suggests a good will and a shared determination among the community of practitioners and researchers to ensure that one of the great possibilities of contemporary technology is realised: the opportunity to bring together people of different cultures so that they can learn alongside each other and from each other.

---

2. The next will place in 2018 in the Pedagogical University of Cracow, Poland.

Telecollaboration demands that practitioners grapple with practical, empirical, and theoretical detail. That is a challenge, and also an attraction, of the field: one inevitably engages not just with intercultural communication, but with the complex relationships between teachers, moderators, students, software interfaces, language, tasks, assessment, institutions and curricula. Online exchange is multifaceted in a way that many areas of Computer-Assisted Language Learning (CALL) are not, and it revolves around the interpersonal in a way that many educational uses of technology do not. While aiming at large-scale objectives, we must also think and research systematically the many other intricate facets of virtual exchange. And so the field attracts – judging by the list of delegates and the programme – colleagues from a range of professional roles, institutional situations, and theoretical perspectives. The diversity of contributions recorded in this volume reflects this complexity.

But there was unity in this diversity: what brought the conference participants together was at least in part a shared conviction that we can use online media to help our students towards a more generous, inclusive but also critical understanding of identity and culture. And we seem to have reason to believe that this conviction is spreading: the response to the conference call suggests that the community of telecollaborative practitioners and researchers is growing. I hope that these selected papers will capture a moment in the development of telecollaboration, but also serve to catalyse further growth.

Acknowledgements

I would like first of all to acknowledge the generosity of the conference sponsors:

- Fáilte Ireland/MeetInIreland.com
- Trinity Long Room Hub Arts & Humanities Research Institute
- Trinity College Dublin Association and Trust
- Faculty of Arts, Humanities, and Social Sciences, Trinity College Dublin

Preface

We were extremely lucky to have three excellent keynote speakers, all of whom contributed greatly to the event. Their engagement with the conference is appreciated very much.

The scientific committee was highly efficient in their work of reviewing contributions both for the conference and for these selected papers. In the run-up to the conference, they were generous in sharing their advice and experience, and a pleasure to work with.

Research-publishing.net have been a tremendously efficient partner in the production of this volume, which has benefitted greatly from their professionalism.

Finally, we are grateful to the authors for their stimulating contributions to the collection.

1 New directions in telecollaborative research and practice: introduction

Sake Jager[1], Malgorzata Kurek[2], and Breffni O'Rourke[3]

1. Introduction

This collection of papers, coming from 'New Directions in Telecollaborative Research and Practice: The Second Conference on Telecollaboration in Higher Education' hosted by Trinity College Dublin from the 21st to the 23rd of April 2016, offers a window on a rapidly evolving form of learning which is used in many formats and contexts, but has as a defining feature the ability to unite learners from classrooms around the world in meaningful computer-mediated tasks and activities.

The papers, with the exception of the keynote addresses, are restricted to 1500 words each, which allowed us to include a fair number (39, together with the three keynote papers), but at the same time posed a significant challenge to authors with regard to the level of detail with which they could report on the telecollaboration projects and the research findings elicited from them. Nevertheless, we hope that the particular collection of papers and format chosen will give both experienced users and newcomers to telecollaboration a glimpse of the breadth and depth of the field and inspire them to apply this innovative form of learning more widely and with more confidence, a stronger sense of purpose, and a greater awareness of good practice.

---

1. University of Groningen, Groningen, the Netherlands; s.jager@rug.nl

2. Jan Dlugosz University, Czestochowa, Poland; gkurka@gmail.com

3. Trinity College Dublin, Dublin, Ireland; orourkeb@tcd.ie

How to cite this chapter: Jager, S., Kurek, M., & O'Rourke, B. (2016). New directions in telecollaborative research and practice: introduction. In S. Jager, M. Kurek & B. O'Rourke (Eds), *New directions in telecollaborative research and practice: selected papers from the second conference on telecollaboration in higher education* (pp. 1-15). Research-publishing.net. https://doi.org/10.14705/rpnet.2016.telecollab2016.486

Chapter 1

From these papers it becomes clear that telecollaboration has long shed its exclusive concern with language and that language and culture are now intricately interwoven in ever more complex contexts of global learning. Nor is the application of telecollaboration any longer the sole domain of language studies. A specific section in this publication has been set aside to describe telecollaboration in other disciplines. The bulk of papers, however, comes from authors with backgrounds in languages, working in a range of disciplines and professions, including language teaching, teacher training, applied linguistics, administration and management, language and media centres, and mobility and internationalisation offices. The papers are based on telecollaborative exchanges between at least 30 different countries (not all countries are specified), covering more than 10 different languages. English, as a foreign language or lingua franca, takes a clear majority: it is mentioned as one of the languages in 26 papers. Spanish (6), German (6) and French (4) are next, followed by the other languages.

Following the theme of the conference, the papers offer an overview of the practical and theoretical considerations that went into the design of the projects and the research started in their wake. Basing ourselves on the original conference strands, we have organised the papers by common themes or threads in telecollaborative research and practice that help to identify distinctive trends and approaches to telecollaboration as a form of learning in higher education. From the comparison and rearrangement of papers, five groups of papers emerged from which we have divided this book into coherent sections. These sections are representative of the main perspectives on telecollaboration presented at the conference. Within each section, however, the research focus or practice described may vary considerably. And many papers could have been included in more than one section.

The papers by our keynote speakers are included in a separate section preceding the other sections. This is not only to honour the speakers who have been kind enough to include their presentations in this publication, but also to emphasise the relevance of the topics they address for the field of telecollaboration as a whole.

2. Keynote papers

2.1. Celeste Kinginger: telecollaboration and student mobility for language learning

Kinginger, in her paper based on the opening keynote address of the conference, explores the potential of telecollaboration in relation to what we know from quantitative and qualitative studies on language learning in student mobility. In a highly relevant, comprehensive review of the literature, she discusses the strong individual differences which have been found in the effectiveness of student stays abroad for language learning. Language development may remain limited due to a range of factors. These include inability to build social networks, retention of strong connections to home, reinforcement of national identities in the face of new cultural or linguistic norms, and failed communication because of overreliance on classroom interaction patterns or incomprehensible language use by the host families. Kinginger sees a key role for telecollaboration in preparing students for the challenges of such exchanges. Telecollaboration may offer a safe environment in which learners have access to expert users of non-pedagogic spoken and written language. Through telecollaboration they may begin to develop the social networks and the language-mediated identities critical for becoming successful language learners during their stay abroad and beyond. She hopes that educators will continue to implement 'articulated curricula' in which telecollaboration is linked with student mobility. By outlining issues that literature and research findings have brought forward with regard to language learning during mobility and by suggesting solutions to help us overcome these, Kinginger's introductory chapter is a valuable resource for educators who want to enhance language learning by setting up telecollaboration, either as a preparation for physical mobility, or as an alternative to it.

2.2. Andreas Müller-Hartmann: a task is a task is a task is a task... or is it?

In his keynote address, **Müller-Hartmann** presents a teacher education perspective and explores the processes that teachers-to-be go through while developing pedagogic competences for telecollaborative task-based language learning. He sees tasks and task design skills as central to creating and assuring a stimulating learning environment. Müller-Hartmann takes the reader from the theoretical considerations of CALL tasks and teacher competence in facilitating rich task-driven interactions to a practical investigation of a case study in which participating student teachers are engaged in task design on the micro-level. As he demonstrates, students' telecollaborative on-task performance offers a window into the processes of developing the competences in focus as well as their agency as future teachers.

While exploring the pedagogical context, the author puts a strong emphasis on the role of qualitative and introspective data in tracking the multilayered processes of competence development. He advocates a mixed-method approach to capture how group members contribute to tasks-as-processes and how, in consequence, they develop a wide range of pedagogical and social competences. This is possible through the analysis of different types of qualitative and retrospective data retrieved from chat transcripts, recorded classroom discourse and students' reflective texts. It is the triangulation of the data that allows a deeper understanding of how teacher trainees become aware of their future role. As the author explains, in this approach tasks become 'exploitable activities' which can generate a wealth of introspective and qualitative data without disturbing the usual classroom procedures and interactions – a flaw hitherto seen as inherent to CALL qualitative research.

2.3. David Little: learner autonomy and telecollaborative language learning

Little's keynote contribution interrogates telecollaboration against the broader background of foreign and second language pedagogy. This analysis encompasses on the one hand a sharp critique of traditional pedagogical practice, and on the other a detailed vision of how classrooms can and should work. Little see the communicative approach as having merely continued the fundamental discourse patterns and roles that have obtained in classrooms for generations, in spite of the failure of these practices to deliver on "the more or less universal goal of L2 education": "to develop learners' communicative repertoires, and by doing so extend their identity and the scope of their agency". He further faults research in instructed SLA for implicitly accepting the pedagogical status quo and failing to construct alternative visions.

The alternative proposed by Little is a classroom driven by language learner autonomy. In such a classroom, learners use the target language from the outset as the medium of planning, executing, monitoring and evaluating their own learning, thereby channelling and extending their agency through the TL. Written language plays a central role in this process, as employed in learner journals, learner-generated learning materials and class posters. This conception of the language learning process prompts a series of questions for telecollaborators, one of the most pointed being the first: "Is your telecollaborative learning embedded in a larger L2 learning dynamic that shares the characteristics of [the autonomy classroom]? If not, why not?".

Implicit in Little's challenge is the argument that telecollaboration cannot by itself be an agent of fundamental change: it can only ever be as effective as the pedagogical environment it is embedded in. Conversely, we might observe that among the promises of telecollaboration is the fact that designing online learning projects obliges us to revisit and interrogate our assumptions about language and intercultural learning, identifying those processes that telecollaboration can best support. Among those processes, of course, is the exercise of learner agency through involved communication. This recognition might in turn stimulate us to critically scrutinise our assumptions about the classroom environment more generally: we might, in other words, find ourselves reshaping our physical classrooms in the image of our virtual ones.

3. Telecollaboration in support of culture and language-oriented education

Telecollaboration in support of culture and language emerged as one of the leading themes from the papers edited. Culture and language have been key foci in telecollaborative practice and research from the early stages, and in light of the background in languages of the majority of authors, it should come as no surprise that a substantial number of contributions centred on how telecollaboration, in different configurations for learners from various language backgrounds, is used to enhance language skills or intercultural communicative competences. All of them have English as one of the languages or as the only language in the exchange.

In the first paper by **Ceo-DiFrancesco, Mora, and Serna Collazos**, English is one of the languages in a tandem exchange including Spanish as the other language. The project, which was set up to offer learners linguistic and cultural interactions which were not readily available in their respective classrooms, suggests that growth in intercultural learning, if any, is partly dependent on the environment in which the learning occurs (Colombia vs. US). The use of Spanish and English and reference to Liddicoat and Scarino (2013) as one of the guiding frameworks links this project to the second paper by **Rojas-Primus**. She finds that telecollaboration can reinforce the experiential, transformative and participatory dimensions of learning by students in Canada who are engaged in telecollaborative activities with learners from Chile. English as a Lingua Franca (ELF) is the language in a project between Spanish and French students, reported on by **Castro and Derivry-Plard**. They seek to engage learners of different L1 backgrounds and cultures in mini-anthropological or sociological tasks along the lines propounded by Kramsch (2014) and others.

Sauro zooms in on intercultural learning in an English teacher education class in Sweden, connected to English teacher programmes in four other countries. She reports that intercultural learning often takes place during in-class discussions and reflections *following* the exchanges, thereby lending support to O'Dowd's (2016) contention that integration in the classroom context is essential for achieving intercultural learning. A qualitative study by **Yang** of student blogs in an English-Korean telecollaboration project also reveals that rich intercultural interactions do indeed occur, providing further support for telecollaboration as a source of intercultural learning.

A less common form of intercultural language learning is presented by **Johnson**. On the basis of an analysis of recorded videos, reflective essays and learner interviews, she discusses the benefits and risks of setting up intergenerational videoconferencing between French learners of English and senior citizens in the US.

On a more practical note, **Abruquah, Dosa, and Duda** examine what is needed to set up intercultural exchanges successfully between students from five European universities. Their study reveals high satisfaction with the exchanges overall, but also provides a word of warning against trying to sustain projects with so many partners. Similarly, **Nicolaou and Sevilla-Pavón**, reporting on telecollaboration projects between students in Cyprus and Spain, find positive development overall of intercultural competence, language skills, and e-literacy; however, in some cases, insufficient commitment and lack of reciprocity may affect students' motivation negatively. Finally, exploring how the motivation for learning English by students from three Asian countries may be enhanced by connecting them to learners in the US, **Shimizu, Pack, Kano, Okazaki, and Yamamura** suggest that telecollaborative classes are indeed effective in providing students increased interaction in English, and helping them recognise the value of language learning via telecollaboration.

4. Training teachers through telecollaboration

One of the recurrent themes in telecollaborative research and practice is training teachers for and through telecollaboration. This trend is reflected in eight papers in which the authors address various dimensions of teacher professional development from teacher-learner interaction through interdisciplinary approaches and task design to teacher competences.

A very interesting perspective has been offered by **Loranc-Paszylk** who, in her study of Polish and Spanish teacher trainees engaged in joint task design, explores the joint potential of cross-cultural videoconferencing and Content and

Language Integrated Learning (CLIL). The author analyses how each of the four pillars of the CLIL conceptual framework can benefit from telecollaboration to conclude that in the context of teacher training it is the cognitive and cultural dimensions that benefit most.

Synchronous online communication is also central to the study by **Wigham and Vidal**, who concentrate on competences required of teachers engaged in videoconferencing. By analysing multimodal transcripts of exchanges recorded between undergraduate learners of French from Dublin and French teacher trainees from Lyon, the authors identify and examine the strategies and semiotic resources that trainee-teachers use to soften potentially face-threatening acts of correcting learners in a videoconferencing mode.

A videoconferencing context has also been explored by **Hoshii and Schumacher**, who offer an asymmetrical study into conversational competence of L2 learners and teachers of German as a Foreign Language (GFL). In the project carried out as part of longitudinal partnership between teacher trainees from Berlin and advanced learners of GFL from Tokyo, the authors investigate participants' interactions and focus on how they signal and then solve problems with comprehension. Based on their findings, Hoshii and Schumacher provide several implications for learning and teacher training.

Interaction is also at the centre of a study by **Loizidou and Mangenot**, who examine formal and informal patterns of communication between learners of French and prospective teachers of French as a foreign language in the context of asynchronous forum discussions. In particular the authors investigate the conditions under which prospective teachers switch between formal instruction and less formal episodes. As the authors conclude, the types of interaction depend on a wide array of environmental and personal factors.

Whyte and Gijsen use an asymmetrical exchange to investigate interaction between teacher trainees and learners. In their study, 35 TEFL teacher trainees from France and the Netherlands collaborated to design interactive tasks for secondary-level English as a Foreign Language (EFL) learners. The authors analyse student-teacher course contributions, the teaching/learning materials they designed, and their reflections on this work. The observations they make reveal wide variation across participating teachers which remain consistent with their differing experience, beliefs, training and institutional cultures.

Using telecollaboration to embrace diversity is a key concept of the paper by **Valcke and Romero Alfaro**. They address the burning issue of growing interculturalism at academic institutions and the consequent need for helping faculty engage in English-Medium Instruction. Importantly, the authors see the value of telecollaborative training in its economy and flexibility to accommodate broadly understood diversities. In their study, academic teachers representing various disciplines from universities in Cadiz (Spain) and Brussels work in intercultural tandems to support each other in the acquisition of English for teaching purposes.

Preparing teachers for telecollaboration is central to the study by **Waldman, Harel, and Schwab**. They provide evidence that experiencing telecollaboration enhances pre-service teachers' self-efficacy to facilitate telecollaborative projects. Following a project in which student teachers from Germany and Israel used videoconferencing to compare and evaluate the ways EFL is taught in their contexts, a survey showed raised feelings of competence in designing, organising, running and assessing online exchanges with their future pupils.

An innovative method of training teachers for telecollaboration is presented by **Melchor-Couto and Jauregi**. The authors use the context of the EU-funded project TILA to explore the role of coaching in enhancing teachers' competences for integrating telecollaboration in their own language courses. In their study the authors report on the remote meetings of the coach and two telecollaborative teachers. They conclude that coaching is successful for integration of complex pedagogical innovations as it assists teachers in adopting and maintaining newly developed skills and practices.

Chapter 1

5. Telecollaboration in service of mobility

As the concept of internationalisation has become prominent in tertiary education, telecollaboration is increasingly used to support mobility programmes as a complementary or preparatory stage, or even as an alternative to mobility. As the studies included in this section demonstrate, participation in telecollaborative exchanges helps learners develop necessary linguistic and intercultural competencies, build social relationships and advance in a range of transversal skills, all of which increase the efficiency of staying abroad.

The preparatory role of telecollaboration for mobility programmes is discussed by **Giralt and Jeanneau**, who investigate a project in which students in Ireland and Spain collaborate online before their study visits. The findings demonstrate that reflection and analysis prompted by students' telecollaboration not only raise their intercultural awareness and promote language practice but also reduce anxiety and increase motivation for the period abroad.

A comparison of various pre-mobility modes and scenarios is offered by **Nissen**, who uses a blended learning approach to analyse those aspects which participating students perceive as assets for their learning. Comparing students' approaches to collaboration with local peers in small groups, local Erasmus students and with telecollaborative partners, Nissen discovers that communication scenarios with external partners, be it face-to-face or telecollaborative, are valued most in terms of perceived learning gains. As the findings show, learner engagement and social presence sustain learning in collaboratively oriented learning situations.

De Martino also focuses on relationships, when he investigates a project in which students of German and Italian work in tandems in the dual roles of native speakers and language learners. Weekly Skype communication on personalised topics serves as preparation for real-life study trips. As the author shows, authentic interaction with native speakers inevitably awakens participants to interculturality issues and helps them establish personal relationships, both of which increase the efficiency of the ensuing study visits.

The impact of virtual versus physical exchanges on the development of personality traits is investigated by **Van der Velden, Millner, and Van der Heijden**. They present a very interesting study based on a large-scale project in which students from ten countries met online in facilitated video conference sessions to discuss current European socio-political issues. The authors investigate the impact of online meetings on participants' transversal skills, relating it to with the Erasmus Impact Study (EIS). They provide evidence that the effects of regular online are comparable to those of the EIS.

Telecollaboration can also be seen as an alternative to physical mobility. **Hagley** provides an account of a large-scale exchange engaging as many as 1500 participants from 21 institutions and six countries. Hagley highlights a unique value of telecollaboration for students from mono-cultural classrooms, where opportunities to engage in authentic communication are scarce. As the author concludes, participation in such a large-scale multi-institutional project frees teachers of the organisational burden and assists learners in attaining cultural acclimatisation, which Hagley sees as preparatory to cultural competence.

6. Telecollaboration for other disciplines and skills

Telecollaboration is increasingly used across disciplines to support the learning of content and transversal skills other than languages. This is reflected in this section, which includes applications in Geography, History, Translation, Public Administration, Political Science, Cultural Studies, and Foreign Relations. Language and intercultural communication are obviously still relevant in these contexts, but the emphasis is on how telecollaboration may enhance content learning by providing a global perspective, prepare students better for functioning in a global society, or increase their intercultural and interreligious tolerance and understanding.

Deutscher examines if and how telecollaboration is used in Germany in geography CLIL courses, where online exchanges can bring in cross-regional perspectives and offer opportunities for authentic language use and integration of digital media, such as charts and maps. In an interdisciplinary project on Latin American history, **Fernández** finds that pre-service history teachers in Argentina and students of Spanish in Denmark employ different Communication Strategies (CS). The recommendations for CS training she provides may be helpful for others responsible for supporting similar asymmetrical collaborations.

In the context of translation studies, **Marczak** reports that telecollaboration may help to increase students' employability by contributing to competences for teamwork, communication, leadership, negotiation, self-management, etc. In view of variation in the degrees to which these skills are developed, he discusses the implications for improving their integration in translator education. Preparing students for working in a global environment is also a key objective in the paper by **Mesh**, who describes how students in an Italian-English tandem project, by working together through wikis and mobile devices, are acquiring the transversal competencies of using digital tools, managing their own learning and communicating effectively in cross-cultural and interpersonal relationships.

Capobianco, Rubaii, and Líppez-De Castro present lessons learnt from a jointly developed course for Master of Public Administration students in the US and Political Science undergraduates in Colombia, intended to prepare students for being successful public affairs practitioners in a highly technological, globalised and diverse environment.

Finally, in the context of a project between students in a Cultural Studies programme in Tunisia and a Foreign Relations course in the US, **Mason** shows that students respond positively overall to telecollaboration as a way of improving intercultural and interreligious understanding and overcoming prejudices and misconceptions, but that deeper discussions of controversial points are sometimes avoided and that slow or no responses, especially from US students, may have had a negative impact on intercultural attitudes.

7. Analysing interaction in telecollaborative exchanges

This section focuses on the analysis of telecollaboration from a range of research perspectives, interaction models and theoretical frameworks. It includes papers informed by discourse analysis, corpus linguistic analysis and conversation analysis, as well as studies looking at telecollaboration through an activity theoretical lens. The studies contribute to enhancing our understanding of what goes on in telecollaborative exchanges both at the micro level of individual utterances and at the macro level of facilitating successful collaborations.

Akiyama, in a discourse analytic study of negotiation turns in a tandem exchange between a Japanese and an American student, shows how valuable opportunities for communication are missed because the American responds to the Japanese student's moments of silence by explaining too much rather than giving him opportunities to speak. Using corpus-based linguistic analysis, **Orsini-Jones, Gazeley-Eke and Leinster** found that the pronoun 'we' as used in asynchronous forum interactions may have different meanings depending on the linguistic and cultural backgrounds of the interlocutors involved. This may be a source of miscommunication between the groups involved.

By analysing conversations and reflective interviews, **Hoffstaedter and Kohn** provide evidence that their task design, based on telecollaboration in which secondary school learners address everyday topics in lingua franca exchanges from their home environments, creates suitable conditions for establishing common ground, exercising empathy and dealing with communication problems.

Drawing on an activity theoretical framework, **Dey-Plissonneau and Blin** report on the affordances emerging during pedagogical interactions in an online videoconferencing session between teacher trainees and learners of French. Looking through a similar activity theoretical lens, **Malerba and Appel** examine the opportunities for tandem language learning in the informal language learning communities Livemocha and Busuu.

Using a faceted classification scheme for computer-mediated discourse, **Batardière and Helm** compare two distinct models of telecollaboration – one synchronous and part of the Soliya Connect Programme, the other asynchronous and part of an intercultural Franco-Irish exchange – with respect to the learning space they afford for politically engaged and reflective pedagogy.

Renner addresses the challenges of applying a conversation analysis framework to data collection in the study of synchronous audio-visual eTandem exchanges. The first cycle of data collection demonstrated the difficulty of capturing all modes of communication, making sure the data are complete and authentic, and getting students to record both on-task and off-task conversations. The same type of data are the focus of the next paper by **Aranha and Leone**, who report on a major initiative to create a databank of oral teletandem interactions of students in Brazil and Italy with students in the US and UK respectively. The Interaction Space Model by Chanier et al. (2014) is used to identify and classify relevant data from the online exchanges.

8. Concluding note

As illustrated above, the papers included in this collection describe telecollaboration from a wide range of perspectives, educational approaches, and research traditions and frameworks. The papers give readers a view of how students experienced telecollaborative projects, how and why teachers and others experts designed the projects and tasks, and how researchers went about analysing them. We hope that this cross-disciplinary, multifaceted approach to practice and research, together with the open access availability of this publication, will bring telecollaboration to the attention of many, including educational administrators and policy makers whose support remains to be fully harnessed to reap the benefits of telecollaboration in HE on a larger scale (Lewis & O'Dowd, 2016). Speaking on behalf of the INTENT/UNICollaboration team, which organised the conference from which these papers have come, we hope that this publication will be followed by a regular stream of papers in the open access journal which this team has planned.

References

Chanier, T., Poudat, C., Sagot, B., Antoniadis, G., Wigham, C. R., Hriba, L., Longhi, J., & Seddah, J. (2014). The CoMeRe corpus for French: structuring and annotating heterogeneous CMC genres. *Journal for Language Technology and Computational Linguistics, 2*(29), 1-30.

Kramsch, C. (2014). Teaching foreign languages in an era of globalization: introduction. *Modern Language Journal, 98*(1), 296–311. https://doi.org/10.1111/j.1540-4781.2014.12057.x

Lewis, T., & O'Dowd, R. (2016). Introduction to online intercultural exchange and this volume. In R. O'Dowd & T. Lewis (Eds), *Online intercultural exchange: policy, pedagogy, practice* (pp. 3-20). New York: Routledge.

Liddicoat, A. J., & Scarino, A. (2013). *Intercultural language teaching and learning*. Malden, MA: Wiley-Blackwell. https://dx.doi.org/10.1002/9781118482070

O'Dowd, R. (2016). Learning from the past and looking to the future of online intercultural exchange. In R. O'Dowd & T. Lewis (Eds), *Online intercultural exchange: policy, pedagogy, practice* (pp. 273-293). New York: Routledge.

Section 1.

Keynote papers

2 Telecollaboration and student mobility for language learning

Celeste Kinginger[1]

Abstract

This paper reviews major findings from qualitative and quantitative research on language learning in student mobility in order to consider how telecollaboration might contribute to the success of student sojourns abroad. Evidence is available to demonstrate the effectiveness of student mobility in every domain of language development. As may be expected, an in-country stay is shown to be particularly beneficial for the social-interactive and pragmatic dimensions of language least amenable to classroom instruction. However, throughout the literature a common finding is of notable individual differences in learning outcomes. To understand why only some, but not all students appear to develop language competence abroad, qualitative research has examined the nature of the experience from a variety of perspectives. This research has shown that students encounter challenges in establishing local social networks and often retain strong ties to home. They also position themselves within newly salient national identities, or are positioned by interlocutors as foreigners with questionable rights to appreciate and to learn local sociolinguistic norms. It has become clear that many learners approach their task with little awareness of diverse language varieties and registers within their host communities. Prior socialization in classrooms can also limit the range of their participation in informal conversations and thus, their development of interactive capacities. Whether implemented as preparation for physical mobility or as

---

1. Pennsylvania State University, University Park, PA, USA; cxk37@psu.edu

How to cite this chapter: Kinginger, C. (2016). Telecollaboration and student mobility for language learning. In S. Jager, M. Kurek & B. O'Rourke (Eds), *New directions in telecollaborative research and practice: selected papers from the second conference on telecollaboration in higher education* (pp. 19-29). Research-publishing.net. https://doi.org/10.14705/rpnet.2016.telecollab2016.487

concurrent support for language learners abroad, telecollaboration holds the potential to address these issues. In telecollaborative pedagogies, students can create social connections with their peers, see themselves through the eyes of others, be exposed to specific attitudes and discourses about foreigner identities, experience and analyze spoken or informal forms, and expand their discourse options beyond the strictly pedagogical.

Keywords: study abroad, student mobility.

1. Introduction

The objective of this paper is to demonstrate how a rationale for telecollaborative pedagogies emerges seamlessly from the literature on language learning in student mobility. Both lay and professional folklore suggest that in-country sojourns involve effortless and "easy learning" (DeKeyser, 2010, p. 89). Moreover, the structure of many language programs suggests that a sojourn abroad is believed to complete the process of language learning such that curricula need no longer address related issues. The findings of research, however, robustly demonstrate that the benefits of student mobility are unevenly distributed among participants, and sometimes quite modest. Moreover, and predictably, it has become clear that a sojourn abroad is most useful for the development of abilities related to social interaction and pragmatics, precisely those capacities least amenable to classroom instruction. Research into the qualities of study abroad experiences has begun to explore the sources of these findings.

2. Understanding language learning and student mobility

Why do some study abroad participants register impressive gains in proficiency scores or documented social-interactive capacities whereas others do not?

Qualitative or hybrid studies have revealed a number of significant challenges that students may encounter during their in-country sojourns. One way to approach this question is by exploring the extent of students' integration into their host communities. The LANG-SNAP project (McManus, Mitchell, & Tracy-Ventura, 2014) followed 56 French or Spanish majors enrolled at a British university through their compulsory year abroad in France, Spain, or Mexico, combining measurements of various aspects of language development with language engagement and social network questionnaires. All of these students were highly motivated to enhance their language ability, expressing strong desires to develop local affiliations. Yet, only a substantial minority met these goals. A subsequent study of high gainers (Mitchell & Tracy-Ventura, 2016) revealed that the contemporary language-related sojourn abroad requires resilience and strategic action: the most successful learners were those who found ways to contribute to their host communities, to barter English for French or Spanish practice, or to develop emotional ties to at least one person, whether a peer, a colleague, or a host parent.

Globalization has exerted a profound influence on the nature of study abroad experiences. Today, study abroad is "a multilingual and intercultural experience involving virtual as well as face-to-face relationships, and the maintenance of long-term social relations alongside those created during the sojourn itself" (McManus et al., 2014, p. 112). On the one hand, students who are overwhelmed by the emotional stress of living abroad may retreat from local involvement almost completely. This was the case, for example, of Deirdre (Kinginger, 2008), an American student in France who devoted all of her free time to online interactions with family and friends at home. On the other, the relative ease of travel enables international "helicopter parenting" or the interpretation of a child's departure as a motivation for tourism by the rest of the family. Another participant in the Kinginger (2008) study, Delaney, was assigned this pseudonym ('daughter of the challenger') because her father visited her in France from the United States three times during her one-semester sojourn to address her complaints about lodging and other aspects of the program. Liza (also from Kinginger, 2008) was accompanied to Strasbourg by her mother, then received visits from her father, sister, and boyfriend, leaving her very little time to learn French.

Another theme emerging from qualitative studies is the potential for students to retreat into discourses of national superiority when encountering new cultural norms. Primed by the resurgence of French-bashing by the American media at the time, Beatrice (Kinginger, 2008) interpreted her Parisian host family's questions about her views on the U.S.-led invasion of Iraq as hostility toward her country, and became estranged from her only willing interlocutors. In the early stages of their sojourn in Australia, the French students portrayed by Patron (2007) were appalled by Australian students' informal dress and manners in class, confused by Australian professors' casual demeanor, and shocked by the prevalence of 'bring your own bottle' festivities involving excessive drinking. Gao (2011) documented the arguments erupting in English classes in Britain when students from mainland China encountered peers from Japan, Taiwan, or Korea who contested their version of Chinese history. Ada, a student from Hong Kong sojourning in Britain (Jackson, 2008), lived with a host family who repeatedly mislabeled her as Japanese, and whose culinary practices, she believed, threatened her health.

In addition to prioritizing their own national identities, students abroad may also be ascribed identities as foreigners with questionable rights or abilities to acquire the local language. Brown (2013) illustrated this process in four case studies involving male sojourners of various national origin in Korea, focusing on these students' mastery of the Korean honorifics system. This system involves choosing between *contaymal*, or 'respect speech', and *panmal*, or 'half-speech', and is strongly associated with the performance of Korean identity. Furthermore, "in every single Korean utterance, the speaker is forced into choices between different honorific verb endings and lexical forms" (Brown, 2013, p. 270). In a discourse completion task, the four advanced learners in the study displayed strong underlying abilities to manipulate honorifics appropriately, for example, in displaying respect to persons older or more senior within organizations. However, in their extracurricular interactions, honorifics were often used in inappropriate ways, either because the students were positioned as outsiders with whom standard politeness need not apply, or because the students themselves believed that the honorifics system "clashed with their identities as Westerners [and] preference for egalitarian language use" (Brown, 2013, p. 295).

The literature also suggests, in various ways, that students abroad could profit from enhanced language awareness. Miller and Ginsburg (1995) scrutinized the folklinguistic theories and conceptual metaphors surrounding language espoused by American learners of Russian. For many, language is analogous to architecture, with words as building blocks and grammar as mortar. Notably, in their reflections on their experiences, the students made no reference to the social interactive abilities, such as pragmatics or interactive competence, best developed in study abroad. Another interesting case comes from a study by Riegelhaupt and Carrasco (2002) investigating the experiences of heritage learners in their ancestral homeland. One of their participants, Lidia, was a second-generation speaker of Mexican Spanish from the Southwestern United States. During her five-week immersion program and homestay in Mexico, she was interpreted by her host family as an inappropriate type of foreigner in comparison with another Euro-American guest. In particular, the host family condemned the non-standard aspects of her Spanish: "the family felt that a 'Mexican' person [...] who spoke Spanish in such a manner was not really welcome in their home" (Riegelhaupt & Carrasco, 2002, p. 336). Although it would not have addressed her hosts' blatant prejudice, some instruction on linguistic concepts such as register or geographic varieties might have assisted Lidia in understanding her predicament. Elsewhere in the literature, in terms of language varieties, we find that the tables are turned when, for example, students travel abroad to learn standard Spanish or Japanese for international communication among the global elite, only to observe with disappointment that their hosts speak Valenciano (Mitchell & Tracy-Ventura, 2016) or Kyoto dialect (Iino, 2006).

Homestay arrangements during study abroad are believed to provide significant access to language learning opportunities. However, several recent microethnographic studies reveal that both the quantity and the quality of these interactions can vary significantly. Pryde (2014) undertook an eleven-month study of intermediate-level Japanese learners of English living with local families in New Zealand, collecting samples of informal conversations at regular intervals throughout the students' sojourn. His findings revealed a strong tendency for all parties to adhere to classroom-style interaction patterns, particularly the infamous IRE sequence (Initiation, Response, Evaluation) and the use of display rather than referential questions, as in the excerpt below from Pryde's unpublished data:

HF:	what are we having for dinner, today?
Miko:	meat pie
HF:	meat pie, yes
HM:	((laughs))
HF:	meat pie, not meet the pie
Miko:	mince pie
HF:	good girl, yes, and
Miko:	carrot
HF:	yes
Miko:	potatoes
HF:	and
Miko:	broccoli
(two response tokens)	
HF:	very good

Most alarming among Pryde's findings is the absence of change over time. Throughout the homestay experience, 'conversations' involved topic choice, initiation and control by the hosts, formulaic patterns, and banal topics. Moreover, it became difficult to collect data as the sojourn continued, since students and hosts spent progressively less time together.

Another study by Kinginger, Wu, Lee, and Tan (2016) suggests that host families may be variably capable of providing learning opportunities to student guests of modest proficiency. The study involved three high school students of Mandarin Chinese and their host families in Beijing in a short-term program (three weeks). Data include audio recordings by the students of situations deemed most useful for language learning. For Sam, who arrived with advanced proficiency developed over a period of 11 years, including a school-sponsored immersion program, the sojourn was an unqualified success. Most interesting here, however, is the contrast between the experiences of students without advanced proficiency, David and Henry. Although David was a beginner, his host family, the Zhaos, displayed considerable skill in using everyday artifacts such as food or photo albums, to render their language use predictable, comprehensible, and thus navigable for David. They also routinely engaged in lighthearted, humorous teasing. Over the quite short period of time he spent with his hosts, David first observed this teasing, then became a target of it, and finally began to participate, as illustrated in the excerpt below. Here the family is examining a photo album containing pictures of David's host sister Zhao Yueman as an infant, as Yueman becomes increasingly annoyed:

Mrs. Zhao:	**zhège shì Yueman**
	this is Yueman
David:	**(LAUGHTER)**
Mrs. Zhao:	**hén xiǎo hén xiǎo**
	very little, very little
	zhè yàng hǎoxiàng dōu bú dào yí- yí- yí suì
	(she) looks to be not even one, one, one year old
	yí suì?
	one year old?
	ha?
	right?
	zhè shì
	this is
	(LAUGHTER) <@ zhèige gèng xiǎo @>
	this one, even younger
David:	**(LAUGHTER)**
Mrs. Zhao:	**tā xiǎoshíhòu jiù zhè yàng**
	when she was little, she already looked like this
	suóyǐ tā xiǎochéng zhè yàng
	so she was this small
David:	**(LAUGHTER)**
Mr. Zhao:	**(LAUGHTER)**
David:	**that's you?** ((referring to Zhao Yueman))
Mr. Zhao:	**(LAUGHTER)**
Mr. Zhao:	**mh**
Zhao Yueman:	**oh (LAUGHTER)**
David:	**méi yóu tōufa**
	no hair
All:	**(LAUGHTER)**

(Kinginger, et al., 2016, p. 47)

The Liu family, Henry's very well-intentioned, conscientious and generous hosts, by contrast, often seemed to be at a loss as to how to interact with a student with

Chapter 2

proficiency estimated as low intermediate. Henry contributed numerous recordings to the project (365 minutes in 8 interactions), but very few of the speaking turns in the data involved him. When the family did attempt to engage him, it was often difficult for Henry to participate because there were no supporting artifacts, making the topic difficult to identify, and there were few attempts to simplify or otherwise accommodate his learning needs. The excerpt below is typical of these data in that the family and Henry's tutor use repetition only in their attempts to communicate, eventually resorting to a translation into English. The party had been discussing the tendency of Chinese parents to be protective of their children's time, doing everything for them from washing their clothes to squeezing out their toothpaste, and decided to ask Henry if the same is true in his family:

Tutor:	**nǐ de yīfushéixǐ**
	who washes your clothes?
Mr. Liu:	**nǐ de yīfushéixǐ**
	who washes your clothes?
Tutor:	**nǐ de suóyǒu de yīfushéixǐ**
	who washes all of your clothes?
Henry:	oh yeah
Mr. Liu:	**nǐ de yīfushéixǐ**
	who washes your clothes?
Henry:	**oh um**
	like um
Liu Boyi:	**wash**
Henry:	**like uhm**
Mrs. Liu:	**who- who wash the clothes for you**
Henry:	**oh ohwǒ de māma**
	oh, oh, my mom
Tutor:	**(LAUGHTER)**
Mr. Liu:	**(LAUGHTER)**
	<@ yíyàng @>
	same

(Kinginger et al., 2016, pp. 49-50)

Students might profit from opportunities to engage in informal interactions prior to study abroad, and all parties might benefit from better understanding of strategies for rendering language comprehensible through the use of physical artifacts to share information or to accomplish tasks.

3. Contributions of telecollaborative approaches

The above-outlined research has demonstrated that study abroad is not a "magical formula" for language learning (DeKeyser, 2010, p. 89). Students abroad can potentially encounter social, ideological, interpersonal, and interactional barriers to their achievement. Telecollaborative pedagogies present considerable potential to overcome these challenges. Most obviously, telecollaboration offers sanctioned access to peers who are expert users of the language under study. In our own experience (e.g. Kinginger, Gourves-Hayward, & Simpson, 1999), students of French who later studied in France had a distinct advantage because they could begin to establish social networks immediately, by reaching out to their former classmates.

In contrast to regular classroom instruction, telecollaboration offers sheltered opportunities to engage in socially consequential second language interactions and to begin crafting a foreign-language mediated identity. Especially in relatively isolated locales, these interactions may be the first in which students come to care sincerely for their own foreign language interactional face and for the impression they convey to their partner class.

Another advantage of telecollaboration can be exposure to ideologies students may encounter abroad, including negotiation of attitudes and stereotypes about foreigner identities and linguistic varieties. As for language *per se*, students engaged in telecollaboration will encounter the ways in which their foreign language is actually used by educated persons, in contrast to the sanitized forms enshrined in textbooks and other official materials. This can include experience and analysis of informal or spoken registers routinely excluded from instruction (Kinginger, 1998) and opportunities to explore the significance of sociolinguistic variants, such as the address form system in many European languages (e.g. *tu* versus *vous* in French, see Kinginger & Belz, 2005). In the future, it is much to be hoped that educators will continue to develop articulated curricula linking telecollaboration with student mobility.

Chapter 2

References

Brown, L. (2013). Identity and honorifics use in Korean study abroad. In C. Kinginger (Ed.), *Social and cultural aspectss of language learning in study abroad* (pp. 269-298). Amsterdam: John Benjamins. https://doi.org/10.1075/lllt.37.11bro

DeKeyser, R. (2010). Monitoring processes in Spanish as a second language during a study abroad program. *Foreign Language Annals, 43*(1), 80-92. https://doi.org/10.1111/j.1944-9720.2010.01061.x

Gao, F. (2011). Exploring the reconstruction of Chinese learners' national identities in their English-language-learning journeys in Britain. *Journal of Language, Identity, and Education, 10*(5), 287-305. https://doi.org/10.1080/15348458.2011.614543

Iino, M. (2006). Norms of interaction in a Japanese homestay setting –Toward two-way flow of linguistic and cultural resources. In M. A. Dufon & E. Churchill (Eds), *Language learner in study abroad contexts* (pp. 151-173). Clevedon, UK: Multilingual Matters.

Jackson, J. (2008). *Language, identity and study abroad: sociocultural perspectives*. London: Equinox.

Kinginger, C. (1998). Videoconferencing as access to spoken French. *Modern Language Journal,82*(4), 502-513. https://doi.org/10.1111/j.1540-4781.1998.tb05537.x

Kinginger, C. (2008). Language learning in study abroad: case studies of Americans in France. *Modern Language Journal, 92*(1), Monograph.

Kinginger, C. (2015). Student mobility and identity-related language learning. *Intercultural Education, 26*(1), 6-15. https://doi.org/10.1080/14675986.2015.992199

Kinginger, C., & Belz, J. (2005). Sociocultural perspectives on pragmatic development in foreign language learning: case studies from telecollaboration and study abroad. *Intercultural Pragmatics, 2*(4), 369-421. https://doi.org/10.1515/iprg.2005.2.4.369

Kinginger, C., Gourves-Hayward, A., & Simpson, V. (1999). A tele-collaborative course on French / American intercultural communication. *French Review, 72*, 853-866.

Kinginger, C., Wu, Q., Lee, H.-S., & Tan, D. (2016). The short-term homestay as a context for language learning: three case studies of high school students and host families. *Study Abroad Research in Second Language Acquisition and International Education, 1*(1), 34-60. https://doi.org/10.1075/sar.1.1.02kin

McManus, K., Mitchell, R., & Tracy-Ventura, N. (2014). Understanding insertion and integration in a study abroad context: the case of English speaking sojourners in France. *Revue Française de Linguistique Appliquée, 19*, 97-116.

Miller, L., & Ginsburg, R. (1995). Folklinguistic theories of language learning. In B. Freed (Ed.), *Second language acquisition in a study abroad context* (pp. 293-315). Amsterdam: John Benjamins. https://doi.org/10.1075/sibil.9.18mil

Mitchell, R., & Tracy-Ventura, N. (2016). Language learning by Anglophones during residence abroad: the contribution of quality in social relationships. *Paper presented at the American Association for Applied Linguistics, Orlando, FL, March.*

Patron, M.-C. (2007). *Culture and identity in study abroad: after Australia, French without France.* Oxford: Peter Lang. https://doi.org/10.3726/978-3-0353-0283-7

Pryde, M. (2014). Conversational patterns of homestay hosts and study abroad students. *Foreign Language Annals, 47*(3), 487-506. https://doi.org/10.1111/flan.12100

Riegelhaupt, F., & Carrasco, R. (2002). Mexico host family reactions to a bilingual Chicana teacher in Mexico: a case study of language and culture clash. *Bilingual Research Journal, 24*, 333-349.

3 A task is a task is a task is a task... or is it? Researching telecollaborative teacher competence development – the need for more qualitative research

Andreas Müller-Hartmann[1]

Abstract

The concept of task has become central not only to an understanding of language learning per se, but also to the design and research of Online Intercultural Exchanges (OIEs). While research on the design of tasks in OIEs has been very productive, we still lack insights into how teachers develop competences in task design on the micro-level. Consequently, this contribution looks at how OIEs allow pre-service teachers to develop such competences when designing telecollaborative task sequences for their future learners. Findings show that the most promising research approach to tackle this question at the interface between telecollaboration, Task-Based Language Teaching (TBLT), and teacher education is a stronger reliance on qualitative research because it helps understand what pre-service teachers do when developing such competences.

Keywords: task-based language teaching, qualitative research, pre-service teacher education.

---

1. Pädagogische Hochschule Heidelberg, Heidelberg, Germany; andreas.mueller-hartmann@ph-heidelberg.de

How to cite this chapter: Müller-Hartmann, A. (2016). A task is a task is a task is a task... or is it? Researching telecollaborative teacher competence development – the need for more qualitative research. In S. Jager, M. Kurek & B. O'Rourke (Eds), *New directions in telecollaborative research and practice: selected papers from the second conference on telecollaboration in higher education* (pp. 31-43). Research-publishing.net. https://doi.org/10.14705/rpnet.2016.telecollab2016.488

Chapter 3

1. Introduction

Historically, tasks and task design have always played an important role when designing OIEs. Already in 1997 Furstenberg wrote that "our main role, then, is to design tasks [...] since the task is what gives meaning to the learners' explorations. Only a well-designed task can ensure the quality of the learning process – which is a teacher's ultimate responsibility" (p. 24; see also Levy & Stockwell, 2006). Chapelle (2001) has been especially influential in CALL task design, suggesting a framework for the evaluation of CALL tasks which has since become prominent in telecollaborative research, but which still professes a Second Language Acquisition (SLA) approach with a strong focus on form. Other researchers, especially Hampel (2010), have put forward a more pedagogic approach to Computer-Assisted Language Learning (CALL) task design by focusing on meaning, task type, and teacher/learner factors.

In the most recent book on technology-mediated TBLT, Gonzalez-Lloret and Ortega (2014) make a strong case for integrating tasks and technology by basing it on existing TBLT theory. They argue for a clear learner focus when they write:

> "Language learning tasks which are mediated by new technologies can help minimize students' fear of failure, embarrassment, or losing face; they can raise students' motivation to take risks and be creative while using language to make meaning" (Gonzalez-Lloret & Ortega, 2014, p. 4).

This is in line with Samuda and Bygate's (2008) call for a more pedagogic approach in TBLT:

> "broader understandings of the ways that tasks can contribute to language learning and teaching [...] must be grounded in understanding of 'task' as a pedagogic tool in different contexts of use" (p. 219, see also Müller-Hartmann & Schocker-von Ditfurth, 2011).

When pursuing a more pedagogic approach to TBLT, the quality of the learning environment is central. Van den Branden and his research group have defined variables at three levels which they represent in three circles each lying inside the other that facilitate a rich task-based interaction, and thus create a "powerful learning environment for language learning" (Devlieger & Goossens, 2007, p. 97). The outer circle (level I) represents the non-threatening, safe classroom atmosphere which is central to any learning, where learners can take risks when using the language. The second circle (level II) is characterized by the design and application of tasks that are motivating, meaningful, relevant, and also challenging. These tasks are learner-oriented, providing a rich interactive language learning experience. This process needs to be monitored by the teacher, which is represented in the innermost or central circle (level III). S/he is central in providing the safe learning atmosphere, designing meaningful and challenging tasks-as-workplans, and facilitating the tasks by providing interactional support. These are key competences teachers also need to develop when teaching OIEs. It is in this innermost circle, when engaging in group formation processes and interacting in their international teams, designing and negotiating tasks, that teachers-to-be begin to develop the central competence of task design. Engaged in a reflective approach to learning, they develop an understanding of what learners (their team partners and by extension their future learners) do. In his teacher competence model O'Dowd (2005) has integrated these pedagogic competences. While most of the competences focus on task design, some also focus on the facilitation of the task-in-process. This brings me to the research question. How can we find out how teachers develop pedagogic TBLT competences in OIEs?

In the methodology section I will argue that a qualitative approach allows us to better understand what pre-service teachers do when developing such competences.

2. Methodology

To understand learners' agency in the ecological contexts of OIE environments, a mere quantitative approach is not sufficient. Instead we need research designs that provide introspective or emic data to be better able to grasp what is happening in the task process. Stickler and Hampel (2015) have called for more qualitative research in CALL contexts because it is connected to what learners are doing. This kind of research approach stresses the importance of trying to understand the learners' actions:

> "We use the term qualitative to mean an approach that favours understanding the subjective world of human experience over explaining objective reality and that may problematize social and political practice as part of their research agenda" (Stickler & Hampel, 2015, p. 380).

The tasks student teachers engage in are what Allwright and Hanks (2009) have called "potentially exploitable pedagogic activities" which facilitate research (p. 154). They are productive because, when triangulated with other data, they allow a deeper understanding of what learners do and think, and they have the advantage of growing out of the teaching itself, the pedagogic activities or tasks, allowing deep insights into the pedagogic process. Allwright and Hanks profess that "good research itself can be good pedagogy" and their main point of exploratory practice – this is how they call their research approach – is "not to get research done, but to get teaching done well" (Allwright & Hanks, 2009, pp. 154-157). This may sound strange at first, but in teacher education contexts, be they face-to-face, online or in blended learning environments, this is paramount.

Consequently, in terms of data collection and analysis, a mixed methods approach was pursued, focusing on one case study to show how data triangulation of chat transcripts of team interaction, classroom discourse in both local contexts (all sessions were filmed) and reflective learner texts allow an understanding of how student teachers developed TBLT competences when trying to facilitate the different levels of Devlieger and Goossens's (2007) 'powerful learning environment' model in their team interaction.

3. Context

The OIE involved 25 teacher trainees from a Master of Arts (M.A.) course in the Teaching English to Speakers of Other Languages (TESOL) teacher training program at the Pädagogische Hochschule in Heidelberg, Germany, and 31 students of an M.A. TESOL at Jan Dlugosz University in Czestochowa, Poland. All students had extensive pedagogical preparation. The group consisted of 39 female and 17 male student teachers. They represented different levels of Intercultural Communicative Competence (ICC), language proficiency and digital competence. Working in a blended learning format over 13 weeks, using English as a lingua franca, participants worked in intercultural dyads, using the online Canvas platform (http://www.instructure.com), which includes wiki, chat and teleconferencing functionalities. To facilitate task design participants used different technology tools (e.g. About.me), including Weebly (http://weebly.com/) – a tool for creating websites to host task sequences for prospective learners. Students completed the following tasks:

- A written and multimodal personal presentation (ice-breaking task) (Task 1).

- A group identity (reflected in its name) (Task 2).

- An ICC activity (Task 3).

- Evaluation of a partnering group's ICC activity (Task 4).

- Design of a sequence of ICC online activities (delivered via a Weebly site) (Task 5).

- Evaluation of the sequence created by a partnering group (Task 6).

- Reflection on one of the critical learning incidents in the course (Task 7).

As case study, a team of two German male students, Dirk and Sven, who worked with Maria, a female student from Poland, was chosen. Dirk and Sven, who were close to their final exams, had already developed quite a few competences in terms of task-based design. They both had teaching experiences from several internships. Maria came across as not very self-confident. She was afraid of making language mistakes when chatting with her partners and she did not have the TBLT background. On the other hand she had quite a bit of technical competence, having already designed a Weebly page in the semester before.

A central approach my partner, Malgorzata Kurek, and I pursue in our classes is model teaching. We try to establish a safe atmosphere in class, be transparent about tasks, design tasks based on pedagogic task criteria and support students during the task-based interaction in a way that they develop their teaching competences through discovery and reflection.

4. Data analysis and discussion

Quantitative data from an end-of-term questionnaire showed that students felt safe and that they realized the importance of the teacher role in creating a safe learning environment, designing meaningful tasks, and facilitating the task-in-process. But these data do not tell anything about the students' task-induced interaction and their learning trajectories. In the following findings, level I (establishing a safe learning atmosphere) and level III (supporting task-based interaction) of the above model will be discussed in light of the triangulated introspective learner data, learner texts, and classroom discourse data.

4.1. Level I: safe atmosphere

In one of their first tasks, each local team had to come up with the rules of conduct in an OIE to help them understand how to establish a safe learning atmosphere. It is illuminating to see to what extent the students realized the importance of this for their competence development.

Rules of conduct (Maria)

    1. Try to be friendly and tolerant
    2. Be in touch with your partner and don't be shy to ask questions :)

3. Have a positive attitude toward the project
4. Express your ideas and expectations in a clear manner
5. Treat this project as a good intercultural experience

Rules of conduct (Dirk and Sven)

1. Always be polite
2. Be open-minded in terms of culture and other opinions
3. Be reliable
4. Be a good teamplayer

(These lists were published in the presentation tool Padlet)

As we can see they are quite different. Maria strongly states that she needs this safe/positive atmosphere by putting it into first place. It is a form of positive self-talk when she writes not to be shy to ask questions. The German group stresses the importance of strong group cohesion by being polite, open-minded and reliable, something that they adhered to in the project. For example, Maria is insecure about her language competence and corrects every misspelling in the chats and sometimes voices her frustration. It is obvious that Maria needs this safe environment where one can make mistakes when communicating to be able to function as a team member.

> **Maria**: It seems to me that you can use different web pages. What tdo you think about using about.me page as a first step?
>
> I look over them but I didn
>
> oh my god.. I can't write. Sorry
>
> I don
>
> wrrr
>
> never mind

Chapter 3

> (Chat transcript, Google Docs, Nov. 16th, 2015)

When asked in a reflective phase by her teacher what problems they have encountered so far Maria concedes:

> **Maria**: For me it's communication because I know I have problems with my language. It is not good enough. [...] By talking with guys I have the opportunity to express my ideas and I try to be correct. I think I can learn a lot from them because Dirk lived in the USA for many years... and his language is very good.
>
> **Teacher**: But I can imagine the pressure on you.
>
> **Maria**: Yeah (chuckle) – I'm very stressed that I have to write something or write a complex sentence.
>
> (Lesson transcript, Poland, Dec. 7th, 2015)

Dirk and Sven realized this need, providing her with the support she needs, as Dirk explains in his end-of-term portfolio:

> **Dirk**: My first impression was that Maria was a little bit shy. She didn't write a lot in the beginning of the collaboration, so I talked to Sven and asked him what he thinks we could do about this. I decided to try to involve her more in our conversations by asking her questions so that she actually HAD to write something back. While we were working on our IC task we had to create, she wrote me this:
>
> > **Maria**: I have to tell you something. Your English is so good. Im;re really impressed! Please forgive me my mistakes.
> >
> > **Dirk**: Thank you very much.
> >
> > **Dirk**: You're English is also very good. I make mistakes too.

Maria wasn't shy, she was just afraid of making mistakes, so I tried to make her feel more comfortable. From this point on, she wrote a little bit more than before. Not as much as Sven and I did, but I thought that she was making progress.

(Portfolio)

As Dirk points out, this polite support bears fruit. It takes them a while to connect and establish group cohesion. When Maria and Dirk wait for Sven in the chat, she relates to their common group identity/name *Busy Heads* (Task 2) and with that expresses her trust in her team, showing that she feels comfortable in terms of social presence:

Maria: Hi not so good. I'm very tired and you ?

Dirk: Sorry to hear that. I'm doing fine but I'm also a little bit exhausted

Maria: So we are really busy heads

(Chat transcript, Google Docs, Nov. 16th, 2015)

In his reflection Dirk stresses that as a teacher he needs this kind of competence to develop a powerful learning environment:

Dirk: It might sound weird, but I had the feeling I should be very sensitive with her and to encourage her from time to time. This seems to me a lot like the relationship between teachers and learners. The teacher always has to encourage his students to make them feel comfortable, so that they are not afraid to make mistakes. Like putting them into the right atmosphere. By the way, I felt comfortable too, because I think it really pushed our work efficiency forward. This makes me very optimistic for my future work with students.

(Portfolio)

Chapter 3

The learners' chat transcripts proved to be very helpful, but the interpretation becomes more valid mainly by triangulating them with the introspective data from Dirk's portfolio and the transcript of Polish classroom discourse which provides Maria's reflective stance.

4.2. Level III: interaction

Let us look at Maria's participation in the task design process. In this interaction – as Dirk reflected in his portfolio – Dirk and Sven try to involve Maria more into the task design process. For the first time in this group's interaction they have a longer exchange about task design (weebly – Task 5), and especially the choice of tool, which Maria is more of an expert on. While she does not have the TBLT knowledge her partners have, she has more competences working with technology. Given the safe learning atmosphere the partners try to create, as well as their attempts to involve her and the fact that she now can use her competences to contribute to the team effort, all of this allows Maria to participate as a full-fledged member of the team, making an important contribution to the task design. This shows how the different levels of the model work together, facilitating productive teamwork.

> **Dirk**: Ok, we already have 2 ideas for the first sequence. Do you have an idea for the second part, Maria? How could the students learn something about their partners' school day?
>
> **Maria**: Maybe they can use storybird in order to write a short book.
>
> **Sven**: What do you mean by writing a short book, Maria?
>
> **Dirk**: Do you mean something like a short text you could write into a diary?
>
> **Maria**: No, it's not a good idea. I thought about sth like that but we should use different tool to do that
>
> **Dirk**: Maybe a different tool but the idea is not bad at all

> **Maria**: I think it gives them the opportunity to develop their writing skills
>
> **Dirk**: Good and important point
>
> **Sven**: Yes! I think that they would need a lot of task support or respectively a lot of pre- teaching in order to be able to perform such a task. But I really like the basic idea as well
>
> **Dirk**: This also depends on their level. A 5th grader would definitely more support than a 9th grader *need
>
> **Maria**: https://penzu.com/ our teacher suggest me this page. We can look into it later.
>
> (Chat transcript, Google Docs, Dec. 7th, 2015)

As Dirk concedes, Maria is considered the expert for this phase.

> **Dirk**: Honestly, I was kind of lost when I first looked at the Weebly homepage. Creating a homepage was new for me, and I was thankful that Maria was in our group because she already created a Weebly page on her own. I still feel confident when I face a new format or interface, but it helped a lot that Maria knew how to do it. It saved us a lot of time.
>
> (Portfolio)

In another reflective phase Maria comments on the relationship between levels I and III:

> **Maria:** It was the time when Dirk and Sven said they really liked our meetings, and they would be really missing this time. That our group is really a group and we did a lot of good work… and it was when I got the feeling they really appreciate our work, our collaboration that maybe we are a real team […].

Chapter 3

>**Teacher**: Was it different at the beginning?

>**Maria**: Yes. Because we didn't talk at all. We didn't talk about our feelings and our opinions. But later on I think they saw I could do something more, that they can also rely on me and that I'm able to help them. And it was a really good feeling. I was so proud of myself.

>(Lesson transcript, Poland, Jan. 25th, 2016)

While Maria is still at the beginning of her TBLT competence development, her comments show how important the learners' emotional stance is, and with that a safe learning atmosphere and trust-building activities in group formation to allow all partners to contribute and develop their TBLT competences; something which Dirk and Sven certainly learned from this exchange.

5. Conclusion

This paper tried to show that by pursuing a mixed method approach with a strong focus on triangulating qualitative, i.e. introspective data, we can succeed in better understanding our student teachers' trajectories when developing task-based competences in OIEs. Using tasks as the possible exploitable pedagogic activities allows us to generate these data without intervening too much into classroom interaction, gaining important insights into student teachers' competence development in terms of pedagogic task design as well as process competences.

References

Allwright, D., & Hanks, J. (2009). *The developing language learner*. Houndmills: Palgrave Macmillan. https://doi.org/10.1057/9780230233690

Chapelle, C. A. (2001). *Computer applications in second language acquisition*. Cambridge: Cambridge University Press. https://doi.org/10.1017/CBO9781139524681

Devlieger, M., & Goossens, G. (2007). An assessment tool for the evaluation of teacher practice in powerful task-based language learning environments. In K. van den Branden, K. van Gorp & M. Verhelst (Eds), (2007), *Tasks in action. Task-based language education from a classroom-based perspective* (pp. 92-130). Cambridge: Cambridge Scholars Publishing.

Furstenberg, G. (1997). Teaching with technology: what is at stake? *ADFL Bulletin, 28*(3), 21-25. https://doi.org/10.1632/adfl.28.3.21

Gonzalez-Lloret, M., & Ortega, L. (2014). *Technology-mediated TBLT: researching technology and tasks*. Amsterdam/Philadelphia: John Benjamins. https://doi.org/10.1075/tblt.6

Hampel, R. (2010). Task design for a virtual learning environment in a distant language course. In M. Thomas & H. Reinders (Eds), *Task-based language learning and teaching with technology* (pp. 131-153). London: Continuum Publishing.

Levy, M., & Stockwell, G. (2006). *CALL dimensions: options and issues in computer-assisted language learning*. New Jersey: Lawrence Erlbaum & Associates.

Müller-Hartmann, A., & Schocker-von Ditfurth, M. (2011). *Teaching English: task-supported language learning*. Paderborn: Schöningh.

O'Dowd, R. (2005). The competences of the telecollaborative teacher. *The Language Learning Journal, 43*(2), 194-207. https://doi.org/10.1080/09571736.2013.853374

Samuda, V., & Bygate, M. (2008). *Tasks in second language learning*. New York: Palgrave Macmillan. https://doi.org/10.1057/9780230596429

Stickler, U., & Hampel, R. (2015). Qualitative research in CALL. *Calico Journal, 32*(2), 380-395. https://doi.org/10.1558/cj.v32i3.27737

4 Learner autonomy and telecollaborative language learning

David Little[1]

Instead of an abstract

When I was invited to give one of the keynote talks at the Second International Conference on Telecollaboration in Higher Education, my first thought was that I should decline. It is true that for thirty years I was responsible for Trinity College Dublin's self-access language learning facilities and resources; true also that around the turn of the millennium I shared in the empirical exploration of tandem language learning via e-mail and in text-based virtual reality. But although I remain interested in these matters, I cannot pretend to have kept abreast of developments since my retirement. On the other hand, I remain research-active thanks to my abiding obsession with learner autonomy, so my second thought was that I should accept the invitation, say something about learner autonomy as the best way of responding to two persistent problems in L2 education, and then raise some questions for telecollaborative language learning. This article summarises the main points of my talk.

1. Introduction: two persistent problems in L2 education

The more or less universal goal of L2 education is to develop learners' communicative repertoires, and by doing so extend their identity and the scope of their agency. This is what lies behind the Council of Europe's notion of plurilingualism, "a communicative competence to which all knowledge

---

1. Trinity College Dublin, Dublin, Ireland; DLITTLE@tcd.ie

How to cite this chapter: Little, D. (2016). Learner autonomy and telecollaborative language learning. In S. Jager, M. Kurek & B. O'Rourke (Eds), *New directions in telecollaborative research and practice: selected papers from the second conference on telecollaboration in higher education* (pp. 45-55). Research-publishing.net. https://doi.org/10.14705/rpnet.2016.telecollab2016.489

and experience of language contributes and in which languages interrelate and interact" (Council of Europe, 2001, p. 4). But formal language learning often fails to meet this target, for two reasons. First, the levels of proficiency achieved fall short of curriculum objectives, as the European Commission's (2012) First European Survey on Language Competences showed; and second, even learners who attain a high level of L2 proficiency, sometimes in several languages, do not think of themselves as plurilingual. This was one of the findings of the city reports compiled by the LUCIDE project (2012–2014; King & Carson, 2015). In reply to the question "Do you consider yourself to be monolingual/bilingual/plurilingual?", a Dublin interviewee, for example, described herself as "monolingual with some French and Irish" (Carson, McMonagle, & Murphy, 2015, p. 50), even though Irish is a compulsory subject from the beginning to the end of schooling in Ireland and she herself had some professional involvement with the language. A possible explanation for this kind of self-concept is provided by an Oslo interviewee's reply to the same question:

> "I regard myself in a narrow sense monolingual because Norwegian is my language. I am multilingual in the way that I speak and write also English, German, and some French, but it's all languages that I have learned in school. I'm not using all the languages every day and it's not part of my everyday life except that I now have to use English a bit more. Because the definition of being bilingual is that you use two languages every day... I'm not bilingual in that way" (Carson, McMonagle, & Skeivig, 2015, p. 75).

According to this interviewee, a sense of oneself as plurilingual depends on regular use of the languages in one's repertoire as an integral part of daily life.

Despite these educational failures, pedagogical traditions roll on unchallenged. First introduced in the 1970s, so-called communicative approaches to L2 teaching have rarely broken out of the initiation-response-feedback dynamic that shaped earlier teaching methods, and successive generations of technology have mostly been used in the service of the same dynamic. What is more, research into 'instructed SLA' tends not to challenge the pedagogical methods that generate the data it analyses and rarely (if ever) attempts to construct a learning-and-teaching dynamic from first principles.

2. Learner autonomy as the means to success in L2 learning

Against this background I make the following claim. The language learning programmes most apt to develop high levels of Target Language (TL) proficiency and integrated plurilingual repertoires are those in which, from the beginning, learners' agency is channelled through the TL; those in which, individually and collaboratively, learners use the TL to plan, execute, monitor and evaluate their own learning. Such programmes are based on the construct of learner autonomy, and the paradigm case is the classroom over which Leni Dam presided for thirty years, from the mid-1970s until her retirement in 2007. She taught English to young Danish teenagers in a middle school near Copenhagen and described her approach in a short book published in 1995; for a more detailed description of her classroom practice and an empirical exploration of its outcomes, see Little, Dam, and Legenhausen (to appear).

Before I summarise Dam's approach in its essentials, I want to illustrate the learning outcomes typical of her classroom. When one of her classes was coming to the end of its fourth year of English (Grade 8, 15 years old), Dam asked each member of the class to write a short text explaining what learning English meant to him or her. The task was immediate: learners were given a sheet of paper and a few minutes in which to collect their thoughts and produce a text. What they wrote was thus close to what they might have said if the task had been to produce an oral text. Here are the (uncorrected) texts produced by two learners, the first a boy and the second a girl:

> "Most important is probably the way we have worked. That we were expected to and given the chance to decide ourselves what to do. That

Chapter 4

we worked independently... And we have learned much more because we have worked with different things. In this way we could help each other because some of us had learned something and others had learned something else. It doesn't mean that we haven't had a teacher to help us. Because we have, and she has helped us. But the day she didn't have the time, we could manage on our own".

"I already make use of the fixed procedures from our diaries when trying to get something done at home. Then I make a list of what to do or remember the following day. That makes things much easier. I have also via English learned to start a conversation with a stranger and ask good questions. And I think that our 'together' session has helped me to become better at listening to other people and to be interested in them. I feel that I have learned to believe in myself and to be independent".

Limitations of space preclude a detailed analysis of these texts. For our present purposes it's enough to note that they both evidence a well-developed capacity to produce reflective discourse that expresses a personal view with unusual fluency. English seems to be a fully integrated part of each learner's communicative repertoire.

3. The autonomy classroom described

In Leni Dam's version of the autonomy classroom, the teacher's goal is to help her learners to become communicatively proficient in the TL. She believes that the surest way of achieving this goal is to engage them from the very beginning in spontaneous and authentic TL use – spontaneous in the sense that it arises unrehearsed from the ebb and flow of classroom activity; authentic in the sense that it focuses on and exploits the interests and aptitudes that the learners bring with them, what Barnes (1976) called their 'action knowledge'. In other words, in the autonomy classroom, students learn the TL by using it to pursue their own interests. As they do so, the capacity for autonomous behaviour that has produced much of their 'action knowledge' is harnessed to the task of L2 learning. Learners' L1 has an essential role to play in all this. It is, after all, the medium in which they first learned to interact with others, the default medium of their discursive thinking, the basis of whatever linguistic intuitions occur to them, and a central component of their identity. Although it is the teacher's aim that as soon as possible her learners should manage all aspects of their language learning in the TL, in the early stages they are likely to use their L1 for purposes of evaluation. This is due partly to the complexity of the task, and partly because it is easier for them to acquire basic skills and underlying concepts of self- and peer-assessment in their L1 before transferring them to the TL.

From the beginning, the teacher herself uses the TL as the medium of classroom communication, translating words and phrases from the learners' L1 on request and scaffolding their attempts to use the TL, in writing as well as speech. Two tools support the learning process: logbooks (the 'diaries' referred to in the second learner text quoted above) and posters (written on sheets of A3 paper and stuck on the classroom wall). Learners use their logbooks (plain notebooks) to record the content of each lesson, make a note of words and phrases they need to remember, plan homework, write short texts of various kinds, and regularly evaluate their progress. Posters, created in real time by the teacher in interaction with the class, serve a wide variety of purposes. They are used, for example, to gather ideas for homework activities; to give learners the words and phrases they need to interact with one another in the TL; to capture – always in the TL – the results of whole-class brainstorming on topics like "Why should we learn English?" or "What can we do to learn English?"; and to record negotiated rules for general classroom conduct or managing group work. For their first homework, learners are required to write a short text 'About myself'. The teacher uses posters to give them a simple template for the task and to translate from their L1 to the TL the words and phrases they need to describe themselves (this activity typically yields words that never occur in textbooks for beginners). In due course the learners themselves use posters to plan group projects.

Learning activities fall into two broad categories, learner-created learning materials and learner-generated texts. Learning materials typically take the form of games –

word cards, picture dominoes, picture lotto, board games. Learner-generated texts begin with 'About myself', move on to 'Picture + text' (learners choose a picture from a magazine, stick it in their logbook, and write a descriptive or narrative text about it), and then to plays, poems, stories, magazines, etc. that are usually produced by groups of learners over several weeks (for examples, see Dam, 1995 and Little, Dam, & Legenhausen, to appear). Because everything happens as far as possible in the TL, the boundaries between intentional learning and creative language use are fuzzy, and traditional distinctions between the skills of listening, speaking, reading and writing are difficult to maintain. The dynamic of the classroom depends crucially on writing in order to speak and speaking in order to write. In their logbooks, their learning materials and the texts they produce, learners use writing to *construct* the TL; and their non-stop use of writing makes learning visible, encourages a focus on form, and provides a basis for reflection and evaluation. As learning progresses, learners become more proficient in performing three interacting roles. They are communicators, using and gradually developing their communicative skills in the TL; experimenters with language, gradually developing an explicit knowledge of the TL system; and intentional learners, gradually developing explicit awareness of language learning.

In what follows I use this brief description of the autonomy classroom to raise some questions for telecollaborative language learning.

4. Some questions for telecollaborative language learning

In the autonomy classroom, learners accept responsibility for their learning, set their own learning targets within the framework provided by the curriculum, choose and create their own learning materials and activities, and evaluate learning outcomes. They do these things in their TL, as committed members of the language learning community to which they belong; and because the learning-and-teaching dynamic is grounded in spontaneous and authentic TL use, autonomous language learning and autonomous language use are inseparable, two sides of the same coin.

Questions for telecollaborative practice:

- Is your telecollaborative L2 learning embedded in a larger L2 learning dynamic that shares the characteristics of the learning environment I have described? If not, why not?

- How do you ensure that your students accept overall responsibility for their learning?

- How do you expect them to keep a cumulative record of their learning?

- Within the constraints of your curriculum, how do you give them choice?

- How do you provide for evaluation and self-assessment?

Language is inescapably dialogic. It evolved out of collaborative interaction, and children acquire it thanks to an 'interactive instinct' (Lee et al., 2009; Trevarthen, 1992); it helps to shape consciousness dialogically – according to Mead (1934), consciousness entails 'becoming other to oneself' (Gillespie, 2005); it also helps to shape cognition dialogically – individual cognition is impregnated with partially shared language, norms, knowledge and conceptual systems (Linell, 2009, p. 79); and when we engage in reflective thinking, 'internal' voices are invoked and interpenetrate (Linell, 2009; cf. Bråten, 1992 and Fernyhough, 2016). The autonomy classroom deliberately exploits the dialogic nature of language in its emphasis on the interactive, interdependent nature of language, language learning, and language use.

Questions for telecollaborative practice:

- How *exactly* do you exploit the dialogic structure of telecollaboration to promote L2 learning?

- How do you make your students aware of the potential of telecollaboration to support their proficiency development?

Chapter 4

- What kinds of discourse initiative are available to your students, and how *exactly* do they take them?

- Telecollaboration exploits digital communication channels that most of your students use in their daily lives: do your telecollaborative projects take sufficient account of this?

The autonomy classroom grounds L2 learning in the learner's 'action knowledge', the complex of knowledge, skills, attitudes and aptitudes that are central to his or her identity. Our subjective identities are partly shaped by the language(s) in which we think about ourselves, present ourselves, and engage with the world; and they are dialogic in the sense that we experience them in relation to others who are similar to or different from us. As Maturana and Varela (1992) put it: "We work out our lives in a mutual linguistic coupling, not because language permits us to reveal ourselves but because we are constituted in language in a continuous becoming that we bring forth with others" (pp. 234-235).

Questions for telecollaborative practice:

- How do you configure the use of telecollaboration to ensure that your students' identity is fully engaged with the process?

- In what ways are the telecollaborative practices you require your students to engage in calculated to draw the TL into their identity?

- Can you find ways of linking telecollaboration for academic purposes with telecollaboration of a more general kind?

In the autonomy classroom, learners are continuously engaged in activities that require them to exploit the 'technology of literacy'. As a process, non-stop writing ensures a focus on linguistic form; in this sense, as Olson (1991) has pointed out, writing *is* metalinguistics. The continuous production of written text also generates learning outcomes. This use of writing is embedded in oral interaction between the teacher and the whole class, between the teacher and groups of learners, between the teacher and individual learners, and among learners working in pairs and small groups. Especially in the early stages, writing supports speaking, while spoken interaction generates written text.

Questions for telecollaborative practice:

- Does your telecollaborative practice combine oral and written communication?

- If yes, how do you use the oral channel to support the development of writing and the written channel to support oral communication?

- If no, how do you link the use of oral or written telecollaboration to students' written or oral activities in non-electronic media?

5. Conclusion

I began by pointing out that although L2 education is characterised by a serious mismatch between curriculum goals and learning outcomes, traditional teaching-and-learning dynamics survive largely unchallenged. I went on to argue that approaches based on the concept of learner autonomy:

- ground L2 learning in spontaneous and authentic TL use that is partly led by the learners;

- require learners to take responsibility for their learning and document both the learning process and its outcomes;

- frame teaching and learning in a recursive dynamic of planning, implementation and evaluation;

- use writing to support speaking and speaking to generate written text;

- and in these ways, ensure that learners' L2 proficiency is part of their developing identity and extends their capacity for agentive behaviour.

This recapitulation prompts a final question:

> Will emerging telecollaborative practice contribute to the evolution of a new learning-and-teaching dynamic that extends learners' identity and their capacity for agentive behaviour, or will it simply add some extra limbs to a pedagogical tradition that has long been sclerotic?

References

Barnes, D. (1976). *From communication to curriculum*. Harmondsworth: Penguin.

Bråten, S. (1992). The virtual other in infants' minds and social feelings. In A. H. Wold (Ed.), *The dialogical alternative: towards a theory of language and mind* (pp. 77-98). Oslo: Scandinavian University Press.

Carson, L., McMonagle, S., & Murphy, D. (2015). *Multilingualism in Dublin: LUCIDE city report*. http://www.urbanlanguages.eu/images/stories/docs/city-reports/Dublin.pdf

Carson, L., McMonagle, S., & Skeivig, A. (2015). *Multilingualism in Oslo: LUCIDE city report*. http://www.urbanlanguages.eu/images/stories/docs/city-reports/Oslo.pdf

Council of Europe. (2001). *Common European framework of reference for languages: learning, teaching, assessment*. Cambridge: Cambridge University Press.

Dam, L. (1995). *Learner autonomy 3: from theory to classroom practice*. Dublin: Authentik.

European Commission. (2012). *First European survey on language competences: final report*. Brussels: European Commission. http://ec.europa.eu/languages/policy/strategic-framework/documents/language-survey-final-report_en.pdf

Fernyhough, C. (2016). *The voices within: the history and science of how we talk to ourselves*. London: Profile.

Gillespie, A. (2005). Theorist of the social act. *Journal of the Theory of Social Behaviour, 35*(1), 19-39. https://doi.org/10.1111/j.0021-8308.2005.00262.x

King, L., & Carson, L. (Eds). (2015). *The multilingual city: vitality, conflict and change*. Bristol: Multilingual Matters.

Lee, N., Mikesell, L., Joaquin, A. D. L., Mates, A. W., & Schumann, J. H. (2009). *The interactional instinct: the evolution and acquisition of language*. Oxford: Oxford University Press. https://doi.org/10.1093/acprof:oso/9780195384246.001.0001

Linell, P. (2009). *Rethinking language, mind and world dialogically*. Charlotte, NC: Information Age Publishing.

Little, D., Dam, L., & Legenhausen, L. (to appear). *Language learner autonomy: a guide for teachers, teacher educators and researchers*. Bristol: Multilingual Matters.

Maturana, H. R., & Varela, F. J. (1992). *The tree of knowledge: the biological roots of human understanding*. Boston & London: Shambhala.

Mead, G. H. (1934). *Mind, self & society*. Chicago: Chicago University Press.

Olson, D. R. (1991). Literacy as metalinguistic activity. In D. R. Olson & N. Torrance (Eds), *Literacy and orality* (pp. 251-270). Cambridge: Cambridge University Press.

Trevarthen, C. (1992). An infant's motive for speaking and thinking in the culture. In A. H. Wold (Ed.), *The dialogical alternative: towards a theory of language and mind* (pp. 99-137). Oslo: Scandinavian University Press.

Section 2.
Telecollaboration in support of culture and language-oriented education

5. Developing intercultural communicative competence across the Americas

Diane Ceo-DiFrancesco[1], Oscar Mora[2], and Andrea Serna Collazos[3]

Abstract

Foreign language telecollaboration offers innovations to enhance language instruction. Previous research has cited its use to develop linguistic skills and intercultural competence (Belz, 2003; Blake, 2013; Chun, 2015; O'Dowd, 2000; Schenker, 2014). This article reports preliminary outcomes of a pedagogical project which leveraged telecollaborative practices in both English and Spanish as a foreign language in order to document the processes of Intercultural Communicative Competence (ICC) development.

Keywords: videoconferencing, oral proficiency, language development, intercultural communicative competence.

1. Introduction

The notion that a cultural and linguistic synchronous exchange can enhance language learning is gaining ground in higher education in the Americas, where

---

1. Xavier University, Cincinnati, Ohio, United States; ceo-difr@xavier.edu

2. Pontificia Universidad Javeriana Cali, Cali, Colombia; oscmoras@javerianacali.edu.co

3. Pontificia Universidad Javeriana Cali, Cali, Colombia; asernac@javerianacali.edu.co

How to cite this chapter: Ceo-DiFrancesco, D., Mora, O., & Serna Collazos, A. (2016). Developing intercultural communicative competence across the Americas. In S. Jager, M. Kurek & B. O'Rourke (Eds), *New directions in telecollaborative research and practice: selected papers from the second conference on telecollaboration in higher education* (pp. 59-67). Research-publishing.net. https://doi.org/10.14705/rpnet.2016.telecollab2016.490

the objective of producing interculturally competent citizens is a necessity. As educators search for ways to provide transformative learning experiences for all students regardless of socioeconomic background, interest in telecollaboration has increased.

The integration of telecollaboration as a pedagogical tool in language teaching expands the treatment of cultures, which, according to Byram (1997), was previously nonexistent or limited to isolated facts and homogenous descriptions. While Lange (2003) found that teachers are often ill-prepared to teach cultures, telecollaboration addresses these limitations. Furthermore, telecollaboration is increasingly theorized to improve language proficiency, cultural knowledge and intercultural awareness (Chun, 2015).

Multiple researchers have defined intercultural competence and ICC (e.g. Bennet, 1997; Byram, 1997; Deardorff, 2006; Sanhueza Henríquez, Paukner Nogués, San Martín, & Friz Carrillo, 2012), with the distinction pertaining to the use of language to build relationships. As telecollaboration practices grow, it is critical to understand how this pedagogical tool contributes to development of ICC.

This article reports preliminary outcomes of a pedagogical project leveraging telecollaborative practices in both English and Spanish, documenting developmental processes of intercultural sensitivity and ICC. The overarching research questions are:

- What is the effect of telecollaboration on students' linguistic development?

- How does student engagement in telecollaboration affect the development of ICC and intercultural sensitivity?

This report focuses on a preliminary set of data, part of a larger study using multiple tools to assess ICC and intercultural sensitivity.

2. Methods

2.1. Context

Instructors of English in Colombia and Spanish in the United States developed a joint program to integrate telecollaboration into course design. The faculty engaged students in synchronous, one to one video conferencing and asynchronous discussion board interactions between September and November 2015. The curricular program focused on the telecollaborative cultural exchange embedded into the course.

2.2. Participants

The participants (N= 38; 25 females, 13 males) were enrolled in an English IV course in Colombia and an Intermediate Spanish I course in the United States. The age range of participants was 18 to 24. Given the nature of self-selection in course matriculation, participants were not assigned at random.

2.3. Structure of telecollaborative sessions

A five step pedagogical design was created, based on the description of ICC development proposed by Liddicoat and Scarino (2013), which highlights noticing, comparing, reflecting and interacting. First, students prepared for telecollaborative sessions with a pre-task assignment, examining their own cultures. The pre-task findings were shared in class. The interactive telecollaborative task was then recorded. Following the session, students posted a reflection to a discussion board. The final step was a class discussion.

2.4. Data collection

Data were collected from surveys, pre and post interviews in the target language, recorded telecollaborative sessions, reflective discussion board posts and self-reflective post surveys. The reflection data from the online forum and recorded

Chapter 5

telecollaborative sessions have not yet been analyzed and do not appear as part of this article.

2.4.1. Pre and post surveys

Two surveys, adapted from Vila (2004), were administered at the commencement of the course of study and at the end of the treatment to measure intercultural sensitivity and ICC. The Scale of Intercultural Sensitivity (SIS) consists of 22 items measuring the affective aspects of ICC and includes five dimensions: engagement in intercultural communication, respect for different cultures, confidence in intercultural communication, enjoyment of intercultural interactions, and attention during intercultural communication. The Test of ICC consists of 18 situations, of which nine measure cognitive competencies and nine behavioral competencies of ICC. The objectives of the test are to evaluate abilities to interpret aspects of verbal and nonverbal communication and levels of flexibility in multicultural contexts. Adaptations to both tools proved necessary to address age and cultural context.

2.4.2. Pre and post target language interview

Structured oral interviews were administered to assess linguistic levels at the commencement of the course and following the treatment. Participants were interviewed by the native speaking professor of their language of study. The interview included elicitations and responses pertaining to self descriptions, justifications of major area of study, comparisons and contrasts between student and best friend, descriptions of family gatherings and opinions regarding national celebrations. All interviews were recorded.

2.5. Data analysis

Qualitative analyses were applied to the test and survey ICC data. The researchers looked at average responses across all participants for the three categories of questions established previously by Vila (2004): non-verbal skills, verbal skills and cultural components. The analyses were performed separately for the two groups in order to qualitatively compare mean responses for each category. Pre and post target language interviews were analyzed according to the illustrative scales in the Common European Framework of Reference for languages (Council of Europe, 2001), specifically global description, self-assessment grid, qualitative aspects of spoken language use, overall listening comprehension, overall spoken interaction, understanding a native speaker interlocutor and conversation. A global assessment was determined and a level assigned for each participant prior to and following the treatment. The interviews were analyzed by the native speaking professor of their language of study.

3. Preliminary results

3.1. Structured oral interview results

Both groups demonstrated changes in oral proficiency development between pre and post treatment. Of the 13 students who completed both pre and post interviews in English, only one remained in level A1 at the end of the study. The remainder of students advanced to a higher level. In Spanish, post evaluation results revealed that only three subjects remained at the A1 level following the treatment (see Figure 1).

Figure 1. Pre and post interview USA and Colombian students

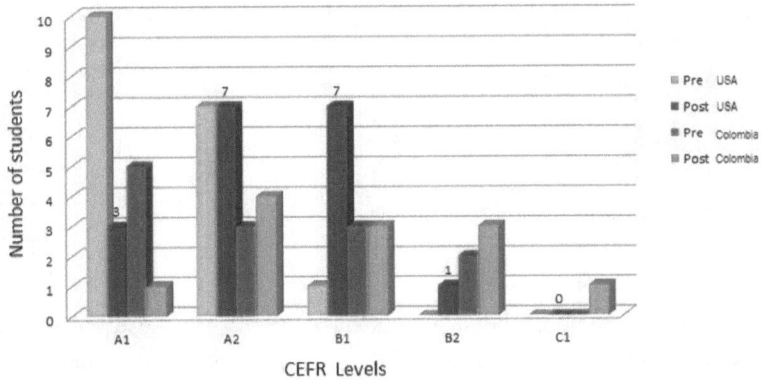

3.2. Survey of intercultural sensitivity and ICC results

A comparison of survey results suggest slight gains overall for both groups and potential growth in the attitudinal, cognitive and behavioral components of ICC. With regards to the affective aspects of ICC, specifically, student disposition to interact with those of other cultures, students showed potential gains in nearly all five dimensions of the SIS. Both groups showed positive growth in two dimensions: implications for interaction with others and level of enjoyment of interaction with others. The United States students scored higher post compared to pre assessment regarding confidence and attention during interactions. Only the Colombia group showed increased scores pertaining to respect for different cultures (see Figure 2).

Figure 2. Intercultural communicative competence

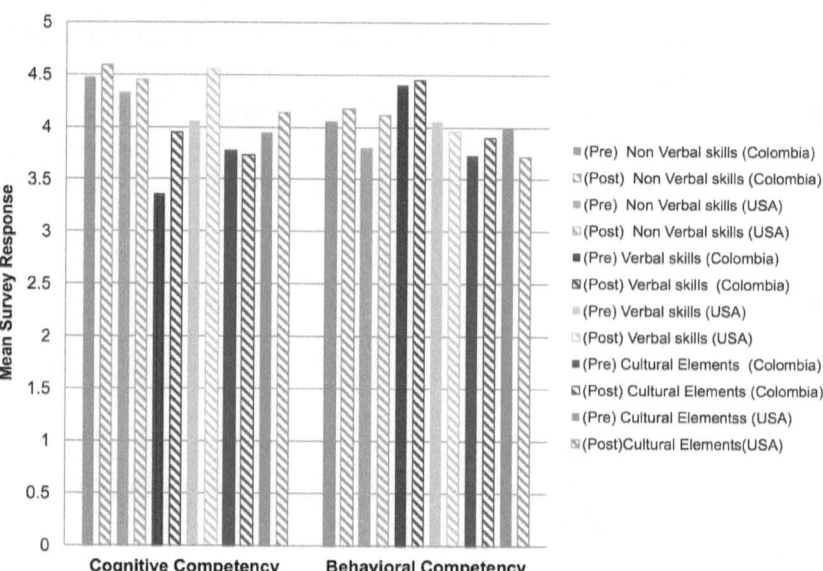

According to pre and post score comparisons of the SIS and the test of ICC, each group showed a tendency toward increased tolerance of other cultures, both in average scores on test items and in average overall test scores.

4. Discussion

Although we report gains in linguistic proficiency, this preliminary report is a limited subset of all data from this project. Data reported here does not include a comparison group, and consequently the gains in linguistic competencies cannot be attributed solely to telecollaboration. However, additional data sources mentioned may provide insights, allowing for a breakdown of components of telecollaboration that led to the gains.

The five step process of the telecollaborative sessions overlapped with classroom activities. Due to this design, telecollaboration was an integral part of the curriculum. Chun (2015) notes that as telecollaboration becomes more crucial to program protocol, the development of ICC cannot be separated from the classroom-based activities that support it.

Group comparisons present some noteworthy tendencies. The U.S. students grew in confidence and attention to others. This may suggest that telecollaboration offers students a means of increasing their confidence level in interactions, specifically ones that cause anxiety in situations beyond their comfort zones. U.S. students made progress in active listening skills necessary for interacting in global settings. Interestingly, Colombian students made gains in the area of respect for others different than themselves. Awareness of others, exploration of difference, respect for peers and reduced anxiety during interactions with peers from foreign lands are reasons that telecollaboration is a useful tool in foreign language higher education.

Despite shortcomings of this report, the data sheds light on the fact that important components of telecollaboration leading to ICC development could be culture specific. Future studies may permit researchers to tease out dimensions of the telecollaborative process that depend on cultural environments. In our case, this preliminary data suggests that ICC growth is possible in an exolingual environment which integrates telecollaboration into course design. Further work is needed in order to document how the cultural settings influence development of ICC.

5. Conclusion

Telecollaboration offers the potential to develop ICC and is particularly useful for populations in which linguistic and cultural interactions outside of the classroom do not readily exist. In this context, telecollaboration becomes a viable if not a necessary strategy to develop ICC. The five step process created for this study serves as a model of practice. Finally, growth differences in ICC development suggest that cultural environments may influence aspects of telecollaboration.

References

Belz, J. A. (2003). Linguistic perspectives on the development of intercultural competence in telecollaboration. *Language Learning and Technology, 7*(2), 68-117.

Bennet, M. J. (1997). How not to be a fluent fool: understanding the cultural dimensions of language. In A. E. Fantini & J. C. Richards (Eds), *New ways in teaching culture. New ways in TESOL series II: Innovative classroom techniques* (pp. 16-21). Alexandria, VA: TESOL.

Blake, R. (2013). *Brave new digital classroom: technology and foreign language learning* (2nd ed.). Washington, D. C.: Georgetown University Press.

Byram, M. (1997). *Teaching and assessing intercultural communicative competence.* Clevedon, UK: Multilingual Matters.

Chun, D. M. (2015). Language and cultural learning in higher education via telecollaboration. *Pedagogies: An International Journal, 10*(1), 5-21. http://dx.doi.org/10.1080/1554480X.2014.999775

Council of Europe. (2001). *Common European framework of reference for languages: learning, teaching, assessment.* Cambridge: Cambridge University Press.

Deardorff, D. K. (2006). Identification and assessment of intercultural competence as a student outcome of internationalization. *Journal of Studies of International Education, 10*(3), 241-266. http://dx.doi.org/10.1177/1028315306287002

Lange, D. L. (2003). Future directions for culture teaching and learning: implications of the new culture standards and theoretical frameworks for curriculum, assessment, instruction and research. In D. L. Lange & R. M. Paige (Eds), *Culture as the core: perspectives on culture in second language learning* (pp. 337-354). Charlotte, NC: Information Age Publishing.

Liddicoat, A. J., & Scarino, A. (2013). *Intercultural language teaching and learning*. Malden, MA: Wiley-Blackwell. http://dx.doi.org/10.1002/9781118482070

O'Dowd, R. (2000). Intercultural learning via videoconferencing: a pilot exchange project. *ReCALL, 12*(1), 49-61. http://dx.doi.org/10.1017/S0958344000000616

Sanhueza Henríquez, S., Paukner Nogués, F., San Martín, V., & Friz Carrillo, M. (2012). Dimensiones de la Competencia Comunicativa Intercultural (CCI) y sus implicaciones para la práctica educativa. *Folios. Segunda época, 36*, 131-151.

Schenker, T. (2014). The effects of a virtual exchange on students' interest in learning about culture. *Foreign Language Annals, 46*(2) 491-507.

Vila, R. (2004). *La comunicación intercultural en educación secundaria obligatoria: test de competencia comunicativa intercultural*. Granada: Investigación Y Sociedad.

6 CHILCAN: a Chilean-Canadian intercultural telecollaborative language exchange

Constanza Rojas-Primus[1]

Abstract

This paper discusses a telecollaborative project between my students of Spanish at Kwantlen Polytechnic University (KPU), Canada and students of English from University of Concepción, Chile in fall 2015. The telecollaborative project was aligned with the intercultural objectives already in place under my current intercultural Spanish language curriculum at KPU. The main purpose was to better understand the relationship of intercultural language teaching and learning and the role telecollaborative language exchanges play in developing students' intercultural competences at my university. Based on discourse analysis of students' reflections, presentations, and in-class discussions, this paper presents my findings.

Keywords: telecollaboration, intercultural language curriculum, intercultural competence, higher education.

1. Introduction

In the context of foreign language education, "telecollaboration […] refers to the application of online communication tools to bring together classes of language learners in geographically distant locations to develop their foreign language skills and intercultural competence through collaborative work" (O'Dowd, 2015, p. 194). Currently, I am working on an inquiry-based research

---

1. Kwantlen Polytechnic University, Surrey-BC, Canada; constanza.rojas-primus@kpu.ca

How to cite this chapter: Rojas-Primus, C. (2016). CHILCAN: a Chilean-Canadian intercultural telecollaborative language exchange. In S. Jager, M. Kurek & B. O'Rourke (Eds), *New directions in telecollaborative research and practice: selected papers from the second conference on telecollaboration in higher education* (pp. 69-75). Research-publishing.net. https://doi.org/10.14705/rpnet.2016.telecollab2016.491

project whose purpose is to test and inform an intercultural Spanish language curriculum in my classes at KPU to facilitate the development of students' Intercultural Communicative Competences (ICC). ICC is the ability to communicate effectively and appropriately with people of other cultures, and it has been increasingly recognised as a priority in effectively engaging diversity in higher education (Byram, 2010; Ghorbani Shemshadsara, 2012). While there is still a need for a deeper understanding of principles and applications on how to effectively teach ICC in the language classroom, research shows that telecollaboration has come to be seen as an important pillar of the intercultural turn in foreign language education (O'Dowd, 2011). My current research supports the vision that "new technologies have significantly contributed to the ways in which language can be taught as culturally contexted practice [… as] they have made other languages and cultures immediately present to language teachers and learners than they have ever been before" (Liddicoat & Scarino, 2013, p. 107). Hence, a telecollaborative language exchange project was conducted in the fall of 2015 between my students of second-semester Spanish at KPU and students of intermediate English from University of Concepción, Chile. The project was entitled CHILCAN: a Chilean-Canadian intercultural telecollaborative language exchange, and aligned with the intercultural objectives of my current intercultural Spanish language curriculum to better understand the relationship and the role telecollaborative language exchanges play in developing students' intercultural competences at KPU.

2. The CHILCAN project: a case study

In fall 2015 the CHILCAN project took place between my students of second-semestre Spanish at KPU and students of intermediate English from University of Concepción, Chile[2]. My colleague at University of Concepción, Prof. Alejandra Deij, and I worked collaboratively to coordinate and supervise the language exchanges among our students via Skype throughout the semester. However, we both assigned and aligned students' telecollaborative tasks to our

---

2. Second semestre students of Spanish at KPU navigate between A1-A2 CEFR level groups and between novice low-mid ACTFL proficiency groups.

respective curricula learning objectives. The CHILCAN tasks for my students were the following:

- 3 bilingual Spanish-English exchanges of 30 minutes per language;

- engage in 30-minute practice of Spanish during each exchange around the themes of conversation studied in class (*the city and the university, sports and spare-time activities, shopping and the cost of living, food and celebrations*);

- take notes (on *language, culture, ask/give feedback*) during each exchange;

- after each exchange, write a structured reflection (on *information learned, feelings, observations, self-awareness, future goals*) in Spanish, in English, or both;

- engage in in-class structured collaborative reflections about evidence of learning from the CHILCAN project;

- present a personal project about the CHILCAN experience (*visual format and presentation in Spanish*).

My students' tasks were aligned with the following intercultural learning objective already in place under my current Spanish language curriculum at KPU:

- intercultural knowledge (*politeness, time, collectivism*);

- intercultural attitude (*curiosity, discovery, openness, willingness, understanding*);

- intercultural skills (*awareness, relating, noticing, comparing, communicating*);

- intercultural behaviours (*adaptability, flexibility, exploration, appropriateness, empathy*).

3. Methodology and analysis

My research question was *what role does telecollaboration play in developing students' intercultural competences in my intercultural Spanish language curriculum at KPU?* To analyse this relationship, I did a discourse analysis of students' reflections, presentation, and in-class discussion. The following is a selection of the analysis:

Students' reflections:

> "Me siento logrado porque entendí más palabras de la conversación (en español) que la primera conversación [I felt accomplished because I understood more words in Spanish than the first conversation][3]. I still had some trouble but I think it's fair to say that I tried to listen past all the Skype glitches".

This reflection is an indicator of openness and willingness (intercultural attitudes) as demonstrated by the student's ability to regard positively and a degree of resilience, despite the difficulties arisen from the language exchange. The student's use of Spanish is also an indicator of exploration in the target language (intercultural behaviour).

> "I like that [my friend][4] says choclo and not maíz, and she told me that she did not have access to cooking classes which is why she learned to cook from her mother. In contrast, I learned to cook both at home and in cooking classes in school, and many people here do the same, if they learn to cook at all".

---

3. The translations in brackets throughout this paper are mine.

4. To protect the identity of students in Chile I have replaced their names by the entry [my friend].

Comfort with diversity is a critical aspect of intercultural development. The student's liking of lexical difference in this reflection is an indication of this comfort, which speaks of the student's degree and level of global understanding (intercultural attitude). Moreover, the choice of words on the student's comparison (intercultural skill), that is "... *did not have access to ...*" and "*many people here ...*" evokes the student's ability to compare with empathy and suspend judgment (intercultural behaviour).

Students' in-class discussion:

> "Ella deja que la conversación termine naturalmente y no es estricta con el tiempo. Mayoría de las veces, nuestra sesión de Skype duran más que una hora. Yo vi que tan importante las relaciones son para los chilenos [She lets the conversation end naturally and is not strict with time. Most of the time our Skype sessions last more than an hour. I realised how important relationships are for Chileans]".

As above, the choice of communicating solely in Spanish is a sign of both intercultural skill and intercultural attitude in respect to the use of the target language. In addition, this opinion shows the student's ability and interest to reflect on the intercultural knowledge learned in class (values and norms about both the concept of time and of human relationship).

Students' presentation:

> "Aprendí que es muy importante practicar un idioma. [My friend] habla puedes aprender un idioma más, si miras las películas en un idioma que quieres aprender, dijo [I learned how important it is to practice a language. My friend told me that we can learn more by watching movies in the language we want to learn]".

This student's presentation is a reflection of appreciation (intercultural attitude) and recognition (intercultural skill) of using a language in meaningful contexts.

This is an important insight because awareness of actions or practical approaches is a vital element for developing and sustaining intercultural growth.

4. Discussion

ICC development is an on-going, lengthy, and often lifelong process (Fantini, 2000) and people, as individuals with uniquely complex experiences of cultural differences, may be in different ICC developmental stages[5]. Research shows that for intercultural learning to occur effectively, students need to have opportunities to reflect consciously on the intercultural knowledge acquired, on their own intercultural skills, and receive feedback on those skills and reflections (Moeller & Nugent, 2014). Hence, my analysis should be understood within the context of the case study under discussion where the intercultural learning that took place through CHILCAN comes within the supporting environment of my intercultural Spanish curriculum. As a result, my evidence suggests that telecollaboration plays the following role in the development of ICC:

- it facilitates experiential learning where the formal intercultural learning of the language classroom is integrated with the natural setting of the online intercultural language exchange;

- it enables transformative learning where students' own beliefs, attitudes, and behaviours surface at a more conscious level as a result of what is happening through the online intercultural experience;

- it is an anchor for participatory learning as the online intercultural experience becomes a situated environment where intercultural learning takes place in collaboration rather than alone, increasing students' ethnorelative views.

---

5. For a discussion on ICC models see Bennett (1993).

5. Conclusion

This CHILCAN case study shows evidence of a relationship between telecollaborative language exchanges and the development of ICC within my intercultural Spanish language curriculum at KPU. Findings of this relationship are (1) students' exploration of intercultural knowledge, (2) student's reflections of personal intercultural skills and behaviours, and (3) student's increase of cultural awareness.

References

Bennett, M. (1993). Towards ethnorelativism: a developmental model of intercultural sensitivity. In M. Paige (Ed.), *Education for the intercultural experience*. Yarmouth, ME: Intercultural Press.

Byram, M. (2010). Linguistic and cultural education for building and citizenship. *The Modern Language Journal, 94*(2), 317-320. http://dx.doi.org/10.1111/j.1540-4781.2010.01024.x

Fantini, A. E. (2000). A central concern: developing intercultural competence. *About Our Institution,* 25-42.

Ghorbani Shemshadsara, Z. (2012). Developing cultural awareness in foreign language teaching. *English Language Teaching, 5*(3), 95-99. http://dx.doi.org/10.5539/elt.v5n3p95

Liddicoat, A. J., & Scarino, A. (2013). *Intercultural language teaching and learning*. Blackwell Publishing. http://dx.doi.org/10.1002/9781118482070

Moeller, A., & Nugent, K. (2014). Building intercultural competence in the classroom. *Faculty Publications: Department of Teaching, Learning and Teacher Education*. Paper 161. http://digitalcommons.unl.edu/teachlearnfacpub/161

O'Dowd, R. (2011). Online foreign language interaction: moving from the periphery to the core of foreign language education? *Language Teaching: Surveys and Studies, 44*(3), 368-380. http://dx.doi.org/10.1017/S0261444810000194

O'Dowd, R. (2015). The competences of the telecollaborative teacher. *Language Learning Journal, 43*(2), 194-207. http://dx.doi.org/10.1080/09571736.2013.853374

7 Multifaceted dimensions of telecollaboration through English as a Lingua Franca (ELF): Paris-Valladolid intercultural telecollaboration project

Paloma Castro[1] and Martine Derivry-Plard[2]

Abstract

Intercultural telecollaboration allows for a radical change in language education. New technologies enable learners of different languages and cultures to practice their intercultural skills. Teachers no longer need to design 'fake' role-plays to develop interaction in the target language. Above all, teachers have the possibility to address the cultural and intercultural dimensions of language education. This paper presents the multifaceted dimensions of a telecollaboration project in English as a Lingua Franca (ELF) with university students in science from UPMC, Sorbonne-Universities, Paris and university students in education from University of Valladolid, opening further questions on the exploration of intercultural telecollaboration in higher education.

Keywords: intercultural telecollaboration, higher education, intercultural education.

1. Introduction

Intercultural telecollaboration allows for a radical change in language education as, for once, the intercultural dimension can be seriously taken into account.

---

1. University of Valladolid, Valladolid, Spain; pcastro@dlyl.uva.es

2. University of Bordeaux, Bordeaux, France; martine.derivry@u-bordeaux.fr

How to cite this chapter: Castro, P., & Derivry-Plard, M. (2016). Multifaceted dimensions of telecollaboration through English as a Lingua Franca (ELF): Paris-Valladolid intercultural telecollaboration project. In S. Jager, M. Kurek & B. O'Rourke (Eds), *New directions in telecollaborative research and practice: selected papers from the second conference on telecollaboration in higher education* (pp. 77-82). Research-publishing.net. https://doi.org/10.14705/rpnet.2016.telecollab2016.492

Online telecollaboration allows learners to develop their language skills directly and authentically. Teachers have the possibility to address the cultural and intercultural dimensions of language education as they mediate 'in vivo' between learners of different languages and cultures thanks to the common platform used. Whereas the linguistic dimension of language education has always been prevailing at the expense of the cultural and intercultural dimension (Byram, 2008; Castro & Sercu, 2005; Chi & Derivry-Plard, 2010; Zarate, Levy, & Kramsch, 2011), online telecollaboration opens up pathways to develop intercultural skills, know-how and knowledge in different cultures (O'Dowd, 2007; Kramsch, 2009; Liddicoat & Scarino, 2013).

To get to know *Others,* as this is one of the leading objectives of language learning in a super-diverse world (Derivry-Plard, 2015), teachers need to tackle the cultural dimensions of language learning and take them earnestly. For instance, engaging learners in mini-anthropological or sociological tasks is a way to deal with the challenge of addressing cultural and intercultural objectives. In language learning, it adds an intercultural dimension to the basic negotiation of meaning-making (Liddicoat & Scarino, 2013) that telecollaboration potentially provides.

Furthermore, the direct link that traditionally binds language and culture – sometimes in a very essentialist approach – is cast aside using ELF with people from different L1s as the medium of negotiating meaning to get to know about cultural perspectives. Prioritising the intercultural dimension allows any language to be used as a lingua franca, and be the medium of getting information, knowledge and access to other cultural environments and people.

2. Methodology

The project was carried out in higher education from January-March 2015. The participants were 10 second-year university students in science from UPMC Sorbonne Universities and 10 third-year university students in education from Valladolid University. Students were asked to design a sociological dossier on the topic of climate change as a group task, and to write their journal of experience as an individual task. The sociological dossier was intended to provide students opportunities to do a joint research, exchange different perspectives and learn about their own culture and the culture of others, whereas the journal of experience aimed at developing awareness in learning skills, cultures and languages. By using Moodle and Google Hangouts, an intercultural learning environment was created, allowing students from both universities to interact and work together under guidance with scaffolding activities designed by the teachers to complete the tasks.

During the first Hangouts meeting, students shared their interests on particular research themes dealing with the broad topic of climate change. Students participated in dyadic interactions using ELF in order to complete the whole project. The activities were organised around the development of a mini-survey: definition of subtopic, research questions, data collection, data analysis, writing the report and powerpoint presentation. Using synchronous and asynchronous communication tools, students fulfilled the tasks required for the mini-survey, which provided opportunities for making joint decisions, solving problems and misunderstandings, and negotiating meaning. During all the process, students were asked to write in their experience journal.

3. Multifaceted dimensions of Paris-Valladolid intercultural telecollaboration

In order to analyse the multifaceted dimensions of our project, we conducted action research using data collected from the following sources: a questionnaire, the students' experience journals and the sociological dossier. Data were analysed according to the language and intercultural dimension, the learning and teaching dimension, and the theoretical and practical dimension.

For the language dimension, telecollaboration seemed to enhance students' communicative competence in the target language as they definitely developed confidence in using English: *"it is an interesting tool to communicate with non English speakers using a foreign language. It is not only good to improve the language, but also to feel comfortable speaking it, know different cultures, different ways of working*". Being engaged in communication with speakers of different L1s allowed students to identify the communicative role of language and to be aware of what they have in common, for example the same difficulties for communicating, rather than their differences: "*I notice that our level of English was different and we had to solve situations of lack of understanding using our mother tongue*". The use of ELF implied using languages as resources and being more at ease in using English with others.

For the intercultural dimension, telecollaboration seemed to enhance students' awareness of intercultural skills for successful communication: "*This experience has taught me to solve situations of misunderstandings with foreigners*". Students identified skills such as the ability to mediate conflict situations, to solve misunderstandings, to negotiate and to make agreements: "*I could mention some learning strategies that I have learnt such as patience, to be able to empathise, to adapt myself to other demands, to make agreements and negotiate with others*". Students also showed awareness of attitudes such as empathy, patience, open-mindedness and confidence in relating with others through another language.

For the learning and teaching dimension, the pedagogical process of the telecollaboration project was based on a socio-constructivist approach of learning that fully took into account the intercultural dimension of communication. In this sense, we linked the target language, the cultural background of speakers and the content of communication by adopting a social science approach to develop de-centering perspectives through viewpoints analysis.

For the theoretical and practical dimension, Paris-Valladolid telecollaboration combined theory and practice as the objective was to test practically the intercultural dimensions that telecollaboration theoretically provides. The practical process was focused on feasible objectives and relevant tasks suited to objectives that needed to be adapted throughout the telecollaborative experience. In this sense, communicative skills were monitored, intercultural skills were put into practice through working together and the social science approach was focused even though it was limited, due to time constraints. The theoretical process was thus constructed from data provided by the multifaceted dimensions of the telecollaboration (English communicative skills, relating to others from a different background, working with others with a common project and deadline, developing a social science approach to deal with better informed differences and similarities in people from different background, developing intercultural know how) in order to inform and describe practice.

4. Conclusion

The analysis of the multifaceted dimensions of Paris-Valladolid telecollaboration suggests that the integrated environment of intercultural telecollaboration allowed for being critical, learning through doing, using ELF, and developing communicative and intercultural skills. In order to be sure of these intercultural multifaceted results, we will need to follow students in further telecollaborations. So, all these *savoir être* and attitudes are potentially there to be developed and sustained, but a 24 hour project face to face in a three month period of time cannot be sufficient to assess these basic intercultural outcomes.

In the context of higher education, the results reveal that the intercultural dimension was potentially present. To evolve further we would need to integrate a coherent set of activities exploring social science approaches. It has been experienced, but for students to be aware, we need more time in a credited course to reach our high educational objectives. This will allow us to monitor more feedback on the different steps of the telecollaboration and better address the challenges of intercultural education within a super-diverse world (Derivry-Plard, 2015; Kramsch, 2009; Zarate et al., 2011).

References

Byram, M. (2008). *From foreign language education to education for intercultural citizenship. Essays and reflections*. Clevedon: Multilingual Matters.

Castro, P., & Sercu, L. (2005). Objectives of foreign language teaching and culture teaching time. In L. Sercu, with E. Bandura, P. Castro, L. Davcheva, C. Laskaridou, U. Lundgren, C. Méndez, & P. Ryan (Eds), *Foreign language teachers and intercultural competence. An international investigation* (pp. 19-38). Clevedon: Multilingual Matters.

Chi, H., & Derivry-Plard, M. (2010). Médiations culturelles à travers une expérience d'e-twinning franco-taïwanaise. *Actes du Colloque de l'ACEDLE : Les langues tout au long de la vie*, 56-73. https://halshs.archives-ouvertes.fr/hal-00832025/document

Derivry-Plard, M. (2015). *Les enseignants de langues dans la mondialisation. La guerre des représentations dans le champ linguistique de l'enseignement* (postface de C. Kramsch). Paris: Éditions des Archives Contemporaines.

Kramsch, C. (2009). *The multilingual subject*. Oxford: Oxford University Press.

Liddicoat, J. A., & Scarino, A. (2013). *Intercultural language teaching and learning*. Chichester: Wiley- Blackwell. http://dx.doi.org/10.1002/9781118482070

O'Dowd, R. (2007). *Online intercultural exchange. An introduction for foreign language teachers*. Clevedon: Multilingual Matters.

Zarate, G., Levy D., & Kramsch, C. (Eds). (2011). *Handbook of multilingualism and multiculturalism*. Paris: Éditions des Archives Contemporaines.

8. Student perspectives on intercultural learning from an online teacher education partnership

Shannon Sauro[1]

Abstract

This study reports on intercultural learning during telecollaboration from the perspective of student participants in a five-country online teacher education partnership. The student perspectives reported here were drawn from one intact class in the partnership, five students who completed this partnership as part of a sociolinguistics course in a secondary school English teacher education program in Sweden. Offline, the telecollaboration served as a discussion point for course themes and as data for a study on a sociolinguistic topic carried out by each student. Findings revealed intercultural learning occurred in three situations: as a result of in-class conflict during discussion of the telecollaboration, through analysis of interactional styles found in the online discussion posts for the sociolinguistics study, and through online discussion with peers in other countries regarding educational practices.

Keywords: teacher education, sociolinguistics, telecollaboration, intercultural learning.

---

1. Malmö University, Malmö, Sweden; shannon.sauro@mah.se

How to cite this chapter: Sauro, S. (2016). Student perspectives on intercultural learning from an online teacher education partnership. In S. Jager, M. Kurek & B. O'Rourke (Eds), *New directions in telecollaborative research and practice: selected papers from the second conference on telecollaboration in higher education* (pp. 83-88). Research-publishing.net. https://doi.org/10.14705/rpnet.2016.telecollab2016.493

Chapter 8

1. Introduction

Telecollaboration has an established history in university foreign language education extending over at least 20 years (O'Dowd, 2016). As is the case with many established language education practices, the effectiveness of telecollaboration to support language and intercultural learning has been the object of both investigation and scrutiny. A recent critique by Liddicoat and Scarino (2013) questions the degree to which the online interactions and tasks used in well-cited studies of telecollaboration truly supported intercultural learning. Specifically, they identify limitations in the online tasks which they defined as cultural tasks, "tasks that focused on factual information" and not intercultural tasks, which "involved learners moving between cultures and reflecting on their own cultural positioning" (Liddicoat & Scarino, 2013, p. 117). As a result, they argue, intercultural learning did not occur automatically out of the online engagement.

O'Dowd (2016), however, points to a growing consensus in the telecollaboration literature which does not assume that intercultural learning occurs as a direct outcome of online interaction. One example can be found in Belz's (2007) discussion of in-class or reflective activities which allow learners to explore what Agar (1994) labels rich points, or points of contact between culturally situated ways of thinking which may result in misunderstanding or tension, that occurred during or around the online interaction.

Telecollaboration is more than a tool for language learning and also represents a means of bringing together distantly located future professionals whose 21st century job demands may benefit from discussion and problem-solving with experts and peers in other contexts. Such was the motivation behind the teacher education partnership, *Innovations in Foreign Language Education*, which brought together language teacher education students in five countries (Canada, Israel, Spain, South Korea and Sweden). This partnership was organized into five modules, each tied to a technology-enhanced theme within language teaching (i.e. flipped classroom, telecollaboration, fandom tasks, social presence online, multimedia materials) and modeled upon the

Sharing Perspectives (2015) model of exchange. Each module incorporated a video lecture, related readings and questions organized and moderated by a different expert, which were viewed, read and discussed by participants in five different multicultural groups. While the emphasis of a such a partnership was not on intercultural learning, the international and multicultural nature of the groupings and the participants potentially provided opportunities for Agar's (1994) rich points to occur around the use of technology in the participants' educational contexts.

Accordingly, this study explores if and when intercultural learning occurred for members of one of the partner classes in this online teacher education partnership.

2. Methodology

The student perspectives from this partnership were drawn from the partner class in Sweden and included all five students, four men and one woman, enrolled in the course. All were in their fifth and final year of a teacher education program preparing them to become secondary school English teachers. The telecollaboration itself was embedded in a sociolinguistics course, with each online module serving as a discussion point for course themes (i.e. language socialization, language ideologies, multimodal literacy, language and ethnicity, gender identities) and as data for a study on a sociolinguistic topic that each student was required to complete (see Sauro, 2016).

Student perspectives were elicited through a semi-structured interview held at the end of the course using a romantic approach "in which the interviewer strives to develop rapport with the interviewees in an effort to generate authentic, in-depth dialog that focuses on participants' meanings" (Roulston, 2011, p. 78). This was augmented by tape analysis (Dörnyei, 2007) of audio recordings of the five one hour in-class discussions of each telecollaboration module, as well as analysis of the students' discussion board posts and the students' completed sociolinguistic studies.

3. Results and discussion

Participants identified three situations where intercultural learning occurred: conflicts that arose during in-class discussion of the telecollaboration, analysis of discussion board posts for the sociolinguistics study, and during the online interaction. Each is illustrated in a vignette below.

3.1. Conflict during in-class discussion

Students identified rich points that resulted in conflict during weekly in-class discussion of the telecollaboration. One in particular concerned a disagreement over the interpretation of an Israel-based U.S. student's post regarding the need to carefully select books of fiction for her future students that would not run afoul of parental disapproval. In class, a conflict arose between Sam, who was dismayed by what he read as unprofessional acquiescence to parental interference, and Andy, who drew upon a gap year spent in the United States to interpret the post as an ironic critique of U.S. politics. Sam, however, drew upon his extensive experience in international online chat communities like Reddit, where irony and sarcasm are indexed through emoticons or other textual markers (e.g. /s to denote sarcasm) to reject Andy's interpretation.

Although neither persuaded the other to change their stance, the disagreement led Sam to observe that "even though we're both Swedes, me and Andy think very different from each other. Culture is as much group as it is individual. You can belong to a lot of different cultures and even though you belong to the same, the others you belong to will color your views so much that it's still not translated perfectly between each other".

3.2. The sociolinguistic study

Students also pointed to analysis of the discussion board postings for their sociolinguistics studies as another site of intercultural learning. Regina, who researched addressivity differences among the members of her online discussion group found that "when we did the research on the Schoology posts [the online platform], I got very aware of how I wrote my own posts".

In particular, a topic raised in the first class meeting regarding Swedish tendency to avoid conflict was revisited in Regina's analysis. She observed how her conflict avoidance strategies in online discussion limited the type of answers she was able to elicit from her peers, and subsequently her level of engagement in the telecollaboration compared to some of her peers: "I realize that I maybe was a bit scared of conflict and I should have just asked more questions or been a bit more pushed towards having an answer".

3.3. Online interaction

Finally, participants identified the online interaction during the telecollaboration as another source of intercultural learning, specifically discussions of educational practices. For Andy, this led to an awareness that what he had previously assumed to be a uniquely Swedish crisis in education was actually a common issue: "There seems to be this shared experience of public educators working in slightly underfunded schools and wanting to do all this stuff, but there just isn't money... And for a long time, I genuinely thought that was just something Swedish".

4. Conclusion

From the perspectives of students in this online teacher education partnership, intercultural learning, in other words, movement between different cultural viewpoints and reflection upon their own culture, occurred in three different situations. The first was as a result of conflict that arose during in-class discussion of the discussion board postings. The second was as a result of analyzing their own and others' interactional strategies in the discussion posts for their sociolinguistic studies. The third was during the online interaction itself and specifically during discussion of educational practices. Taken together, these reflect O'Dowd's (2016) argument that such learning occurs not necessarily as a direct result of online discussion but rather out of scaffolded offline discussion or structured reflection activities.

References

Agar, M. (1994). *Language shock: understanding the culture of conversation*. New York: William Morrow.

Belz, J. A. (2007). The development of intercultural communicative competence in telecollaborative partnerships. In R. O'Dowd (Ed.), *Online intercultural exchange* (pp. 127-166). Clevedon, UK: Multilingual Matters.

Dörnyei, Z. (2007). *Research methods in applied linguistics*. Oxford: Oxford University Press.

Liddicoat, A. J., & Scarino, A. (2013). *Intercultural language teaching and learning*. Malden, MA: Wiley-Blackwell. http://dx.doi.org/10.1002/9781118482070

O'Dowd, R. (2016). Learning from the past and looking to the future of online intercultural exchange. In R. O'Dowd & T. Lewis (Eds.), *Online intercultural exchange: policy, pedagogy, practice* (pp. 273-293). New York: Routledge.

Roulston, K. (2011). Interview 'problems' as topics for analysis. *Applied Linguistics, 32*(1), 77-94. http://dx.doi.org/10.1093/applin/amq036

Sauro, S. (2016). *Sociolinguistics popular science piece instructions*. https://www.academia.edu/25685629/Sociolinguistics_Popular_Sicence_Piece_Instructions

Sharing Perspectives. (2015). *Sharing perspectives foundation*. http://www.sharingperspectivesfoundation.com/

9 Blogging as a tool for intercultural learning in a telecollaborative study

Se Jeong Yang[1]

Abstract

This paper is based on an analysis of blog writings from an English-Korean telecollaborative project. This research found that rich intercultural interactions occur between Korean learners and English learners. Through a discursive analysis of the blog writings in which participants compared Korean and American cultures, this paper elucidates participants' intercultural learning in a process of conversing with target language speakers online.

Keywords: blogging, intercultural learning, qualitative approach.

1. Introduction

Many telecollaborative studies have explored language learners' intercultural learning (Belz, 2003; O'Dowd, 2003), but it is rather unclear how to identify and assess it (Helm, 2009). In order to provide detailed accounts of intercultural learning, many studies have used qualitative approaches based on the analysis of participants' writing (Menard-Warwick, 2009). For example, Helm's (2009) telecollaborative study showed that diaries could be used as a valuable resource for identifying intercultural understanding. For the current study, blog writing is used to analyze participants' intercultural learning. Blogs, especially shared blogs, are acknowledged as a space for developing critical ideas based on its sharedness and openness (Bloch, 2007). While posting new entries and commenting on other

1. The Ohio State University, Columbus, Ohio; yang.1876@osu.edu

How to cite this chapter: Yang, S. (2016). Blogging as a tool for intercultural learning in a telecollaborative study. In S. Jager, M. Kurek & B. O'Rourke (Eds), *New directions in telecollaborative research and practice: selected papers from the second conference on telecollaboration in higher education* (pp. 89-95). Research-publishing.net. https://doi.org/10.14705/rpnet.2016.telecollab2016.494

posts, participants exchange, share their ideas, and can develop their cultural knowledge. The current study aims to provide a deeper qualitative description of intercultural learning in a telecollaborative project. The study addresses the following research question: what evidence of intercultural attitudes, knowledge, skills, and critical awareness (Byram, 1997) can be identified in the blog writings?

2. Methodology

The current telecollaborative study was conducted in an out-of-school context with two adult language learning groups (aged 21 to 45). Based on the participants' interests and self-rated target language proficiency, a total of eight pairs of Korean speakers learning English (who are referred to as ELL) and English speakers learning Korean (who are referred to as KLL) were formed by the researcher. For 11 weeks, the participants engaged in personal and group blog writings while exchanging their cultural and linguistic knowledge. The researcher posted a new topic every week in the group blog. The participants wrote their ideas and experiences about the topics in their personal blog in an L2, which were commented on by their partner in his/her L1. In order for participants to discuss the topics with multiple people, the participants were also invited to discuss their ideas in the group blog. The participants posted a new entry or left comments on other participants' posts in either L1 or L2. The participants' Korean writings were translated into English by the researcher. Drawing on inductive qualitative data analysis, all the data was transcribed, organized, and then coded (Miles & Huberman, 1994). In this process, Byram's (1997) Intercultural Communicative Competence (ICC) model was adopted for identification of intercultural learning.

3. Result

In this section, the analysis of five blog excerpts that illustrate Byram's (1997) ICC model will be presented. These samples are not the only evidence of intercultural understanding in participants' writings. These examples were chosen because they clearly show the five components.

3.1. Attitudes

Attitudes refer to individuals' openness and readiness to change their previous belief about their own and other cultures (Byram, 1997). When the participants had the discussion on eating dog meat in Korea, Sara (KLL) seemed to be unsettled and uncomfortable with the idea of eating dog meat at first. However, as she discussed with other participants, she revisited this issue and changed her opinion:

> "China eats monkey brains… Cambodia eats fried tarantulas… Mexico eats ant larvae… we can't call things barbaric just because we haven't tried them" (4/27/2015, group blog).

As seen in the above writing, she defended other food cultures which people may consider to be "barbaric". After considering other nations' food cultures, she seemed to accept the Korean food culture of eating dog meat.

3.2. Knowledge

Knowledge refers to information about social groups and practices (Byram, 1997). Amanda's (KLL) knowledge of Korean culture seemed to be generated from her experience in Korea and seemed later to be converted into her own knowledge through communication with other participants. In her previous communication with her partner, Amanda raised questions about Koreans' respect for elders and her partner confirmed that there is a high social expectation for Koreans. Based on this conversation, she then used a blog as a space for developing and sharing her ideas of Korean culture:

> "Americans don't really have the same mentality for elder people. In Korea I see people give up their seat for older people. It doesn't happen that often here in the States" (4/28/2015, personal blog).

This statement includes not only her observation about Korean culture but also her awareness of American culture. By posting her idea, Amanda displays her knowledge about both cultures and attempts to share with others.

3.3. Skills of interpreting and relating

Skills of interpreting and relating refer to an ability to interpret other cultures and to relate it to individual's own culture (Byram, 1997). Haeun (ELL) wrote the difference between Korean and American cultures regarding discrimination.

> "Koreans discriminate more against foreigners [compared to Americans], I think. I feel Americans are more used to having foreigners around since people from different countries immigrated to the U.S. and have lived together for a long time" (6/5/2015, personal blog, translated).

The use of "more" indicates that Haeun compared Korean culture to American culture. More importantly, her reflection of Koreans' discrimination moved beyond a superficial idea. She attempted to interpret the reasons behind Koreans' discrimination by referencing her knowledge of American history. The comparison of two cultures seemed to enrich her understanding of both cultures.

3.4. Skills of discovery and interaction

Skills of discovery and interaction refer to the ability to acquire new knowledge (Byram, 1997). In the fourth week, participants discussed the popularity of Korean pop culture and its impact on the economic and political status of Korea in the world. Many participants expressed that Hallyu (i.e. the Korean Wave[2]) is widespread and its impact is significant. David (KLL) showed his interest in Hallyu after communicating with other participants:

---

2. The Korean Wave refers to the increasing popularity of Korean popular culture around the world.

"I wonder if people do like Korean things because it is truly high quality or because people are hooked on this tidal wave effect. Perhaps one day the Hallyu wave will be gone and I wonder if it will shift to a different country" (5/9/2015, group blog).

David's statement "I wonder if it will shift..." implies that he did not just assume a value for the target culture but rather he approached it critically, indicating that his interest may turn into further exploration. *Skills of discovery and interaction*, thus, seem to originate from interest in a culture which is inspired by others' ideas and drives learners to explore.

3.5. Critical cultural awareness

Critical cultural awareness refers to an ability to evaluate an individual's own culture and the target culture (Byram, 1997). Haeun (ELL) displayed her opinion regarding Koreans' aspiration for English learning:

"I agree that [Korean people] spend a lot of money and time in English learning. In fact, I think there may not be many situations where people have to use English in their social lives except for tasks within a particular company" (5/30/2015, personal blog, translated).

Haeun, who before argued that learning English is necessary for everyone, adjusted her opinion after her partner posted her opinion about Koreans' abnormal enthusiasm for English learning. Haeun agreed with her partner's idea and her statement "there may not be many situations" indicates her awareness of the problem. Haeun seemed to develop her cultural awareness through communicating with her partner.

4. Discussion and conclusion

Based on Byram's (1997) ICC model, the current research explores intercultural learning in a telecollaborative project.

First, *attitudes* comprise not only positive or negative feelings but curiosity and willingness to change misconceptions (Byram, 1997). In this sense, *attitudes* include a more active agency, which is seen in Sara's case. She changed her attitudes regarding Koreans eating dog meat. Second, *knowledge* seems to be socially constructed in that it is based on previous experience, but it can change or evolve through interaction with others. Amanda's understanding of Korean culture about respect for the elderly was derived from her observation in Korea, but was confirmed through interaction with her partner. Third and fourth, *skills of interpreting and discovery* may be more advanced levels of intercultural learning since they seem to involve participants' active exploration of finding out the reasons or background beyond stereotypical ideas. As Haeun and David showed, they did not just accept surface level knowledge. Rather, they attempted to interpret or seek deeper understanding. Fifth, *critical cultural awareness* seems to be derived from interactions with others, which is evidenced in participants' writings. For example, many writing examples started with a phrase of reflection on another person's post as seen in Haeun's writing "I agree that..." This implies that Haeun built on another's idea. In fact, communications with different people allowed participants to construct new viewpoints which may further develop as a critical awareness.

The results of the current study corroborate the findings of previous research that in using blogs, participants can share their intercultural ideas and participants' writing samples are important evidence to show their intercultural learning (Helm, 2009).

References

Belz, J. A. (2003). Linguistic perspectives on the development of intercultural competence in telecollaboration. *Language Learning & Technology, 7*(2), 68-99.

Bloch, J. (2007). Abdullah's blogging: a generation 1.5 student enters the blogsphere. *Language Learning & Technology, 11*(2), 128-141.

Byram, M. (1997). *Teaching and assessing intercultural communicative competence*. Clevedon, UK: Multilingual Matters.

Helm, F. (2009). Language and culture in an online context: what can learner diaries tell us about intercultural competence? *Language and Intercultural Communication, 9*(2), 91-104. http://dx.doi.org/10.1080/14708470802140260

Menard-Warwick, J. (2009). Comparing protest movements in Chile and California: interculturality in an Internet chat exchange. *Language and Intercultural Communication, 9*(2), 105-119. http://dx.doi.org/10.1080/14708470802450487

Miles, M. B, & Huberman, A. M. (1994). *Qualitative data analysis* (2nd ed.). Thousand Oaks, CA: Sage.

O'Dowd, R. (2003). Understanding the "other side": intercultural learning in a Spanish English e-mail exchange. *Language Learning & Technology, 7*(2), 118-144.

10. Intergenerational telecollaboration: what risks for what rewards?

Erica Johnson[1]

Abstract

Foreign language telecollaboration pairs learners so that they may improve their language and intercultural skills. A lesser known model, intergenerational telecollaboration, uses senior citizens as native language partners instead of peers. This paper presents the results of an intergenerational videoconferencing project between learners in second-year non-specialist English classes at a French university and senior citizens in Massachusetts. Between September 2014 and June 2016, seven learners were partnered with seniors in order to practice their speaking skills. Based on the data collected over two years, this paper analyses the risks and rewards of intergenerational telecollaboration.

Keywords: intergenerational, seniors, videoconferencing, language learning.

1. Introduction

Telecollaboration links students who are either learning a common foreign language or who are learning the other's language in order to develop linguistic and intercultural competences (O'Dowd & Ritter, 2006). While most telecollaboration has focused on this peer model (Develotte, Guichon, & Vincent, 2010; Helm,

---

1. Université Lumière Lyon 2, Lyon, France; e.johnson@univ-lyon2.fr

How to cite this chapter: Johnson, E. (2016). Intergenerational telecollaboration: what risks for what rewards? In S. Jager, M. Kurek & B. O'Rourke (Eds), *New directions in telecollaborative research and practice: selected papers from the second conference on telecollaboration in higher education* (pp. 97-103). Research-publishing.net. https://doi.org/10.14705/rpnet.2016.telecollab2016.495

Chapter 10

2015; O'Dowd, 2015), a lesser-known model, intergenerational telecollaboration, uses seniors as language partners for learners (FCB Brasil, 2014).

Seniors are ideal partners because they have more time to devote to their communities (Holtgrave, Norrick, Teufel, & Gilbert, 2014). Intergenerational projects also allow students to work through any pre-existing attitudes about seniors (Jones, 2011) while providing seniors the opportunity to develop a better understanding of young people and to participate in more meaningful social interactions (Roodin, Brown, & Shedlock, 2013). Cordella et al. (2012) also found that in intergenerational language partnerships, seniors corrected learners and provided feedback.

This paper examines the risks and rewards of an intergenerational videoconferencing project between learners in non-specialist English classes at a French university and seniors in Massachusetts.

2. Methodology

Project *Dynamic Interactions between Senior Citizens and University Students through Skype* (DISCUSS), started in the fall of 2014, pairs second-year non-specialist English learners at a French university with seniors in Massachusetts for one-on-one videoconferencing exchanges via Skype (Skype, n.d.).

Data for this paper was collected between September 2014 and June 2016. During the 2014-2015 academic year, learners from one advanced (C1) English class volunteered to participate, and a total of five students over two semesters worked with a senior. Data from that year consisted of recorded video of the exchanges between learners and seniors, students' end-of-semester reflective essays, and individual end-of-project interviews with all participants.

For the 2015-2016 academic year, learners from two English classes – one upper-intermediate (B2) and one advanced (C1) – were selected based on their answers to two questionnaires: the first focused on their personal background, their computer skills and their foreign language experience, whereas the second covered learners' opinions about videoconferencing with peers and seniors. Data from that year consisted of learner responses to the two questionnaires, recorded video of the sessions between learners and seniors, and end-of-semester reflective essays written by students.

3. L2 learner attitudes and motivation

Intergenerational telecollaboration involves many risks. One central risk is motivation: do learners even want to work with seniors? To elicit their pre-project opinions, learners were asked about speaking with peers and with seniors. The results presented in Figure 1 show that almost all students agreed that speaking with either a student or a senior would be a positive experience. However, more learners strongly agreed that it would be a positive experience to speak with a student rather than with a senior, indicating a preference of working with peers. Only one learner responded that speaking with a senior would be a negative experience, explaining that he "would be disappointed" and might find it "boring".

Figure 1. Learner pre-project opinions about speaking with American peers and American seniors

It would be a positive experience to speak with ...

	B2 (23 students)		C1 level (21 students)	
	American students	American seniors	American students	American seniors
Strongly agree	12	4	14	2
Agree	10	17	7	18
Disagree	0	0	0	0
Strongly disagree	0	1	0	0
No answer	1	1	0	1

Another question related to motivation asked learners to choose between a student and a senior and to justify their choice. The responses appear in Figure 2. Most students would prefer to work with a student, reinforcing the previous conclusion that learners would prefer to work with a peer. The main justifications provided by students involved being the same age and having things in common.

Figure 2. Learner pre-project preference regarding their choice of videoconferencing partner

If you had the choice between an American student and an American senior citizen, what would you choose?

	B2 (23 students)	C1 (21 students)
Student	13	17
Senior citizen	3	3
Doesn't matter	7	1

However, a few students expressed a preference to be partnered with a senior: three B2 students and three C1 students would actually prefer to work with a senior instead of a student, and for seven B2 students and one C1 student, either possibility was acceptable. Some reasons included learning more with a senior than with a peer, the unexpected experience of working with a senior, and being able to ask seniors for life advice. The objective of this questionnaire was merely to determine learners' pre-project attitudes about videoconferencing with peers and with seniors, as the two learners in the 2015-2016 project had already been selected based on their answers to the first questionnaire.

4. Logistical issues in intergenerational videoconferencing

Having addressed the risks pertaining to learner attitudes and motivation, the remaining difficulties that emerged from this project were logistical. One such challenge is not finding seniors to participate. Partnering with a senior center to help recruit seniors has not been as successful as anticipated. The objective during the fall 2015 semester was to have six students working with seniors, but no seniors signed up. The same objective was maintained the following spring, but only two seniors registered, so the project was downsized. One B2 student who finally exchanged with a senior at the end of the spring semester lamented in his end-of-semester reflective essay that it is "too bad that the exchanges with seniors seem so complicated to set up".

Understanding language learners can be problematic, and this is an issue in intergenerational videoconferencing, especially if seniors are hard of hearing or are not accustomed to speaking with foreigners. Higher-level students were selected to mitigate this risk, but one senior citizen chose to abandon the project because she found it too challenging to understand her learner. To minimize this risk, participants should be given information sheets which provide suggestions for overcoming language difficulties.

Seniors sometimes encounter technological difficulties, which can be very discouraging. Some seniors had expressed interest but eventually gave up when they encountered technical problems. Hopefully, as videoconferencing becomes more widely used, more seniors will be familiar with the technological tools necessary to participate.

Since exchanges take place outside of class, learners must be able to record their exchanges for research, which is sometimes difficult or even impossible. For example, one student was unable to record her exchanges because her laptop had broken and she could only use her tablet. She still managed to talk with her senior, but no data from her exchanges was collected.

Seniors may also have health issues. One 92-year-old senior was not replying to her learner, and it turned out that she had been in the hospital. Her health improved, but due to the university calendar, her learner was partnered with a different senior.

5. Rewards of intergenerationalvideoconferencing

Despite these risks, intergenerational videoconferencing is very rewarding for both learners and seniors. In end-of-project interviews, all participants expressed satisfaction with their exchanges. One learner expressed how happy she was to work with a senior because it allowed her to work on "one of the skills [she lacked] the most" with a native speaker. Another learner talked about providing companionship – albeit virtual – to her senior. She also stressed that they always found topics to discuss despite their age difference. Interestingly, the fear of not having anything in common was one of the potential negative aspects expressed by learners in the questionnaire.

One senior taught two learners how to make origami peace cranes by giving them verbal instructions and using the webcam to show them how to fold the paper. The learners helped and corrected each other to accomplish the task. When the learners successfully finished their peace cranes, it was rewarding to see their expressions of joy. The senior was thrilled as well, calling it "a miracle of modern science".

After the end of the data collection for the 2014-2015 project, one learner started videoconferencing with her senior on Sundays in order to complete the *New York Times* crossword puzzle together. The learner explained that her senior would explain vocabulary that she did not understand, and when they were unable to figure out the answer together, the learner used her technology skills to search for the answer on the Internet. The learner added that she was happy to be able to teach her senior slang terms that younger people use. This interaction is specific to an intergenerational exchange, as it seems highly unlikely that an L2 learner would be able to teach slang terms to a native speaker of the same age.

6.   Conclusion

The analysis of project DISCUSS has shown that while not all language learners are interested in videoconferencing with seniors, a certain number are curious and see the potential of such a project; some would even prefer to work with a senior. Intergenerational videoconference is inherently risky though, with difficulties ranging from finding willing seniors with the necessary technology skills to language-related issues. Despite encountering difficulties, seniors and learners alike were delighted with their exchanges and found them to be beneficial, which indicates that the rewards outweigh the risks in intergenerational telecollaboration.

References

Cordella, M., Radermacher, H., Huang, H., Browning, C. J., Baumgartner, R., De Soysa, T., & Feldman, S. (2012). Intergenerational and intercultural encounters: connecting students and older people through language learning. *Journal of Intergenerational Relationships, 10*(1), 80-85. http://dx.doi.org/10.1080/15350770.2012.646536

Develotte, C., Guichon, N., & Vincent, C. (2010). The use of the webcam for teaching a foreign language in a desktop videoconferencing environment. *Recall, 22*(3), 293-312. http://dx.doi.org/10.1017/S0958344010000170

FCB Brasil. (2014, May 7). CNA - Speaking exchange [Video file]. https://www.youtube.com/watch?v=-S-5EfwpFOk

Helm, F. (2015). The practices and challenges of telecollaboration in higher education in Europe. *Language Learning & Technology, 19*(2), 197-217.

Holtgrave, P., Norrick, C., Teufel, J., & Gilbert, P. (2014). Building community and social capital by engaging capacity-building volunteers in intergenerational programs. *Journal Of Intergenerational Relationships, 12*(2), 192-196. http://dx.doi.org/10.1080/15350770.2014.899836

Jones, S. H. (2011). Life is experienced until we die: effects of service-learning on gerontology competencies and attitudes toward aging. *Advances in Social Work, 12*(1), 94-112.

O'Dowd, R. (2015). Supporting in-service language educators in learning to telecollaborate. *Language Learning & Technology, 19*(1), 64-83.

O'Dowd, R., & Ritter, M. (2006). Understanding and working with 'failed communication' in telecollaborative exchanges. *CALICO Journal, 23*(3), 623-642.

Roodin, P., Brown, L. H., & Shedlock, D. (2013). Intergenerational service-learning: a review of recent literature and directions for the future. *Gerontology and Geriatrics Education, 34*, 3-25. http://dx.doi.org/10.1080/02701960.2012.755624

Skype. (n.d.). *About Skype*. http://www.skype.com/en/about/

11 Telecollaboration, challenges and oppportunities

Emmanuel Abruquah[1], Ildiko Dosa[2], and Grażyna Duda[3]

Abstract

This article discusses some practical ideas associated with a pilot intercultural telecollaboration project. The aim of the project was to connect students from five countries: Estonia, Finland, Hungary, Poland and Spain, and to make them interact using social media, such as Facebook, Skype, Google Hangouts, etc. There were success stories connected with the project outcomes, as well as some challenges and problems, such as students' motivation and the available technology. This paper presents the project's objectives, methods and results.

Keywords: intercultural communication, telecollaboration, social media tools, motivation, active learning.

1. Introduction

Nowadays, more and more universities broaden their syllabi with intercultural education reinterpreting communicative skills into intercultural communicative skills which have become a must. Although academic syllabi of these courses may differ, they always have the learning goal of making students sensitive

---

1. Tampere University of Applied Sciences, Tampere, Finland; emmanuel.abruquah@tamk.fi

2. Budapest Business School, Budapest, Hungary; dosa.ildiko@uni-bge.hu

3. Silesian University of Technology, Gliwice, Poland; grazyna.duda@polsl.pl

How to cite this chapter: Abruquah, E., Dosa, I., & Duda, G. (2016). Telecollaboration, challenges and oppportunities. In S. Jager, M. Kurek & B. O'Rourke (Eds), *New directions in telecollaborative research and practice: selected papers from the second conference on telecollaboration in higher education* (pp. 105-111). Research-publishing.net. https://doi.org/10.14705/rpnet.2016.telecollab2016.496

to intercultural issues and cooperation. In the global working environment, employers expect fresh graduates to be able to work together with colleagues from other cultures and become global citizens. As not every student has the opportunity to study abroad, it remains an important task of universities to provide them with courses that might replace a longer period spent abroad (Jones, 2011).

2. Project objectives

The purpose of the collaboration was to establish an interaction between the students of five universities to encourage them to use the English language and to share information about their different cultures. By creating international learning communities and calling their attention to the basics of cultural differences, we aimed to have the students realize and question their own values and habits (Alred, Byram, & Fleming, 2006) by making them aware of differences to increase their European multicultural, social consciousness and mutual understanding (Dominguez, 2007). Our primary long-term goal was for the students to be able to study and work abroad, and to cooperate in multinational communities.

3. Research questions

As this was a pilot project, there were several issues whose results could not be anticipated at all. The first question was whether it is possible for five participating institutions to work together efficiently. Right from the beginning it seemed quite a challenge to coordinate the different syllabi and especially the different teaching periods. The second question was what task to design for the students to be interested in, to bring the planned results and to fit into the curricula. There were several other issues which at the beginning were seen as minor problems, such as the most preferable way of communication for the students, how detailed the instructions should be, how many tasks to give them, and how much to control the teams.

4. Project design

The participants were students of five universities: BGF-PSZK (Hungary), TAMK University, Tampere (Finland), Silesian University of Technology, Gliwice (Poland), Polytechnic University, Valencia (Spain), and Pärnu College, University of Tartu (Estonia). They studied different subject areas and attended different university courses, including media and art, economics, finance and engineering, though there was one thing in common; they were learning English as a second language.

4.1. Tasks

Task 1. The introductory task was completed by two or three students from the participating institutions. Students were asked to make a five-minute video that would describe their native cultures. Students had to select specific aspects of their lives that were significantly influenced by culture, like food, leisure time, national holidays, and traditions. The videos were uploaded to a designated YouTube channel for the students to watch and discuss.

Task 2. The task focused on teamwork and telecollaboration. All universities delegated two students to each team, compiled by the teachers. The teams were assigned different topics based on the popular concept of cultural dimensions (e.g. Hall, 1976; Hofstede, Hofstede, & Minkov, 2010). The dimensions included 'power distance', 'uncertainty avoidance', 'high context and low context', or themes mining the cultural differences found in non-verbal communication and business etiquette. The teams researched their own topics and together they prepared a questionnaire, to which they collected the answers in their home groups and from the team members. The results were presented to their course mates within a few weeks.

4.2. Organization

The participating teachers started with the creation of their own Google Drive interface for sharing various documents, including related articles, questionnaires, task descriptions, objectives, recommended schedules, suggested tests, and lesson plans.

After the first introductory task, 13 international teams were compiled with two students each from the same course. The reason behind this was on the one hand to not have too many teams, and on the other hand it appeared a good idea to have two students from one country in each international team, so that they would be able to support each other. Finland participated with a total of 56 people. Estonia generated two groups of 16 persons each. Spain had 29 participants, Poland 19, and Hungary 30. Altogether, the teams had a relatively high average headcount, i.e. 12-13 students each. The students received the team members' names, e-mail addresses and task descriptions, but the way of communication was not prescribed.

5. Challenges and results

We were faced with two kinds of challenges; technical and motivational. The first concerned common starting and ending dates that would suit all participating universities, and some technical issues regarding the use of social media tools. The second motivational challenge became evident during group activities where leadership and time management were in need. This created frustration among some students and affected their participation.

We created an evaluation questionnaire for the participants from four countries (Spain left the project): Finland (47) Hungary (27), Estonia (19) and Poland (14). A 5-point Likert Scale was used, where five was the best, and one was the weakest evaluation. In addition, the students had to answer some open-ended questions such as: 'Explain your choice', 'What did not work well?' or 'Please, propose suggestions for improving cooperation'. The questionnaires were collected by each country's tutors, and summarized into a table.

At the end of the project we invited six Hungarian and eight Finnish students to give us more information about their experiences in order to be able to refine the project. The interview answers, suggestions, and opinions were incorporated into the project results.

Figure 1. The results of the survey

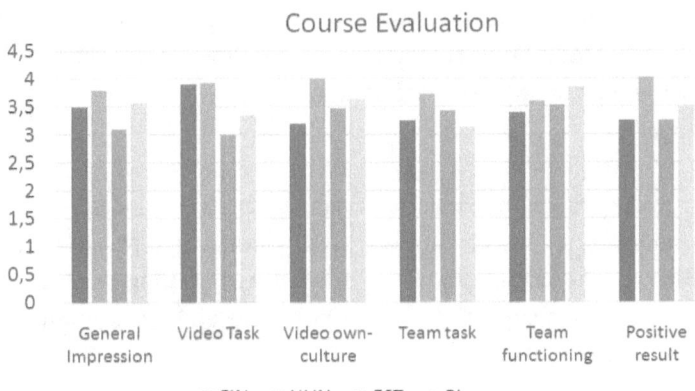

Figure 1 summarizes the opinions given by the four groups of international students. The results of the survey depict that students were satisfied with the project. On the whole Hungarian students gave the most positive feedback, Finnish, Estonian and Polish students gave lower ratings which seemed to be more realistic, as there were several critical remarks about timing, teamwork, not clear enough instructions, etc. The positive ratings of the Hungarian students could be attributed to the fact that they were either less critical or more motivated.

When asked whether the telecollaboration task ended on a positive note, the highest ratings were given by the Hungarians: 4.03. The Finnish, Estonian and Polish students' results were lower: 3.25, 3.26, and 3.5, respectively.

6. Conclusions and perspectives

In conclusion, we can say that the project was a great initiative. Despite their early objections to the additional workload, students enjoyed the program, describing it as special and unique because of the international teamwork, unconventional tasks and methods.

As suspected, it was not easy to synchronize the five countries' different courses and their original syllabi. As the Spanish participant's objectives were different, they quit after the first task without saying so, which meant a lot of frustration for the other four countries' students. It was also a huge challenge to organize groups of several students in a way in which they would be able to work together.

In answer to the original research questions, it can be concluded that, however exciting and colourful it seems to have five countries in a project, it creates a huge burden for the organizers. Even if every participating teacher is highly motivated, it is almost impossible to coordinate five different semesters, syllabi and so many students.

Harris (1999) summarizes the viewpoints on a successful telecollaboration project by mentioning requirements of the participation, deadlines, interim deadlines, and concrete instructions. In our case, the importance of those criteria was proven. It will be necessary at the launch of a next telecollaborative project to concentrate on precise planning of the aims and objectives, as well as on requirements and timing.

As regards the second research question it is worth planning the tasks in a way that they are simple, attractive and can offer a chance for discussions. The intercultural questions in the questionnaires that students had to ask and answer in Task 2 exaggeratedly fixed the direction of the relations on that special content only, which took away the spontaneity and curiosity of a free conversation. In our future telecollaborative projects, we should find a task where students need to use their own special knowledge and which needs a lot of discussion and cooperation.

Building on our current experience we would like to continue telecollaboration in the future since it is not simply a useful and enjoyable activity for students, it is also a great opportunity for the instructors to restructure their courses, and it amplifies our European identity (Dominguez, 2007).

References

Alred, G., Byram, M., & Fleming, M. (Eds). (2006). *Education for intercultural citizenship: concepts and comparisons.* Clevedon, GBR: Multilingual Matters.

Dominguez, A. M. (2007). Models of telecollaboration. In R. O'Dowd (Ed.), *Online intercultural exchange. An introduction for foreign language teachers.* Clevedon, Buffalo: Multilingual Matters. pp 85-104.

Hall, E. T. (1976). *Beyond culture.* Garden City, N.Y: Anchor Press.

Harris, J. (1999). First steps in telecollaboration. *Learning & Leading with Technology, 27*(3). http://virtual-architecture.wm.edu/Foundation/Articles/First-Steps.pdf

Hofstede, G., Hofstede, G. J., & Minkov, M. (2010). *Cultures and organizations: software of the mind* (3rd ed.). USA: McGraw-Hill.

Jones, E. (2011). *Global perspectives and the role of language. Shaping the Future.* University Council of Modern Languages (UCML).

12. Exploring telecollaboration through the lens of university students: a Spanish-Cypriot telecollaborative exchange

Anna Nicolaou[1] and Ana Sevilla-Pavón[2]

Abstract

This paper examines university students' views about a Cypriot-Spanish telecollaboration project through which participants used Google+ Communities for intercultural exchange over the course of one semester. The project was established through the UNICollaboration platform and it involved first-year students at the Cyprus University of Technology (CUT) and the University of Valencia (UV). The telecollaboration tasks and activities were embedded in the students' English for Specific Purposes modules. The project aimed at developing students' cultural awareness and competence learning, as well as at enhancing their motivation to learn English at university level. This paper outlines the pedagogical goals of the project, the design of tasks, the communication modes, the digital tools used for interaction and task completion, and the targeted competences. Using qualitative data through focus groups interviews with the students who participated in the project, the paper aims at exploring telecollaboration from the student experience perspective, demonstrating the benefits and challenges of online intercultural exchanges.

Keywords: telecollaboration, design-based research, students' views.

---

1. Cyprus University of Technology, Limassol, Cyprus; anna.nicolaou@cut.ac.cy

2. Universitat de València, Valencia, Spain; Ana.M.Sevilla@uv.es

How to cite this chapter: Nicolaou, A., & Sevilla-Pavón, A. (2016). Exploring telecollaboration through the lens of university students: a Spanish-Cypriot telecollaborative exchange. In S. Jager, M. Kurek & B. O'Rourke (Eds), *New directions in telecollaborative research and practice: selected papers from the second conference on telecollaboration in higher education* (pp. 113-119). Research-publishing.net. https://doi.org/10.14705/rpnet.2016.telecollab2016.497

Chapter 12

1. Introduction

In this era of globalization and unending technological growth, telecollaborative learning can provide a fertile background for crossing global boundaries and meeting the demands of 21st century learners as universal citizens. Telecollaboration (Guth & Helm, 2010), or Online Intercultural Exchange (OIE) (O'Dowd, 2007) is

> "[a] form of virtual mobility which is being increasingly [adopted] by university educators in Europe and elsewhere [as a substitute for physical student mobility]. Foreign language telecollaboration refers to virtual intercultural interaction and exchange projects between classes of foreign language learners in geographically distant locations" (O'Dowd, 2013, p. 47).

A total of 115 students participated in this Cypriot-Spanish telecollaboration exchange using Google+ Communities for interacting and collaborating over the course of one semester. The exchange was twofold as it included two projects: The Spain Cyprus Intercultural Telecollaboration (SCI-TEL) project which connected 27 first-year students at the UV and 32 first-year students at the CUT, and the Cyprus Spain Intercultural Telecollaboration (CSI-TEL) project which connected 31 first-year students at the CUT and 25 first-year students at the UV. The interventions designed were embedded in the participants' English for Specific Purposes modules and were benchmarked to the Common European Framework of Reference for languages (CEFR) and the related course syllabi. The two instructors agreed on a monolingual language configuration with English being used as a lingua franca. Communication modes included synchronous and asynchronous interaction in a blended learning environment. Web 2.0 tools included the use of Google+ Communities for asynchronous interaction, Google Hangouts for synchronous communication, and Google Drive for collaborative completion of tasks.

Target competences of the telecollaboration project included intercultural communicative competence, language competence and media literacy. A learner-centered, socio-constructivist, task-based approach to computer-assisted language learning and teaching was adopted. The tasks supported collaborative inquiry and the co-construction of knowledge and were designed so as to be authentic, challenging, meaningful and enjoyable while capable of enabling students to develop linguistic, intercultural, problem-solving and digital skills. The design of tasks followed O'Dowd and Ware's (2009) typology. These included interactions on the Google+ Community to discuss and complete activities about stereotypes, experiences communicating in the L2, enrollment and student life in their respective institutions, culture shock, the creation of a digital story and the delivery of an oral presentation about an innovative product or technology.

2. Methodology

This paper reports on the first cycle of an on-going Design-Based Research (DBR) study. DBR is an emerging educational paradigm situated in a real educational context where an intervention takes place. It involves continuous cycles of design, enactment, analysis, and redesign and leads to the development of practical design principles, patterns or grounded theorizing (Anderson & Shattuck, 2012; Brown, 1992; Collins, 1992). The study combined a mixed methods approach with quantitative and qualitative data collection. For the purposes of this paper, qualitative data collected from focus groups interviews with students will be presented. Focus groups interviews were conducted with students-participants in the telecollaboration exchange at both universities upon completion of the project. Questions asked were semi-structured and open-ended, specifically related to the main issues under investigation, exploring topics such as the students' experience with telecollaboration with foreign students as part of their language course at the University; the issues which had arisen and how they had dealt with them; the strategies they had used for successful communication; their overall views on language learning, collaboration, culture, online interaction and technology in education; the contributions of the project to the development of different competences; and the elements they would add to or remove from the project. Forty-six students from CUT and 46 students from the UV participated in the interviews. Topics discussed included students' attitudes and feelings, communication modes, peer feedback, time constraints, personal commitment and the affordances of the digital tools used. Data were analyzed qualitatively on NVivo.

3. Results

The telecollaboration project was well received by most students, and participants exhibited positive attitudes towards the exchange, as shown by their responses. An interesting quote articulated by a student at the CUT is:

> "Our collaboration with the Spanish students through this project was very important as we got closer to a new culture that we didn't know before. We learned about their way of life and different elements about Spain in general. We used various applications, such as Google+ and we did different tasks".

Students' feelings towards the exchange presented fluctuations as they either evolved positively or negatively, as expressed by students in the final focus groups interviews. Nevertheless, positive perceptions were more common than negative ones. Reasons reported that may have led to a positive evolution of students' feelings were participants' progressive familiarization with the concept of the telecollaboration, with their partners and the digital tools used, as well as the incremental complexity of tasks and activities which made the whole project more interesting to them. A student from the UV expresses this positive evolution of feelings during the exchange:

> "Well, I felt kind of weird at the beginning because I had to work with someone I didn't know, but then when I started to talk to her it was like really interesting because we had a lot of things in common so it was nice to meet people from other countries and know more about their culture".

Factors mentioned that may have led to a negative evolution of students' feelings were low commitment and responsiveness levels on behalf of some participants who did not appear to be adequately engaged, as well as the complexity of certain collaborative tasks which required reciprocity among partners and mutual respect of deadlines. A student from the UV mentions:

> "At the beginning it was exciting but then it was… a boring thing because they were not responding".

Similarly, a student from the CUT refers to how communication broke down in the course of the exchange and how this had an impact on the evolution of feelings:

> "It started off with great enthusiasm… that we would speak with students from a different country, but after a while, communication broke down because they wouldn't log in".

Despite the challenges of lack of mutuality and low commitment levels, the majority of participants acknowledged the value of telecollaboration as a situation whereby certain competences can be developed. Specifically, students referred to the project's linguistic and communicative gains, such as negotiating meaning, vocabulary building, the development of listening, oral, reading and writing skills, as well as other skills such as adaptability, flexibility, and responsibility. Furthermore, students valued the project from an intercultural point of view, emphasizing that the project provided them with access to different opinions and diverse viewpoints while at the same time it helped them position themselves and project their own cultural orientation onto others. Students also highly emphasized the digital competences attained through the project. Motivation levels for language learning at tertiary education appeared to have risen according to students' responses.

Focus groups interviews also provided an insight to the challenges involved in telecollaboration exchanges which may have led to a communication breakdown and failure to reach the pedagogical goals set at the onset of the project. Such challenges include issues of level mismatch, limited time for too many assigned tasks, different expectations, language level gap, and personal commitment, among others.

4. Discussion

Research studies have reported on various gains but also on the pitfalls of telecollaboration projects. This project has been perceived to be beneficial in many respects, yet at the same time it has been challenged by many participants. In this project, some partnerships maintained steady interaction and kept motivation levels and positive feelings at high levels till the closure of the exchange, yet other partnerships demonstrated low levels of commitment and mutuality which led to communication breakdown and negative feelings towards the project. One of the students' suggestions to ensure commitment was to make the participation voluntary for those who are really interested and willing to collaborate. Another suggestion was to increase the amount of synchronous in-class activities as a means to establish more personal rapport, connectivity, interactivity and responsiveness. Overall, the telecollaboration exchange was positively received as a concept, and its multiple gains were acknowledged by most participants.

5. Conclusion

Telecollaboration exchanges, if successful, may be a constructive and beneficial experience for students, but they have also been found to be a complicated process. Success or failure in telecollaboration revolves around various interrelated factors pertaining to the learners themselves, the task design, or the context in which the telecollaboration takes place. For this reason, continuous iterations of refined and redesigned interventions might prove useful in making the telecollaborative learning environment more effective and beneficial to the learners involved.

References

Anderson, T., & Shattuck, J. (2012). Design-based research. A decade of progress in education research? *Educational researcher, 41*(1), 16-25.

Brown, A. L. (1992). Design experiments: theoretical and methodological challenges in creating complex interventions in classroom settings. *The journal of the learning sciences, 2*(2), 141-178. http://dx.doi.org/10.1207/s15327809jls0202_2

Collins, A. (1992). Towards a design science in educatio. In E. Scanlon & T. O'Shea (Eds), *New directions in educational technology.* Nato ASI Series.

Guth, S., & Helm, F. (2010). *Telecollaboration 2.0: language, literacies and intercultural learning in the 21st century* (Vol. 1). Peter Lang.

O'Dowd, R. (Ed.). (2007). *Online intercultural exchange: an introduction for foreign language teachers*. Clevedon: Multilingual Matters.

O'Dowd, R. (2013). Telecollaborative networks in university higher education: overcoming barriers to integration. *The Internet and Higher Education, 18,* 47-53. http://dx.doi.org/10.1016/j.iheduc.2013.02.001

O'Dowd, R., & Ware, P. (2009). Critical issues in telecollaborative task design. *Computer Assisted Language Learning, 22*(2), 173-188. http://dx.doi.org/10.1080/09588220902778369

13 A comparison of telecollaborative classes between Japan and Asian-Pacific countries – Asian-Pacific Exchange Collaboration (APEC) project

Yoshihiko Shimizu[1], Dwayne Pack[2], Mikio Kano[3], Hiroyuki Okazaki[4], and Hiroto Yamamura[5]

Abstract

The purpose of this report is to compare the effects of 'telecollaborative classes' between students in Japan and those in Asian-Pacific countries such as Taiwan, Thailand, and the United States (Hawaii). The telecollaborative classes are part of the Asian-Pacific Exchange Collaboration (APEC) project, a 4-year project involving students in elementary school through junior and senior high school (age range, 10–18 years). All Japanese students have been studying English since the age of 10. The focus of the present research is on awareness of English learning and communication among Japanese students before and after video chat sessions. The results suggest that telecollaborative classes improve student awareness and motivation toward English learning and communication. This is the first report of the telecollaborative APEC project.

Keywords: international exchange, telecollaboration, student awareness, APEC.

1. Toyama Prefectural University, Imizu, Japan; shimizu@pu-toyama.ac.jp

2. University of California, Irvine, The United States of America; dwayne.pack@uci.edu

3. Gifu Shotoku Gakuen University, Gifu, Japan; mkano@gifu.shotoku.ac.jp

4. University of Toyama, Toyama, Japan; hokazaki@edu.u-toyama.ac.jp

5. National Institute of Technology, Toyama College, Imizu, Japan; Yamamura@nc-toyama.ac.jp

How to cite this chapter: Shimizu, Y., Pack, D., Kano, M., Okazaki, H., & Yamamura, H. (2016). A Comparison of telecollaborative classes between Japan and Asian-Pacific countries – Asian-Pacific Exchange Collaboration (APEC) project. In S. Jager, M. Kurek & B. O'Rourke (Eds), *New directions in telecollaborative research and practice: selected papers from the second conference on telecollaboration in higher education* (pp. 121-128). Research-publishing.net. https://doi.org/10.14705/rpnet.2016.telecollab2016.498

Chapter 13

1. Introduction

1.1. Background

Although the Japanese media routinely emphasizes the importance of English-speaking ability, it generally seems as though insufficient time is allocated to English learning in the classroom in Japan. Japanese teachers of English often attempt to engage in language input activities during English lessons at school, but in the current educational environment, effectively motivating students to learn English remains difficult, particularly in terms of speaking and listening. In 2011, the Ministry of Education, Culture, Sports, Science, and Technology of Japan introduced an action plan entitled 'Five Proposals and Specific Measures for Developing Proficiency in English for International Communication', with the aims of providing students with more opportunities to interact with native speakers of English and encouraging teachers to adopt 'collaborative learning' with foreigners using information and communication technology.

1.2. Previous studies

Shimizu (2005) found that previous studies on this topic reported that real-time communication with native English speakers via videoconferencing tended to take the form of lengthy group discussions, which could be difficult for Japanese students, who are often reluctant to speak out loud in front of others. Shimizu (2005) also reported that one-on-one communication activities using Skype (Microsoft Skype Division, Luxembourg City, Luxembourg), a free Voice over Internet Protocol (VoIP) application, may allow students to speak more freely and comfortably. He also found that the use of Skype led to a rapid increase in the number of words spoken. Regarding collaborative learning, Johnson, Johnson, and Holubec (2002) reported the following merits of collaborative learning: "It is obvious that pair-work or group-work are superior to individual activities when various skills or judgments are required for better achievement" (p. 8).

1.3. Objectives

As described above, collaborative learning via Skype, so-called 'telecollaboration', has tremendous potential to enhance students' positive attitudes toward English learning and communication. Therefore, the objective of this study was to compare the effects of 'telecollaborative classes' in the APEC project between students in Japan and those in Asian-Pacific countries such as Taiwan, Thailand, and the United States (Hawaii). In the schools participating in the project, English is a primary communication tool, and students are expected to be aware of the importance of English learning. Therefore, student awareness toward English learning was investigated. Telecollaboration was adopted as a strategy to increase student motivation and inspire positivity toward English learning and communication.

2. Methodology

2.1. Experiment

A total of 20 schools in Asian-Pacific countries, 10 of which are located in the cities of Imizu, Namerikawa, and Toyama in Toyama Prefecture in Japan, participated in the present study (Figure 1 below).

An elementary school, a junior high school, and a senior high school in each city in Toyama Prefecture participated in the project. Teachers at the schools in each city started a team in which they could exchange information about the schedule and the lesson plans at each school. Each city in Toyama Prefecture has a partner city, and each school has a partner school. Key teachers at each school can directly discuss with each other over the Internet what they want to do in their telecollaborative classes. Students in Japanese classrooms, where English learning starts from the fifth grade onward, number about 40. Elementary school teachers want to start Skype sessions with all students in order to make the class easier to control. All elementary students are

Chapter 13

beginners. On the other hand, junior and senior high school teachers want to provide students with one-on-one or one-on-two communication activities via Skype in order to provide more speaking opportunities in English. The primary devices for junior and senior high school students in Toyama Prefecture are 20 handheld PCs (iPod Touch; Apple Inc., California, United States), two wireless routers (UQ WiMAX; UQ Communications, Tokyo, Japan), and Skype for oral communication (Figure 2).

Schools in Toyama Prefecture can freely use these devices for their collaborative activities. By using these devices, students are able to communicate orally in regular English classes (Figure 3). The yearly telecollaborative class schedules are different for each school, but when the sessions are held, students can engage in mostly one-on-one oral communication for 40 minutes. Every school shown in Figure 1 had just started their sessions, so the main tasks for students during telecollaborative classes were activities such as self, school, and community introductions.

Figure 1. APEC project school link

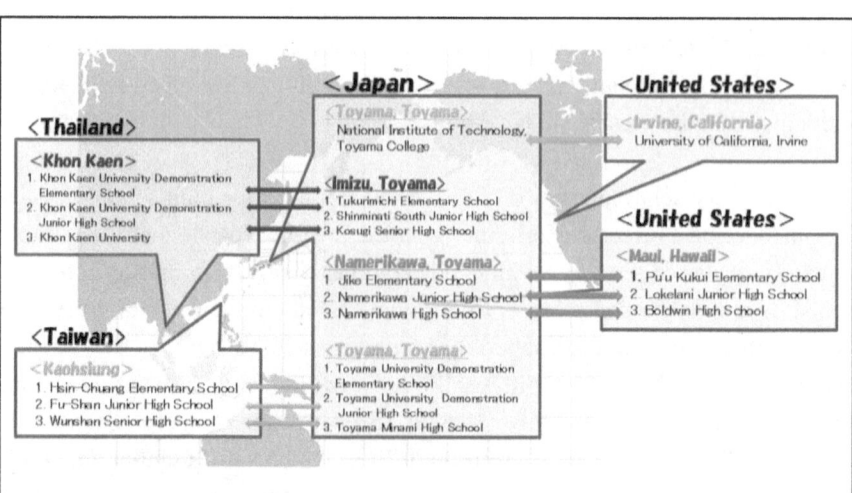

Figure 2. Devices used in telecollaborative classes

Figure 3. Telecollaborative classes

2.2. Assessment procedure

In order to assess the development of student awareness toward English learning and communication through telecollaborative classes, pre- and post-questionnaires were conducted. The pre- and post-questionnaires each have 13 questions with responses ratable on a 5-point Likert scale. All items are written in Japanese to ensure that the students can fully comprehend the meaning of each question.

3. Results

A *t*-test was conducted to analyze changes in student awareness toward English learning and communication as a result of telecollaborative classes. Results from one high school in Toyama Prefecture are shown in Table 1.

Table 1. Changes in student awareness toward English learning and communication as a result of telecollaborative classes at a high school in Toyama (N=20)

Item		Pre		Post		Difference		t	df	p		d
		M	SD	M	SD	M	SD					
37	I would like to join Skype activities more often.	4.14	2.39	7.06	2.30	2.91	2.39	7.20	34	.000	***	1.24
32	I would like to communicate with people in foreign countries via Skype.	3.97	2.35	6.94	2.45	2.97	2.58	6.80	34	.000	***	1.24
28	I would like to study abroad.	3.17	2.39	5.46	2.38	2.29	2.07	6.54	34	.000	***	0.96
33	I would like to communicate with people in foreign countries via SNS.	4.49	2.49	7.11	2.42	2.63	2.46	6.32	34	.000	***	1.07
29	People can realize the importance of studying English through conversations on Skype.	4.43	2.50	6.77	1.99	2.34	2.30	6.03	34	.000	***	1.04
36	I would like to join international exchange projects more often.	4.66	2.25	6.94	2.50	2.29	2.48	5.45	34	.000	***	0.96

34	I am highly motivated to learn English.	4.20	2.39	6.26	2.06	2.06	2.45	4.97	34	.000	***	0.92
25	Conversations with people who live in other countries are fun!	5.63	2.16	7.11	2.17	1.49	1.90	4.63	34	.000	***	0.69
30	I would like to take an English proficiency test regularly to evaluate my progress.	3.40	2.60	5.00	2.00	1.60	2.10	4.50	34	.000	***	0.69
27	People can become good English speakers after a 1-year stay in an English-speaking country.	4.83	2.13	6.09	1.96	1.26	2.06	3.61	34	.001	**	0.61
26	English will be an important communication tool in my future career.	7.06	2.03	8.14	1.31	1.09	2.08	3.09	34	.004	**	0.64
31	English conversations through Skype are fun!	5.63	2.73	7.11	2.42	1.49	3.04	2.89	34	.007	**	0.58
35	I would like to become a good English speaker.	7.11	1.94	7.91	1.84	0.80	1.89	2.50	34	.017	*	0.42

***p<0.001; **p<0.01; *p<0.05

4. Discussion

As shown in Table 1, significant improvements were observed for all 13 items on the post-questionnaire. These findings suggest that telecollaborative classes are effective in providing students with increased opportunities for interaction in English, and help them recognize the value of language learning via Skype.

5. Conclusion

The findings of this study indicate that the APEC project has produced positive early results. They also suggest that telecollaborative classes improve student awareness and motivation toward English learning and communication. The APEC project will continue until 2019. In future research, this model will be implemented into classes from elementary to high school throughout Toyama Prefecture.

6. Acknowledgments

This research was supported in part by a Grant-in-Aid for Scientific Research (No. 15K02742) from the Ministry of Education, Culture, Sports, Science, and Technology of Japan.

References

Johnson, D. W., Johnson, R. T., & Holubec, E. J. (2002). *Circle of learning: cooperation in the classroom* (5th ed.). Minneapolis, MN: Interaction Book Company.

Shimizu, Y. (2005). Study to establish an appropriate learning environment for students to converse freely for long period of time – synergistic effect of combination videoconference systems and computer software, "Net-meeting". *Japan Association for Educational Technology, 30*, 75-78.

Section 3.

Training teachers through telecollaboration

14 Incorporating cross-cultural videoconferencing to enhance Content and Language Integrated Learning (CLIL) at the tertiary level

Barbara Loranc-Paszylk[1]

Abstract

This paper attempts to provide evidence of cross-cultural videoconferencing affordances with reference to a Content and Language Integrated Learning (CLIL) context at the tertiary level. At the core of CLIL lie student-centered paradigms of teaching methodologies that invite task and project work and authentic and meaningful communication, while also providing numerous opportunities for intercultural learning. The aim of this paper is to discuss the results of collaboration that took place in spring 2015 between two cohorts, namely post-primary English as a Foreign Language (EFL) teacher trainees at two universities: the University of Bielsko-Biala in Poland and the University of León in Spain. The main objective of the task was to develop lesson plans and EFL teaching materials that included Polish and Spanish cultural content, respectively, and in addition, to provide feedback on the work sent by the partner university team during videoconferencing sessions. The results of the project illustrated in the self-reported data suggest that within the CLIL methodological framework it was the cultural and cognitive dimension that appeared to benefit most from incorporating the cross-cultural videoconferencing into the course.

Keywords: telecollaboration, videoconferencing, CLIL, teacher training, English as a lingua franca.

1. University of Bielsko-Biala, Bielsko-Biała, Poland; bloranc@ath.edu.pl

How to cite this chapter: Loranc-Paszylk, B. (2016). Incorporating cross-cultural videoconferencing to enhance Content and Language Integrated Learning (CLIL) at the tertiary level. In S. Jager, M. Kurek & B. O'Rourke (Eds), *New directions in telecollaborative research and practice: selected papers from the second conference on telecollaboration in higher education* (pp. 131-137). Research-publishing.net. https://doi.org/10.14705/rpnet.2016.telecollab2016.499

Chapter 14

1. Introduction

Cross-cultural telecollaboration as an innovative educational experience is becoming more and more popular in the higher education area. It has influenced teaching practices at many different levels as it may be implemented with a great deal of flexibility in various learning contexts. For example, Bueno-Alastuey and Kleban (2014) discuss their telecollaboration project, emphasizing benefits which such an experience could bring despite the fact that students had completely different educational needs.

Almost a decade ago, O'Dowd (2007) enumerated the main goals of telecollaborative exchanges: achieving target language linguistic development and intercultural communicative competence. However, as can be seen in the research agenda nowadays, along with their typical goals, telecollaborative projects are also thought to add new value to "general educational goals, internationalization of education, and electronic/digital literacies in higher education" (Chun, 2015, pp. 11-12). There are therefore premises for integrating cross-cultural telecollaboration into various educational settings, and the aim of this article is to provide indications of the potential benefits that can be derived from engaging in telecollaborative projects in the CLIL context, since these inherently entail development of linguistic and intercultural skills.

2. CLIL and telecollaboration

The conceptual framework of CLIL is based on the four Cs curriculum, that is, Content, Communication, Cognition and Culture (Coyle, 1999). CLIL learning objectives typically focus on the following: progress in knowledge, skills and competences related to subject curriculum (Content dimension), learning and using a foreign language to learn about content (Communication), "'self' and 'other' awareness" achieved through the learners being exposed to the local and global context and consequently acquiring alternative perspectives (Culture) and finally, Cognition, which is thought to involve not only development of high order thinking skills but also fostering independent analysis and students' own understandings with respect to culture and content (Coyle, Hood, & Marsh, 2010, pp. 56-57).

The rationale for incorporating telecollaboration into the CLIL classroom can be found at several levels where areas of interest of CLIL and telecollaboration overlap.

Firstly, intercultural teaching in CLIL, which includes "articulating alternative interpretations of content rooted in different cultures" (Coyle, 1999, p. 60) and promotes cross-cultural sensitivity (Coyle, Holmes, & King, 2009), may become more meaningful thanks to personalized intercultural encounters facilitated by online exchanges.

Secondly, telecollaborative projects, by juxtaposing participants' different cultural backgrounds and thus reinforcing comparative perspectives, invite reflection and critical thinking and, as a result, may enhance CLIL students' gains within the cognitive dimension.

Furthermore, online exchanges increase the amount of language exposure and interaction allowing for "a new realm of collaborative inquiry" (Kern, Ware, & Warschauer, 2004, p. 254), and therefore possibly contribute to the development of linguistic skills and collaborative construction of content knowledge among CLIL students.

Next, by addressing the learning needs of contemporary generations of students, focus on immediacy and personalized hands-on experience with integrated digital technologies and online exchanges may enhance the progressive aspect of the CLIL educational context that has already been described as "an innovative methodology that has emerged to cater to this new age" (Mehisto, Marsh, & Frigols, 2008, p. 11).

Finally, telecollaborative exchanges may help CLIL students, especially those at university level, become global citizens who are culturally aware and fluent in today's lingua franca, as English is the dominant language of communication used in telecollaborative projects, and at the same time, the most frequently used language of instruction in CLIL (Dalton-Puffer, 2011).

3. Methodology

In this action research study of cross-cultural telecollaboration, the MA study program for post-primary teachers was selected as the CLIL context, since it includes a number of non-linguistic courses delivered in English, along with classes that offer English language support.

3.1. Aim of the study

The focus of the study was to investigate a repertoire of CLIL students' self-perceived gains resulting from the telecollaboration. The following research question was formulated: To what extent will telecollaboration enhance the gains related to the CLIL four Cs conceptual framework: content expertise, communication in English language, development of (critical) thinking skills and intercultural competence?

3.2. Participants and the task

The participants were Master of Arts (MA) students at two partner universities: 14 students from the University of Bielsko-Biala (Poland) and 11 students from the University of León (Spain). Both cohorts were homogenous with respect to age and L1, level and profile of studies. Their level of English language proficiency ranged from B2 to C1. The task involved preparation of a detailed plan for one lesson unit with teaching materials, exchanging it via e-mail and finally discussing it during videoconferencing sessions. The telecollaboration exchange primarily focused on content learning – that is, on developing expertise in devising teaching materials by completing a task as part of a regular university course on *Teaching FL skills*.

4. Results and conclusions

For the purposes of the study, qualitative data was used. Data was collected by means of 22 participant-recall surveys using an identical sample of both Polish and Spanish participants – all 11 Spanish participants and 11 out of the 14 Polish participants completed the survey, answering open-ended questions such as: *What aspect of the telecollaboration project did you find most useful?*; and *Can you describe gains resulting from the project?* The students' reports were analyzed and the dominating tendencies related to self-perceived gains were classified into categories.

Students' answers which were classified into the culture category included the following themes: interacting with peers from another country (mentioned by 20 out of the 22 respondents), learning about the foreign peers' teaching ideas/ learning styles (18 out of the 22 respondents), and finding out about educational solutions typical in the respective country (11 out of the 22 respondents). One Polish participant wrote: "I liked the fact that I could see how the students in Spain prepare lesson plans and didactic materials. What is more, I have learned more about Spanish culture and how the students from the partner university perceive Poland".

Gains within the cognitive dimension were also reported: 15 out of the 22 participants' surveys reflected thoughts suggesting some development of a comparative perspective and critical reflection. Themes that were classified under this category include: being able to compare and contrast different teaching procedures and educational solutions, and developing awareness of differences between the two countries. An illustrative quote from a Spanish student may serve as an example: "The most interesting aspect of the project was the ability to compare the procedures used during FL teaching in both countries. It gave me a new perspective on teaching English". Another Spanish student wrote: "It was a great experience because I could compare Polish and Spanish ways of teaching and learning English".

As a result, a repertoire of self-perceived gains reported by the participants from both cohorts could be classified mostly into the respective categories of culture and cognition dimensions. Gains related strictly to content and linguistic development were mentioned by only eight and three out of the 22 respondents, respectively. This might be explained by the fact that the task to perform was more a revision of already acquired knowledge rather than a new topic in the content curriculum. As far as the language development is concerned, the participants from both cohorts were probably not prioritizing linguistic gains because, while being relatively advanced language users, yet not native speakers of English, they might have perceived using English as a lingua franca to communicate with peers with another country more as a language practice than as a language learning experience.

The findings of this study cannot be generalized due to the small sample of participants; however, they may indicate that cross-cultural telecollaboration could enhance the CLIL educational experience since they signal that through authentic interaction in the intercultural context facilitated by new technologies the development of intercultural learning and some critical reflection may be fostered.

References

Bueno-Alastuey, M. C., & Kleban, M. (2014). Matching linguistic and pedagogical objectives in a telecollaboration project: a case study. *Computer Assisted Language Learning, 29*(1), 148-166. https://doi.org/10.1080/09588221.2014.904360

Chun, D. M. (2015). Language and culture learning in higher education via telecollaboration. *Pedagogies: An International Journal, 10*(1), 5-21. https://doi.org/10.1080/1554480X.2014.999775

Coyle, D. (1999). Theory and planning for effective classrooms: supporting students in content and language integrated learning contexts. In J. Masih (Ed.), *Learning through a foreign language* (pp. 46-52). London: CILT.

Coyle, D., Holmes, B., & King, L. (2009). *Towards an integrated curriculum: CLIL national statement and guidelines*. London: The Languages Company.

Coyle, D., Hood, P., & Marsh, D. (2010). *Content and language integrated learning*. Cambridge: Cambridge University Press.

Dalton-Puffer, C. (2011). Content and language integrated learning: from practice to principle? *Annual Review of Applied Linguistics, 31*(1), 182-204. https://doi.org/10.1017/S0267190511000092

Kern, R., Ware, P., & Warschauer, M. (2004). Crossing frontiers: new directions in online pedagogy and research. *Annual Review of Applied Linguistics, 24*, 243-260. https://doi.org/10.1017/s0267190504000091

Mehisto, D., Marsh, D., & Frigols, M. J. (2008). *Uncovering CLIL*. Oxford: Macmillan.

O'Dowd, R. (Ed.). (2007). *Online intercultural exchange: an introduction for foreign language teachers*. Clevedon: Multilingual Matters.

15. Multimodal strategies allowing corrective feedback to be softened during webconferencing-supported interactions

Ciara R. Wigham[1] and Julie Vidal[2]

Abstract

This paper focuses on corrective feedback and examines how trainee-teachers use different semiotic resources to soften feedback sequences during synchronous online interactions. The ISMAEL corpus of webconferencing-supported L2 interactions in French provided data for this qualitative study. Using multimodal transcriptions, the analysis describes multimodal strategies used both in the error and resolution phases of the corrective sequences and in face work during these. These include combining visual and verbal modes in mitigation/remedial strategies and in role-switching cues.

Keywords: corrective feedback, videoconferencing, face work, multimodality, teacher-training.

1. Introduction

In language teaching-learning situations, the provision of corrective feedback that indicates to a learner that his/her use of the target language is incorrect (Lightbown & Spada, 1999) forms part of the didactic contract. The interactionist approach to Second Language Acquisition sees corrective feedback as an

---

1. Clermont Université – LRL, Clermont-Ferrand, France; ciara.wigham@univ-bpclermont.fr

2. Université de Lyon – ICAR, Lyon, France; vidal_julie@yahoo.fr

How to cite this chapter: Wigham, C. R., & Vidal, J. (2016). Multimodal strategies allowing corrective feedback to be softened during webconferencing-supported interactions. In S. Jager, M. Kurek & B. O'Rourke (Eds), *New directions in telecollaborative research and practice: selected papers from the second conference on telecollaboration in higher education* (pp. 139-146). Research-publishing.net. https://doi.org/10.14705/rpnet.2016.telecollab2016.500

important component of the learning process, as it allows learners to integrate attention to meaning and form (Loewen, 2012). However, for trainee-teachers (henceforth trainees) involved in telecollaborative exchanges, the initiation of corrective feedback sequences during which participants divert from the main topic to deal with a communication/linguistic problem can be difficult to manage. Firstly, because the interaction genre of 'pedagogical conversations' (Guichon & Drissi, 2008) requires trainees to alternate between the roles of conversational partner and teacher. Secondly, because the sequences are potentially 'delicate' moments in the interaction and there is a risk of threatening the learner's social face and, in turn, creating a serious risk for the smooth interaction (Kerbrat-Orecchioni, 2011). This paper examines the multimodal strategies adopted by trainees when providing corrective feedback to soften the potentially face-threatening act of correction for the faces of their interaction partners.

2. Methodology

This study draws on the ISMAEL corpus (Guichon, Blin, Wigham, & Thouësny, 2014) that structured data from a telecollaboration project between Business undergraduates at Dublin City University (DCU) and trainees at Université Lyon 2 (Lyon2) on a French as a foreign language Master's programme. DCU students were following a Business French module (CEFR exit-level B1.2) to prepare for future internships in France. The trainees were taking an online teaching module.

Due to differently sized groups in Lyon and Dublin, each trainee led six weekly online interactions with either one or two DCU learners using the webconferencing platform *Visu* (Guichon, Bétrancourt, & Prié, 2012). Interactions were thematic, focusing on Business French. After each 40-minute interaction, the trainees both viewed their online sessions to produce multimodal feedback reports and participated in group debriefings led by a teacher trainer.

The study examined four interactions. Verbal transcriptions had previously been completed. Using *ELAN* (Sloetjes & Wittenburg, 2008), corrective feedback sequences were isolated using Varonis and Gass's (1985) model for non-understandings. This model includes a *trigger phase* and a *resolution phase* that consists of an *indicator, response* and *reaction to response.* Co-verbal elements were also annotated (gestures, facial expressions, proximity to screen, posture). Two colleagues coded the sequences independently on a scale ranging from zero (very face-threatening) to five (highly softened). On this scale, three represented a neutral correction. Corrective sequences identified as being softened were then analysed with reference to Kerbrat-Orecchioni's (1992) framework of face work and differences between highly-softened and sequences coded as slightly or very face-threatening were examined.

3. Analysis

Due to space constraints, one corrective feedback sequence representative of the data is analysed here. The sequence occurs during a discussion about the usefulness of the trainee's feedback report. The *trigger* is the learner Alannah's pronunciation of the lexical item *pronończiation*. The trainee's reception of the non target-like item is communicated in the visual mode: Although Adèle previously had her hands on her headphones, she closes her eyelids to focus more closely on the audio channel then moves proxemically closer to her webcam (Figure 1a).

Figure 1. Semiotic resources to signal error and during resolution phase

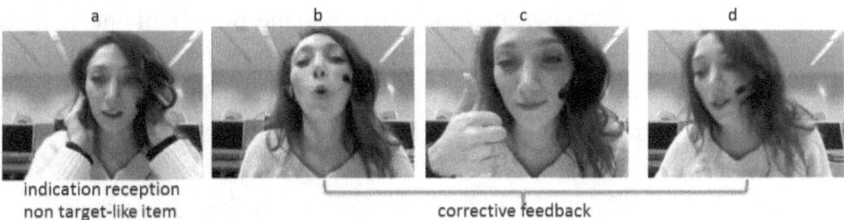

A range of semiotic resources in the visual mode are then employed by the trainee in coordination with the audio modality during the *resolution phase*. These include exaggerating and holding facial expressions in order to illustrate

the mouth's position (Figure 1b); employing gestures to isolate the different syllables (Figure 1c), and using different body postures, moving diagonally across the screen, to accompany the syllabic rhythm whilst the learner repeats the target item (Figure 1d).

During the *resolution phase,* the learner expresses a more delicate face, perhaps because the sequence represents a relatively long parenthesis within the main interaction (1m38s), or because her repetitions did not immediately align with the target form. This is communicated visually through posture changes (head on desk) and facial expressions of frustration, and verbally through L1 exclamations (oh/ ma:n).

To soften the feedback, the trainee uses mitigation as a remedial strategy to repair the damage done to the learner's face. Utterances that place the problem on the difficulty of the lexical item itself, rather than the learner (Figure 2a), are employed. Here, the rate of speech was slower and was accompanied in the visual mode by a slight head inclination and a smile. The trainee also used flattery as a softening device (Figure 2b) to gain the confidence of the learner. In the visual mode, the trainee adopted a more caring posture by changing her gaze directly towards the webcam, smiling and inclining her head.

The trainee provides 'breathing spaces' by using gaze-change as a hesitation device when the learner was repeating or reincorporating the correction (Figure 2c). This slows down the interaction and gives the learner space to repeat the correction for herself rather than for the benefit of the trainee. Indeed, close webcam shots can be intrusive for learners if they last too long. The trainee, in moving her gaze away from focusing intently on her learner's image, contributes towards relieving the tension: the micro pause allows the learner to laugh at herself and this laughter is then shared between participants. It also allows the trainee to structure her thoughts, prompting a change in strategy and a signal to the learner that the text chat modality will be foregrounded (Figure 2d). Typing into the text chat allows the introduction of another pause that helps ease any tension.

Figure 2. Mitigation strategies and breathers

a	Adèle	[it's difficult to say][a] PRO-[N]UN-[CIA]-TION [the-] [the p-] the pronu[nas- hm]
	Alannah	[proNUNcia]tion: [((laughs))]
	Adèle	[pronunna:] ["i don't (inaud.)"] [p`o:/ nun:/] [(na-
	Alannah	ci)]
b	Adèle	[that's CUTE [even like that\] [b]
	Catriona	[((laughs))]
		[...]
c	Alannah	[p`o- pronon/] [proNUNnation/][c] [euh: ((laughs))] [oh ma:n[((laughs))]
	Adèle	pro- [no\ no\ hang on hang on][d] [watch wat- ((laughs))] [PRO/]
	Chat (Adèle)	pro
d	Alannah	p`o-
	Chat (Adèle)	nun
	Adèle	NUN/

The clear closing phase of the sequence contributes to softening the feedback. *Role-switching cues* (Vidal & Wigham, in press) signal to learners that the trainee is moving between her roles of teacher and conversational partner. In this example, Adèle firstly closes the sequence visually by using a gesture to encourage the learner and recognise the progress made (Figure 3a). This gesture is for the learner: it is clearly framed and held close to the webcam. However, in the audio modality there is overlap because the learner continues to attempt to pronounce the target form. Adèle then further encourages the learner, using a gesture (Figure 3b) and a mitigation strategy to distance the learner from the difficulty (it's hard to say isn't it). The learner announces she is tired, perhaps to ask for the correcting parenthesis to be closed. The trainee immediately reacts by moving to her more symmetrical role of conversational partner and stating she understands that the learner works a lot. Accompanied by an empathetic pout in the visual mode, this closes the corrective sequence.

Figure 3.   Role-switching cues

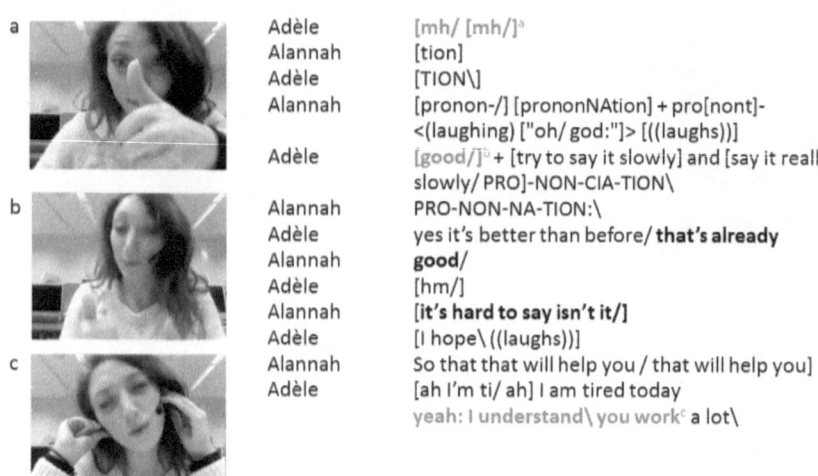

a	Adèle	[mh/ [mh/]ᵃ
	Alannah	[tion]
	Adèle	[TION\]
	Alannah	[pronon-/] [prononNAtion] + pro[nont]-<(laughing) ["oh/ god:"]> [((laughs))]
	Adèle	[good/]ᵇ + [try to say it slowly] and [say it really slowly/ PRO]-NON-CIA-TION\
b	Alannah	PRO-NON-NA-TION:\
	Adèle	yes it's better than before/ **that's already**
	Alannah	**good**/
	Adèle	[hm/]
	Alannah	**[it's hard to say isn't it/]**
	Adèle	[I hope\ ((laughs))]
c	Alannah	So that that will help you / that will help you]
	Adèle	[ah I'm ti/ ah] I am tired today
		yeah: I understand\ you workᶜ a lot\

4.   Conclusion

The analysis of the four different interactions revealed some initial multimodal strategies to soften corrective feedback. These included the use of role-switching cues in opening and closing phases of the correction: introducing the corrective phase with preliminary utterances to indicate the change in interactional posture and using gestures to move back into the role of conversational partner. Gestures were also used to suggest that the trigger was technical and not language-related. This use of the visual mode helped prompt self-correction. Gaze change and the text chat modality also allowed the introduction of 'breathers' into the correction phase, reducing pressure on the learner. In the verbal mode, mitigation as a remedial strategy, accompanied by changes in proximity and posture helped trainees show empathy with the learner. A follow-up study is planned to examine, with reference to Lyster and Ranta's (1997) corrective feedback taxonomy, whether feedback type affects the extent to which the feedback is softened and the semiotic resources used.

5. Acknowledgements

The authors are grateful to the ASLAN project (ANR-10-LABX-0081, Université de Lyon), for its financial support within the program "Investissements d'Avenir" (ANR-11-IDEX-0007), operated by the National Research Agency (ANR). This research was also supported by the Ulysses programme.

References

Guichon, N., Bétrancourt, M., & Prié, Y. (2012). Managing written and oral negative feedback in a synchronous online teaching situation. *CALL, 25*(2), 181-197. https://doi.org/10.108 0/09588221.2011.636054

Guichon, N., Blin, F., Wigham, C. R., & Thouësny, S. (2014). *ISMAEL learning and teaching corpus*. Dublin, Ireland: Center for Translation and Textual Studies & Lyon, France: Laboratoire ICAR.

Guichon, N., & Drissi, S. (2008). Tutorat de langue par visioconférences : comment former aux régulations pédagogiques ? *Les Cahiers de l'Acedle, 5*(1), 185-217.

Kerbrat-Orecchioni, C. (1992). *Les interactions verbales* (vol. II). Paris: Collin.

Kerbrat-Orecchioni, C. (2011). L'impolitesse en interaction : aperçus théoriques et étude de cas. *Philiogy Studies and Research. Romance Language Series, 9*, 142-178.

Lightbown, P., & Spada, N. (1999). *How languages are learned*. Oxford: Oxford University Press.

Loewen, S. (2012). The role of feedback. In S. M. Gass & A. Mackey (Eds.), *The Routledge handbook of second language acquisition* (pp. 24-40). London & New York: Routledge.

Lyster, R., & Ranta, L. (1997). Corrective feedback and learner uptake: negotiation of form in communicative classrooms. *Studies in Second Language Acquisition, 19*, 37-66. https://doi.org/10.1017/S0272263197001034

Sloetjes, H., & Wittenburg, P. (2008). Annotation by category – ELAN and ISO DCR. In *Proceedings of the 6th International Conference on Language Resources and Evaluation* (LREC 2008).

Varonis, E. M., & Gass, S. (1985). Non-native/non-native conversations: a model for negotiation of meaning. *Applied Linguistics, 6*(1), 71-90. https://doi.org/10.1093/applin/6.1.71

Chapter 15

Vidal, J., & Wigham, C. R. (in press). Fournir des rétroactions correctives. In N. Guichon & M. Tellier (Eds), *Enseigner l'oral en ligne. Une perspective multimodale.* Paris: Didier.

16. Problem-solving interaction in GFL videoconferencing

Makiko Hoshii[1] and Nicole Schumacher[2]

Abstract

This paper reports on the interaction between upper intermediate German as a Foreign Language (GFL) learners in Tokyo and prospective GFL teachers in Berlin in an online videoconferencing environment. It focuses on the way problems in comprehension and production are brought up and solved in the subsequent interaction. Our findings illustrate that our synchronous online medium supports a balanced interaction between Second Language (L2) learners and prospective teachers, the main feature of which is joint utterance construction within scaffolding processes. We will show implications for L2 learning and teacher training.

Keywords: interaction, German as a foreign language, group-to-group video conferencing, questions, non-lexical cues, scaffolding.

1. Introduction

Conversational interaction is one of the most important factors for successful L2 learning (Mackey, 2012). Spontaneous questions in particular, asked to clarify and confirm one's understanding, provide interactional benefits in initiating negotiation of meaning. In traditional teacher-centred classrooms, however, questions often occur in an asymmetrical way: Teachers typically ask display

---

1. Waseda University, Tokyo, Japan; mhoshii@waseda.jp

2. Humboldt-Universität zu Berlin, Berlin, Germany; nicole.schumacher@hu-berlin.de

How to cite this chapter: Hoshii, M., & Schumacher, N. (2016). Problem-solving interaction in GFL videoconferencing. In S. Jager, M. Kurek & B. O'Rourke (Eds), *New directions in telecollaborative research and practice: selected papers from the second conference on telecollaboration in higher education* (pp. 147-153). Research-publishing.net.
https://doi.org/10.14705/rpnet.2016.telecollab2016.501

questions as first turns of Initiation-Response-Feedback (IRF) exchanges whereas referential questions by teachers or spontaneous questions asked by learners occur rather rarely (Ellis, 2012; Seedhouse, 2004). In this paper, we will report on a group-to-group videoconferencing setting in joint German courses between Waseda University in Tokyo and Humboldt-Universität zu Berlin, in which GFL learners and prospective GFL teachers participate. We will address the following research questions:

- How do the interlocutors signal the difficulties they face in comprehension and production?

- How do they solve these difficulties in their interaction?

With our article, we would like to contribute to the discussion on the use of videoconferencing to support L2 learning and teaching (Bahlo, Paul, Topaj, & Steckbauer, 2014; Hampel & Stickler, 2012).

2. Data and methodology

We collected our data in joint GFL courses, conducted from 2004 until 2014 (see Hoshii & Schumacher, 2010, for more details). At Waseda University, the course was titled 'Videoconferences in German'. The participants were undergraduate students of different subjects (upper intermediate learners of German). The course aimed at promoting the learners' oral skills in L2 communication as well as their abilities to debate and give presentations in German[3]. At Humboldt-Universität zu Berlin, the course was called 'Teaching via videoconferences'. The participants were graduate students of German as a foreign language and therefore prospective teachers. They trained how to promote learners' oral skills by reflecting on their own talk through observations and transcriptions of the recordings.

---

3. Since 2015, the course has been continued in cooperation with the University of Vienna.

In this paper, we will present representative oral data collected during the first three videoconferences (80 minutes each) of the summer term 2014, produced by five Japanese and six German students[4].

We used an essentially explorative approach. While assorting interactional sequences containing questions in our data, we also found non-lexical units with interrogative functions. We then classified the questions and non-lexical units with regard to their function and analysed the subsequent interaction.

To gain insight into the characteristics of our interaction with regard to the question of who controls the discourse, we additionally looked at the frequency of questions and non-lexical cues in the two groups (for more details, see Hoshii & Schumacher, forthcoming a).

3. Results and discussion

In our data, there are no display questions. All questions and signals are open-ended and referential, based on the interlocutors' own intentions. Four categories are pivotal for our analysis: refocusing questions (RF-questions) and refocusing non-lexical cues (RF-cues) indicating problems in comprehension, as well as questions and non-lexical cues revealing problems in production (P-questions, P-cues).

3.1. RF-questions

Following Rost-Roth (2006), refocusing questions refer to previous utterances, focusing on (parts of) the utterances in order to secure understanding. In (1), a learner (non-native speaker) requests clarification of the word *Schulstufe* (level of education), refocusing on the word in the previous utterance of a native speaker. In doing so, she initiates negotiation of meaning.

---

[4]. All participants gave us permission in written form to use their oral and visual data for academic purposes.

(1)

      498 NS 5   und in welcher schulstufe warst du dort?
                          and in which level of education were you there?
→ 499 NNS 1   schulstufe?
                          level of education? (VC03_2014)

130 of 242 RF-questions (54%) are asked by the students in Berlin, 112 (46%) are asked by the students in Tokyo. The discourse control is thus evenly balanced since both groups of interlocutors initiate negotiation of meaning sequences (see Hoshii & Schumacher, forthcoming a, b, for more details).

3.2. RF-cues

Refocusing cues are non-lexical utterances indicating a comprehension problem with the previous utterance. They may function as clarification requests just like RF-questions, often causing the interlocutor to modify his/her original utterance and thus initiating negotiating of meaning. This non-lexical refocusing can be observed in (2), where the learner's *hm?* causes the native speaker to reduce her original sentence to only the subject and the verb, expressed twice, thus tailoring her utterance to the learner's needs.

(2)

      1193 NS 5   sie spart darauf ins ausland zu gehen
                         she is saving money to travel abroad
→ 1194 NN 3   hm?
                         hm?
      1195 NS 5   sie spart – sie spart
                         she is saving – she is saving (VC03_2014)

3.3. P-questions

In questions indicating planning phases of production (P-questions), internal thoughts are produced in utterances like "How do I say…?", often in line with disfluency and hesitation phenomena. In (3), we see a question indicating that the learner is searching for a word. P-questions are not necessarily directed to the other interlocutors and may involve code switching to the L1 or a previous learned L2 (English), both of which can be seen in (3). Here, it leads to self-initiated other-repair.

(3)

→ 189 NNS 3   nur-<<eng>men.> ah nur; <<jap>nan to iu, otoko?=was heißt otoko?>
                only <<eng>men.> ah only; <<jap>nan to iu, otoko?=what is otoko?>

  190 NNS1   [männer?]
                [men?] (VC02_2014)

3.4. P-cues

Non-lexical cues indicating the planning phase of production often occur as hesitation phenomena in form of filled pauses, indicating that the speaker needs time for production or repair (Schwitalla, 2012, p. 90). In our data, such cues often initiate joint utterance constructions, as in (4). Here, one learner (NNS 5) scaffolds another learner's (NNS 3) utterance, thus reacting to her disfluency marker *hm*, that follows the beginning utterance of the comparative form *mehr* (more). The self-initiated other-repair *leichter* leads to a confirmation by the first speakers (*ja, leichter, einfacher*), thus completing the collaborative utterance.

(4)

  258 NNS 3   zum beispiel; diese prüfung für wase-waseda ist ganz schwer
                For example; this exam for wase-waseda is very difficult

→ 259 NNS 3   aber für andere universitäten vielleicht; mehr-hm
                but for other universities perhaps; more-hm

  260 NNS 5   leichter
                easier

  261 NNS 3   ja, leichter, einfacher
                yes, easier, simpler (VC02_2014)

Interestingly, only the learners use non-lexical (RF- or P-) cues. This reveals that their speech is quite natural and spontaneous. The absence of these cues in the native speaker data, on the other hand, indicates that they are aware of their role as prospective teachers. They try to control their speech in a way to provide the learners with comprehensible input to offer them learning opportunities.

4. Conclusion

Videoconferencing in joint foreign language courses enables conversational interaction in institutional settings. Two features are pivotal to the interaction in our GFL videoconferences: First, interlocutors on both sides initiate problem-solving interaction, hence the control of the discourse is evenly distributed. Secondly, problems in comprehension and production are solved collaboratively and the learners' utterances are scaffolded and tailored to their needs (see Hoshii & Schumacher, forthcoming b, for more details). For learners, this setting therefore facilitates authentic L2 communication and promotes their autonomy. Within teacher training, it may raise the prospective teachers' awareness of their own speech. Videoconferencing in joint foreign language courses may thus promote the interactional competence of both L2 learners and L2 teachers.

5. Acknowledgements

We would like to thank the CCDL Support Office of Waseda University and the CMS of Humboldt-Universität zu Berlin for their technical support, Christoph Gube for his transcriptions and the participants of our videoconferences for their commitment.

This article presents partial results of research projects supported by the Waseda University Grant for Special Research Projects (project numbers: 2014K-6019, 2015K-26).

References

Bahlo, N., Paul, C., Topaj, N., & Steckbauer, D. (2014). Videokonferenzen im DaF-Bereich? Überlegungen zu Möglichkeiten und Grenzen am Beispiel "Skype in the classroom". *Info DaF* 1, 55-69. http://www.daf.de/downloads/InfoDaF_2014_Heft_1.pdf

Ellis, R. (2012). *Language teaching research & language pedagogy*. Malden, MA: Wiley-Blackwell. http://dx.doi.org/10.1002/9781118271643

Hampel, R., & Stickler, U. (2012). The use of videoconferencing to support multimodal interaction in an online language classroom. *ReCALL, 24*(2), 116-137. http://dx.doi.org/10.1017/S095834401200002X

Hoshii, M., & Schumacher, N. (2010). Videokonferenz als interaktive Lernumgebung – am Beispiel eines Kooperationsprojekts zwischen japanischen Deutschlernenden und deutschen DaF-Studierenden. *GFL* 2.2010, 71-91. https://docs.google.com/viewer?url=http://gfl-journal.de/1-2010/Hoshii_Schumacher.pdf

Hoshii, M., & Schumacher, N. (forthcoming a). Fragen in der Interaktion per Videokonferenz. In J. Appel, S. Jeuk, & J. Mertens (Eds.), *Sprachen lehren. Beiträge zur Fremdsprachenforschung* (Band 14). Baltmannsweiler: Schneider.

Hoshii, M., & Schumacher, N. (forthcoming b). Verständnissicherung und gemeinsamer Äußerungsaufbau in der Interaktion per Videokonferenz. In G. Schwab, S. Hoffmann, & A. Schön (Eds.), *Empirische Forschung zur Unterrichtsinteraktion*. Münster: LIT-Verlag.

Mackey, A. (2012). *Input, interaction, and corrective feedback in L2 learning*. Oxford: Oxford University Press.

Rost-Roth, M. (2006). *Nachfragen. Formen und Funktionen äußerungsbezogener Interrogationen*. Berlin: de Gruyter. http://dx.doi.org/10.1515/9783110912630

Schwitalla, J. (2012). *Gesprochenes Deutsch. Eine Einführung*. Berlin: Erich Schmidt Verlag.

Seedhouse, P. (2004). *The interactional architecture of the language classroom*. Malden: Blackwell.

17 Interactional dimension of online asynchronous exchange in an asymmetric telecollaboration

Dora Loizidou[1] and François Mangenot[2]

Abstract

The telecollaborative project under study involves, on the one hand, Masters students who are studying to become teachers and who design the tasks as well as tutor them, and, on the other hand, French language students. The relationship in this type of telecollaboration has been shown to be both asymmetric and symmetric. The hypothesis this paper seeks to examine is that designing tasks and providing corrective feedback by the 'native' partners tends to take precedence over less formal exchanges. We thus analyse the patterns of communicative exchange between tutors and learners in the forum and we examine if there are less formal episodes between them. We are interested in the conditions under which they appear.

Keywords: forum exchanges, informal communication, IRF pattern, telecollaboration.

1. Introduction

As stated by Ware (2005), "research has shown that telecollaboration does not automatically promote the kinds of language learning that educators often anticipate" (p. 64). As in many other projects, one of the aims of the

---

1. Université Grenoble Alpes, LIDILEM, Grenoble, France; dora.loizidou@univ-grenoble-alpes.fr

2. Université Grenoble Alpes, LIDILEM, Grenoble, France; francois.mangenot@univ-grenoble-alpes.fr

How to cite this chapter: Loizidou, D., & Mangenot, F. (2016). Interactional dimension of online asynchronous exchange in an asymmetric telecollaboration. In S. Jager, M. Kurek & B. O'Rourke (Eds), *New directions in telecollaborative research and practice: selected papers from the second conference on telecollaboration in higher education* (pp. 155-161). Research-publishing.net. https://doi.org/10.14705/rpnet.2016.telecollab2016.502

telecollaboration which will be analysed in this article is to offer university learners of French a greater variety of language practices than what is usually the case in textbooks or in the language classroom (Mangenot & Salam, 2010). But the telecollaborative project we are analysing here has a specific feature: it involves, on the one hand, Masters students who are studying to become teachers and who design the tasks as well as tutor them, and, on the other hand, French language students. The relationship in this type of telecollaboration has been shown to be both asymmetric and symmetric: tutors are in a teacher as well as a peer/interlocutor role (Dejean & Mangenot, 2006; Mangenot & Salam, 2010). Hence our research questions: which one of these two roles tends to prevail in this particular context? Which patterns of communicative exchange between tutors and learners appear in the forums? Under which conditions do less formal episodes appear?

2. Methodology

2.1. A task-based approach within forums

We take as a premise the fact that a task-based approach is necessary in order to elicit the communicative process. In our case, pedagogical scenarios composed of two or three pre-tasks and a final task were designed and tutored by four future language teachers from Grenoble University (Masters students, hence 'tutors'), and carried out by 15 students of French from the University of Cyprus ('learners') on a weekly basis with a new topic each week. Moodle forums were the main communication tool. As a result, there are 14 scenarios and the ten week exchange led to 35 tasks (21 pre-tasks, 14 final tasks), all requiring verbal production[3]. Our data set consists in task instructions and forum online interaction between the tutors and the learners.

---

3. As we are studying the communication patterns, we eliminated from our corpus the six pre-tasks which did not require any production.

2.2. Analysis of communicative patterns

Our analysis relies on a comparison with the Initiation-Response-Feedback (IRF) pattern, long ago described by classroom interaction researchers (British Council, n.d.). As shown by Celik and Mangenot (2004), who studied forum exchanges resulting from tasks assigned by the course instructor, an IRF structure can be observed in most cases: Task instruction/Student answers/ Instructor feedback. But some important differences with IRF structure in face to face situations should be noted: there is less time pressure to react, there may be a quasi-unlimited number of responses, the tutor feedback may be given either for each message or globally, and peers may also react to some productions.

Another factor which influences the communicative pattern in forums is the possibility of creating discussion threads (Kear, 2001; Mangenot, 2008). Moodle allows different types of forums, some with a single discussion thread, some with predefined threads (which the learners cannot modify), and some which allow learners to create new threads.

We built a table of all pre- and final tasks, with the number of threads and messages they contained. A short version of this table is given below. Thanks to this table, we could infer some quantitative results, and identify for a qualitative analysis exchanges where the structure differed from the IRF pattern. We will examine the conditions in which these exchanges appear and question the degree and type of interactivity they present.

3. Results

We used a bottom-up/top-down approach to classify the 617 forum messages into three patterns (see Table 1). The first striking observation is the high proportion of *feedback patterns* (66.9% of the messages, 66.7% of the threads). We find most of these IRF patterns in the forums dedicated to the final productions.

A second observation is the low number of *independent messages* (n=41, 6.6%), which shows a certain degree of interactivity.

A third finding is the very high number of threads (n=186); a thread contains on average 3.3 messages (617: 186), which is a low value, especially if a discussion is expected. According to Ware (2005), "the online medium itself supports a range of avoidance strategies that would not otherwise be available to students communicating face to face" (p. 64). The overuse of thread creation by the learners could be interpreted as an avoidance strategy.

A final observation regards the distribution of the *non IRF* threads (n=37): these are mainly (81%) to be found in the pre-task phase.

Table 1. Classification of the forum messages

Exchange pattern	Forums			Discussion threads			Messages (in threads)		
	pre	final	total	pre	final	total	pre	final	total
Independent messages	9	3	12	21	4	25	37	4	41
Feedback (IRF)	7	15	22	39	85	124	90	323	413
Non IRF	9	1	10	30	7	37	146	17	163
Total	25	19	44	90	96	186	273	344	617

Regarding the qualitative analysis of *non IRF* exchanges, we selected one *non IRF* exchange from our corpus. The task topic deals with stereotypes about love; the forum under study corresponds to a pre-task in which learners were asked about the difference between a French and a Cypriot lover and requested to post their respective opinion in a new discussion thread.

In this forum, threads created by the learners contain a one to one exchange learner/tutor. The learners reply to their tutors' task instructions. Their messages deal with the topic, but there is no reference to other messages posted in the other threads and no explicit addressee in their messages (as if the recipient was obviously their tutor). Then, a tutor replies; the tutors do not give any evaluative feedback, but they build on the learners' contributions (see Figure 1). After the tutors' comments, we observed that the learners reply by also building on their response (see Figure 2).

Figure 1. Tutor's response

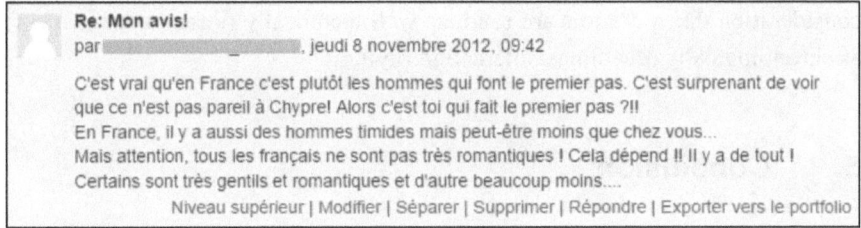

Figure 2. Learner's response

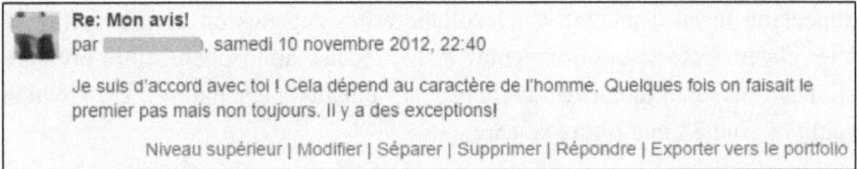

4. Discussion

The quantitative and qualitative analysis above reveals some conditions under which the exchange structure differs from the IRF pattern. First, pre-tasks seem to elicit more casual exchanges. Second, some topics seem to foster a more symmetric relationship. In the forum presented above, the beginning of the exchange structure is close to the IRF pattern, but there is no feedback from the tutors and the exchange is a symmetric one.

Globally, we observed that there is more interactivity between the learners when they are asked to contribute to the same discussion thread as opposed to creating a new one, and that the greatest interactivity between peers is reached when instructions require a collaborative interaction in order to accomplish the task.

There was one such task in our corpus; collaboration showed nevertheless to remain incomplete and thus unsatisfactory, due to the rapid (weekly) succession of the tasks and the slow rhythm of forum interaction. Therefore, we assume that proposing meaningful and relevant tasks is not sufficient to lead to an interactive and more symmetric exchange; the learning scenario should also take into consideration the way tools are used, as well technically (thread management) as chronologically (deadlines, interaction rhythm).

5. Conclusion

In this paper, we studied exchanges in an asymmetric telecollaboration and examined the conditions under which less formal exchanges appear; in addition to the factors we discussed here, we consider that the interactional dimension in an asymmetric telecollaboration depends on a wider array of interrelated factors: environmental factors (class atmosphere, time pressure etc.) and personal factors (motivation, participants' personalities, etc.), which could be studied in a future research.

References

British Council. (n.d.). *Teaching English, initiation-response-feedback (IRF)*. https://www.teachingenglish.org.uk/article/initiation-response-feedback-irf

Celik, C., & Mangenot, F. (2004). La communication pédagogique par forum : caractéristiques discursives. *Les Carnets du Cediscor. Publication du Centre de recherches sur la didacticité des discours ordinaires, 8*, 75-88.

Dejean, C., & Mangenot, F. (2006). Tâches et scénario de communication dans les classes virtuelles. *Les Cahiers de l'ASDIFLE, 17,* 310-321.

Kear, K. (2001). Following the thread in computer conferences. *Computers & Education, 37*(1), 81-99. http://doi.org/10.1016/S0360-1315(01)00036-7

Mangenot, F. (2008). La question du scénario de communication dans les interactions pédagogiques en ligne. In M. Sidir, E. Baron, & G.-L. Bruillard (Eds), *Journées communication et apprentissage instrumenté en réseaux* (pp. 13-26). Paris: Hermès, Lavoisier.

Mangenot, F., & Salam, P.-L. (2010). Quelles normes langagières dans les échanges pédagogiques en ligne ? Une étude de cas. In O. Bertrand & I. Schaffner (Eds), *Quel français enseigner ? La question de la norme dans l'enseignement / apprentissage* (pp. 53-72). Palaiseau: Les Editions de l'Ecole polytechnique.

Ware, P. (2005). 'Missed' communication in online communication: tensions in a German-American telecollabotation. *Language Learning & Technology, 9*(2), 64-89.

18. Telecollaboration in secondary EFL: a blended teacher education course

Shona Whyte[1] and Linda Gijsen[2]

Abstract

Telecollaborative research often focuses on intercultural objectives rather than language learning, and highlights limitations due to technical difficulties and poor task design. This study redresses the balance by focusing on language and learner interaction in an exchange involving the English as a Foreign Language (EFL) learners of 35 secondary school student-teachers in two European countries. The teachers were enrolled in courses on technology for language education, and collaborated in a virtual environment to devise interactive tasks for their learners. Analyses of student-teacher course contributions, the teaching/learning materials they designed, and their reflections on this work shed light on the affordances of telecollaboration from a task-based language teaching perspective.

Keywords: task-based language teaching, teacher education, interaction, telecollaboration.

1. Introduction

O'Dowd (2016) identifies two purposes for telecollaborative exchange: "'authentic' interaction with native speakers or with learners from other countries"

---

1. Université Nice Sophia Antipolis, Nice, France; whyte@unice.fr

2. Fontys University of Applied Sciences, Tilburg, the Netherlands; l.gijsen@fontys.nl

How to cite this chapter: Whyte, S., & Gijsen, L. (2016). Telecollaboration in secondary EFL: a blended teacher education course. In S. Jager, M. Kurek & B. O'Rourke (Eds), *New directions in telecollaborative research and practice: selected papers from the second conference on telecollaboration in higher education* (pp. 163-170). Research-publishing.net. https://doi.org/10.14705/rpnet.2016.telecollab2016.503

and "first-hand experience of 'real' intercultural communication" (p. 275). Much work (Guth & Helm, 2010; Kramsch, 2014) has focused on the second goal, while projects focusing on the first highlight difficulties due to technical constraints and task design (Belz & Reinhardt, 2004; Hanna & de Nooy, 2009; O'Dowd & Ware, 2009). However, telecollaboration offers unique opportunities for purposeful interaction in a communicative context with interlocutors outside the classroom as recommended by second language research (De Bot, 2007). It thus merits further attention.

The present study involved secondary school EFL classes taught by 35 student-teachers in France and the Netherlands. The teachers were enrolled in courses on technology for language education in their respective institutions, and collaborated in a virtual environment to devise learning tasks involving interaction between their learners.

2. Methodology

2.1. Teacher education course

Masters in Teaching English students at two universities took a blended course in their second (final) year of graduate studies (eight hours in the Netherlands, 12 in France). The Dutch teachers taught some 20h/week, while the French trainees had a 9h/week placement plus academic and pedagogical training. After an online kick-off meeting, participants completed introductory tasks, then formed nine cross-cultural teams of three to five teachers. The six to eight week course included weekly face-to-face meetings plus group work using Google applications; teams' results and reflections were shared in a final joint session.

2.2. Participants

A pre-course questionnaire on background profiles and attitudes to language learning/teaching and technology use yielded the information in Table 1.

Table 1. Background data on FR and NL teachers

		FRENCH % (N=20)[3]	DUTCH % (N=13)
L1	national language	85	69
	English	10	23
AGE	27 or under	50	38
	over 37	15	38
TRAINING	EFL	3	77
	English studies	65	0
EXPERIENCE	under 5 years	85	54
	over 10 years	5	31

The French participants thus formed a younger, more homogeneous group, with less specialised training and experience than the Dutch. Attitudes to foreign language teaching and learning were tested on nine questionnaire items from Lightbown and Spada (2000), using a 5-point Likert scale where scores over three reflect conservative/misguided beliefs. The French group displayed slightly more conservative attitudes than the Dutch (3.18/2.89). Scores on a further 14 items concerning self-efficacy perceptions with respect to technology use also revealed a slight advantage to the Dutch (3.92/4.15, scores > 3 reflect greater confidence).

2.3. Teaching/learning activities

Table 2 gives details of the activities designed by each team. The majority used e-mail communication, and met only some of Erlam's (2015) four task criteria in terms of (1) focusing on meaning rather than linguistic form, (2) closing some kind of gap in understanding or knowledge across learners, (3) requiring learners to use their own linguistic resources rather than pre-taught structures or expressions, and (4) leading to an outcome other than language use. Successful accomplishment of task criteria is indicated in boldface in Table 2.

---

[3]. In the interests of focus and space, only the most important figures are reported (so percentage totals do not always equal 100).

Table 2. Teaching/learning tasks by team

Team	Learner activities	Task criteria			
		1. Meaning focus	2. Gap	3. Own resources	4. Outcome
1	group e-mail exchange (Skype)	No	Information exchange	Pre-task	final message, presentations
2	e-mail exchange in self-selected pairs (video selfies)	Yes	Information exchange	Pre-task	e-mail summary
3	exchange video presentation in groups to devise quizzes (learner videos)	Yes	**Reasoning gap**	Pre-task	**class quiz**
4	e-mail exchange for hotel reservations (tourism vocational education) (YouTube)	Yes	Information exchange	Pre-task	e-mail confirmation
5	group e-mail exchange (separate final quiz/ video presentations) (learner video)	Yes	Information exchange	Pre-task	e-mail feedback, learner presentations
6	e-mail in pairs to plan weekend in partner country	Yes	Information exchange	**Yes**	written reports
7	e-mails in groups for writing skills (digital poster, slides)	Yes	Information exchange	Pre-task	learner presentations
8	common production in groups (Padlet)	Yes	**Reasoning gap**	Pre-task	**A4 poster presentation**
9	collaborative short story in groups (Google Docs, Padlet, website)	Yes	**Reasoning gap**	**Yes**	**class discussion**

Teachers had most difficulty meeting the third criterion, with many pre-teaching the required material instead of encouraging learners to rely on their own resources, and the fourth, with most teams failing to plan a collaborative outcome beyond language use. Interestingly, the most successful teams were among either the most motivated (Team 3) or least engaged participants (Teams 8 and 9) at the start of the project.

3. Participant reflection

Teachers' reflections on their telecollaborative experience, derived from a summary of French class discussion with reactions from the Dutch group, are shown in Table 3.

Table 3. Themes in teacher reflection

	FRENCH	DUTCH
learner perspectives	pupils enjoyed exchange	same opinion
	parents/schools also supportive	same opinion
social relations	greater learner freedom in project activities allowed more personalised teacher-learner relations	same opinion
intercultural concerns	some reticence about non-target cultural exchange	no such reticence
	pupil insights about own culture and similarities with Dutch	greater experience with English as Lingua Franca (ELF) exchanges
classroom management and discipline	concerns about lack of motivation and/or inappropriate behaviour	novice teachers agreed
	difficulties concerning grading (usual incentive)	others underlined difficulty of implementing task-based language teaching without good class management
using versus learning English	difficulties deciding when to correct learners	focus on meaning rather than accuracy
	limited exploitation of learner productions	desire for outcome (joint production)
	satisfied with process rather than product	
technical issues	minor difficulties	avoidance of interactive tasks due to lack of internet access and privacy issues
	choice of familiar tools	
	anticipation of problems	
transitions from digital to face-to-face environments	teachers spent time reformatting/printing online work for classroom exploitation	no reformatting
	some found Padlet collaborations 'messy'	untidiness viewed as part of learning process

teacher collaboration	difficulty of scheduling and updating planned activities	success attributed to similarities in goals and attitudes (e.g. creating fun activities)
	some misunderstandings only apparent once activities were underway	less successful teams were imbalanced, with one side more committed
innovation and project-based learning	not always easy to fit telecollaborative tasks into ongoing teaching units	greater interest/experience/incentive for innovation and project-based learning
	not immediate professional priority	would have preferred more flexibility regarding timing

In sum, for the more successful teams whose classroom projects met more task criteria and who reported greater satisfaction with the telecollaborative experience, pupils were enthusiastic and sought to extend contact via additional tasks or independent means. Technical problems were minor, perhaps because teachers deliberately limited risks. While some French teachers expressed concerns about language accuracy and reported difficulty fitting project activities into ongoing teaching units, the Dutch teachers focused more on communication and did not see errors as problematic. Some French teachers felt it was not intrinsically useful to focus on Dutch/French culture, though the Dutch, with greater ELF experience, disagreed. Teacher perceptions seemed to reflect the perceived success of class exchanges. Those involved in less successful telecollaborations cited difficulties in coordination; some felt that projects of this type did not reflect their priorities for professional development. Those teachers who 'clicked', or worked together well, cited factors such as good communication, effective feedback, common aims and an open attitude.

4. Conclusion

The study revealed wide variation across participants, consistent with their different training, experience, and beliefs. The value of (inter)cultural exchange seemed to be different for English studies versus EFL graduates, and learning tasks were also evaluated differently by novice and experienced teachers. Some of the cross-group differences may stem from institutional factors: Dutch universities combine in-service and pre-service teacher education, and teachers are offered incentives for project-based learning and innovation. In France, the integration of university and school-based components of teacher education is more recent and there is less practical support for task-based language teaching or innovation in general. The project goals were partially met in the sense that teachers did focus on language use, although their tasks generally offered limited opportunities for interaction. To technical difficulties and task design problems, which were already identified in the introduction as challenges for telecollaboration, we can add teacher beliefs and the wide variation therein which this study has revealed. For some teachers, the project raised questions about the role of telecollaboration in formal teacher education programmes and how much can realistically be achieved in pre-service versus in-service training. For others, the experience was the occasion for rich, nuanced reflection on telecollaboration as an irreplaceable component of technology integration training.

References

Belz, J. A., & Reinhardt, J. (2004). Aspects of advanced foreign language proficiency: Internet-mediated German language play. *International Journal of Applied Linguistics, 14*(3), 324-362. http://dx.doi.org/10.1111/j.1473-4192.2004.00069.x

De Bot, K. (2007). Language teaching in a changing world. *The Modern Language Journal, 91*(2), 274-276. http://dx.doi.org/10.1111/j.1540-4781.2007.00543_12.x

Erlam, R. (2015). 'I'm still not sure what a task is': teachers designing language tasks. *Language Teaching Research, 20*(3), 279-99. http://dx.doi.org/10.1177/1362168814566087

Guth, S., & Helm, F. (2010). (Eds). *Telecollaboration 2.0: language, literacy and intercultural learning in the 21st Century*. Bern: Peter Lang.

Hanna, B., & de Nooy, J. (2009). *Learning language and culture via public internet discussion forums*. New York: Palgrave Macmillan. http://dx.doi.org/10.1057/9780230235823

Kramsch, C. (2014). Teaching foreign languages in an era of globalization: introduction. *The Modern Language Journal, 98*(1), 296-311. http://dx.doi.org/10.1111/j.1540-4781.2014.12057.x

Lightbown, P. M., & Spada, N. (2000). *How languages are learned*. Oxford: Oxford University Press.

Chapter 18

O'Dowd, R. (2016). Learning from the past and looking to the future of online intercultural exchange. In R. O'Dowd & T. Lewis (Eds), *Online intercultural exchange: policy, pedagogy, practice*. London: Routledge.

O'Dowd, R., & Ware, P. (2009). Critical issues in telecollaborative task design. *Computer Assisted Language Learning, 22*(2), 173-188. http://dx.doi.org/10.1080/09588220902778369

19. It takes two to tango: online teacher tandems for teaching in English

Jennifer Valcke[1] and Elena Romero Alfaro[2]

Abstract

Due to the increasing internationalisation of higher education, universities must ensure the professional development of their teaching staff in English-Medium Instruction (EMI). Nevertheless, very few universities have the means to invest in teacher training and offer their teachers the opportunity to develop the competences that will ensure best practice in teaching and learning. In order to find a low-cost and flexible solution, two universities, Universidad de Cadiz (Spain) and the Université Libre de Bruxelles (Belgium) piloted an online tandem teacher training programme in 2014-2015. This programme was designed to help teachers face the challenges and opportunities of the multilingual and multicultural learning space (Lauridsen & Lillemose, 2015).

Keywords: teacher training, EMI, online collaboration, MMLS.

1. Introduction

Within the context of EMI, the universities of Cadiz (Spain) and Brussels (Belgium) faced a common dilemma: how should non-native speaking university lecturers be trained to deal with the challenges and opportunities of teaching through English? Both universities shared the same vision of EMI embedded

---

1. Karolinska Institutet, Stockholm, Sweden; jennifer.valcke@ki.se

2. Universidad de Cadiz, Cadiz, Spain; elena.romero@uca.es

How to cite this chapter: Valcke, J., & Romero Alfaro, E. (2016). It takes two to tango: online teacher tandems for teaching in English. In S. Jager, M. Kurek & B. O'Rourke (Eds), *New directions in telecollaborative research and practice: selected papers from the second conference on telecollaboration in higher education* (pp. 171-177). Research-publishing.net. https://doi.org/10.14705/rpnet.2016.telecollab2016.504

within a broader internationalisation perspective, where changing the medium of instruction not only implied a shift in language use within classrooms, but also a need to deal with cultural diversity and the professional development of their respective teaching staff (Lauridsen & Lillemose, 2015).

Each institution offered either formal or informal pedagogical support programmes for EMI, led by two experts in the field of Integrating Content and Language in Higher Education (ICLHE). They decided to pilot an online training programme for academic staff in order to enhance transnational collaboration within EMI, since "[i]nternational and intercultural interaction and collaboration has the potential to develop cultural insight and exchange that is enriching and enabling for individuals and through them for local, national, and global communities" (Leask, 2015, p. 72).

The online option seemed appealing for many reasons, including the fact that it would allow sufficient adaptability to be integrated within the two institutional contexts; with different cultural beliefs and values, different teaching styles and beliefs about learner identity, different disciplines and disciplinary cultures, and different linguistic contexts (French for Brussels, and Spanish for Cadiz). It provided the coordinators with a flexible solution to cater for the need of professional development that can fit into teachers' busy schedules. Finally, it also provided low cost and low maintenance solutions for both institutions.

This exchange project was set up to achieve the

> "potential benefits of online communities of practice among teachers, such as the opportunities for reflection offered by asynchronous interaction; the contributions of teachers who tend to be silent in face-to-face settings but 'find their voice' in mediated interaction; and the unique affordances for learning of immersive virtual simulations, among others" (Dede et al., 2009, p. 9).

The main intended learning objectives for participants were to improve the English language skills for teaching purposes; reflect on the roles of teachers in EMI contexts; create situations where English is a meaningful means to exchange ideas about teaching and learning; learn about different teaching strategies for EMI; share ideas about teaching and learning in higher education; and also discuss the role of language in learning.

2. Course design

Teachers were asked to perform six tasks over seven months; each task consisted of asynchronous preparation (reading texts or watching videos) followed by a synchronous Skype conversation of 20 minutes minimum (with specific questions to answer), which had to be summarised in writing by each participant individually after the online exchange. The initial task featured an ice-breaking activity to allow participants to get to know one another. All the pre-tasks, tasks, and post-tasks were detailed in an online logbook, which the participants had to keep updated throughout the project. All post-task summaries had to be posted on a Moodle platform which all participants had access to. It must be noted that a large amount of time was initially spent planning and setting up the tasks online.

Table 1 below shows the timeline of the project's discussion activities over the academic year 2014-2015.

Table 1. Timeline of the project's discussion activities

Oct-Nov 2014	Getting ready: Moodle, Skype and logbook
Dec 2014	Discussion 1 – Getting to know one another
Jan 2015	Discussion 2 – Reflections on teaching
Feb 2015	Discussion 3 – Where is English taking universities?
Apr 2015	Discussion 4 – Content and Language Integrated Learning
May 2015	Discussion 5 – Student goal-orientation, motivation & learning
June 2015	Discussion 6 – Active and experiential learning
Sept 2015	We all meet in Brussels

Initially, the coordinators thought that teachers would work in tandems, one teacher from each different institution. In fact, 34 content teachers applied to join the project: 20 from Cadiz and 14 from Brussels. The coordinators therefore felt that, in order to satisfy all teachers, that there would be 11 tandems and three groups of three. Additionally, certain teachers felt so inhibited by their low language levels that they asked if an individual working solution could be provided, and the coordinators decided on allowing three content teachers to carry out reflective audio journals. In this last possibility, teachers worked alone on the pre-task and prepared the questions of each task, but recorded their answers as audio files which had to be uploaded on the Moodle platform.

It was decided to privilege groupings where participants had similar language levels, and also similar disciplinary backgrounds. Fulfilling this last criterion proved impossible, very few teachers taught in the same disciplines: law, linguistics, business studies, engineering, political science, education, psychology, and architecture. This had a positive effect, albeit fortuitously. Mixing teachers from different disciplines together proved productive since teachers had to talk of their disciplines and research in layman's terms. This allowed teachers to practise a wider range of language skills, which were similar to the language they used in their classrooms to explain academic content to students with no or little previous knowledge.

Since there was a conference organised in Brussels on ICLHE in September 2015, the coordinators decided to offer the possibility to participants to meet physically by organising an Erasmus Training Mobility. 27 of the 34 teachers travelled to Brussels. The coordinators observed that the physical meeting at the end of the project was in itself a large motivational factor for teachers and contributed to their international mobility and intercultural experience, while also contributing to the development of their teaching skills.

3. Evaluation

Teachers were asked to self-assess their language skills using the Common European Framework of Reference for languages (CEFR) before the first task and after the last task, as well as fill in a participant experience survey. Of the 34 content teachers who took part in the project, only 19 responded fully to all tasks (14 from Cadiz and five from Brussels), including the self-assessment of language.

Although teachers described improvements in their use of English, only six of the 19 respondents reported a clear increase in English proficiency from one CEFR scale to the next: two teachers reported going from B1 to B1+, two teachers from B2+ to C1, and two teachers from C1 to C1+. Although most teachers did not report a change from one CEFR scale to another, they did self-report improved spoken interaction (seven teachers), spoken production (seven teachers), and listening skills (four teachers). All respondents reported improvements in confidence (18 teachers), fluency (17 teachers), and vocabulary range (13 teachers).

Many participants recalled feeling comfortable with their tandem or group of three partners, which led the teachers to develop a community of practice:

> "The success of telecollaboration and e-tandem learning activities tends to rely on the quality of the relationship that develops between geographically separated participants. [I]t is an exchange between a pair of individuals, already positioned as friends" (Hanna & de Nooy, 2009, p. 88).

From the participant experience survey, teachers especially highlighted as beneficial the fact that they exchanged ideas and resources on EMI, discussed their research, the role of language in learning, teaching in university contexts, and educational development for EMI.

4. Conclusion

When embarking on a teacher training online exchange, Dede et al. (2009, p. 10) recommended that coordinators consider the following questions:

- How should the professional development programme be designed (content, pedagogical strategies, methods of delivery, and identification of good practices) to maximize its effectiveness?

- What measures of effectiveness and means of evaluation should be used to document the outcomes and impacts of the professional development program? What specific tools, if any, should teachers experience as part of the professional development?

- What types of learner interactions should the programme foster through its methodology and its infrastructure for delivery?

The coordinators of the present online exchange wish to pursue the experiment further and have reflected on the above questions. A number of possible improvements should therefore be implemented for the next iteration of the project in 2016-2017.

A more robust online platform will be set up, using a website for communication between teachers and the dissemination of tasks, and Adobe Connect meeting rooms for synchronous discussions.

The groupings will only be in pairs, as it seemed that it was difficult for groups of three to find suitable times for their synchronous online discussions.

In addition to Cadiz and Brussels universities, other partner universities have shown interest and initial contact has already been established with Karolinska Institutet (Sweden), Université Catholique de Louvain (Belgium), and Université de Mons.

In terms of the topics addressed in each task, there will be a stronger focus on international education, intercultural education, pronunciation and ICLHE. Each written assignment will have to be posted on the online discussion forum to allow for peer review with clear descriptors.

Finally, the coordinators also decided to maintain the physical mobility at the end of the next iteration since it was such a powerful motivational factor for teachers to develop professionally.

References

Dede, C., Jass Ketelhut, D., Whitehouse, P., Breit, L., & McCloskey, E. M. (2009). A research agenda for online teacher professional development. *Journal of Teacher Education, 60*(1), 8-19. http://dx.doi.org/10.1177/0022487108327554

Hanna, B., & de Nooy, J. (2009). *Learning language and culture via public Internet discussion forums*. New York: Palgrave Macmillan. http://dx.doi.org/10.1057/9780230235823

Lauridsen, K. M. & Lillemose, M. K. (Eds). (2015). *Opportunities and challenges in the multilingual and multicultural learning space*. http://intluni.eu/uploads/media/The_opportunities_and_challenges_of_the_MMLS_Final_report_sept_2015.pdf

Leask, B. (2015). *Internationalizing the curriculum*. New York: Routledge.

20. Getting their feet wet: trainee EFL teachers in Germany and Israel collaborate online to promote their telecollaboration competence through experiential learning

Tina Waldman[1], Efrat Harel[2], and Götz Schwab[3]

Abstract

The paper presents a telecollaboration project between 54 pre-service teachers of English as a Foreign Language (EFL) studying at a teacher training college in Israel and a university in Germany. The telecollaboration involved a collaborative Project Based Learning Task (PBLT) in which the students compared and evaluated the ways EFL is taught in their respective contexts. The purpose of this ongoing study is to provide pre-service EFL teachers with an apprenticeship of learning ways that technology can be used to transcend classroom walls for virtual mobility and cooperation. It specifically intends to determine how such an apprenticeship can strengthen student teachers' belief in their ability to implement telecollaboration in their own teaching. Data for the study were gathered through a pre-post quantitative survey. The findings indicate that telecollaboration experience integrated into teacher training can raise students' perceived self-efficacy to implement telecollaborative exchange projects into their future teaching.

Keywords: telecollaboration, teacher education, project based learning tasks, PBLT, self-efficacy.

1. Kibbutzim College of Education, Tel Aviv, Israel; Tina.waldman@smkb.ac.il

2. Kibbutzim College of Education, Tel Aviv, Israel; Efiharel@gmail.com

3. Karlsruhe University of Education, Karlsruhe, Germany; goetz.schwab@ph-karlsruhe.de

How to cite this chapter: Waldman, T., Harel, E., & Schwab, G. (2016). Getting their feet wet: trainee EFL teachers in Germany and Israel collaborate online to promote their telecollaboration competence through experiential learning. In S. Jager, M. Kurek & B. O'Rourke (Eds), *New directions in telecollaborative research and practice: selected papers from the second conference on telecollaboration in higher education* (pp. 179-184). Research-publishing.net. https://doi.org/10.14705/rpnet.2016.telecollab2016.505

Chapter 20

1. Introduction

Despite some criticism (Hanna & De Nooy, 2009; Kramsch, 2009), telecollaboration is acknowledged as a versatile tool which foreign language educators can implement to encourage not only the practice of language skills, but also to raise intercultural awareness, enhance collaborative learning practices, and increase learner motivation by providing opportunities for authentic language use through the activity of online task collaboration.

While telecollaboration is becoming an established tool in higher education, it is found less commonly in K12 educational contexts, mainly because school teachers lack the experience, competences and confidence to integrate telecollaborative projects into their teaching. Teacher confidence or self-efficacy "relates to the beliefs teachers hold about their perceived capability in undertaking certain teaching tasks" (Bandura, 1997, reported in Pendergast, Garvis, & Keogh, 2011, p. 47). "Supporting the development of teachers' self-efficacy is essential for producing […] committed and [pioneering] teachers" (Tschannen-Moran & Woolfolk Hoy, 2001, reported in Pendergast et al., 2011, p. 47) who are willing to take creative steps like introducing telecollaborative exchanges into their own classrooms. However, telecollaboration projects rely heavily on instructor guidance (Belz, 2003). Furthermore, multiple skills are necessary to organize, design, assess and run a telecollaborative exchange. As a result, self-doubt regarding these competences may pose an obstacle to pre-service teachers entering the field.

O'Dowd (2015) has defined the mind-set for running telecollaborative activities in a model comprising 40 descriptors defined mostly in terms of 'can do' statements. These statements refer to organizational, pedagogical, and digital competences as well as attitudes and beliefs of the telecollaborative teacher (O'Dowd, 2015, pp. 67-68). This model has informed our study, in which we created an apprenticeship of the skills necessary for the telecollaborative instructor through systematic learning in practice.

This study was guided by the main research question: does experiencing a telecollaboration enhance the pre-service teachers' self-efficacy to facilitate telecollaborative projects? The original study contained additional questions, but due to limited space they cannot be discussed here.

2. Methodology

2.1. Participants

Participants were 54 pre-service teachers of EFL studying at a teacher training college in Israel and university in Germany. Participants from Israel were 33 student teachers in the third year of their Bachelor of Education (B.Ed.) program. The Hebrew and Arabic mother tongue participants had high English matriculation scores, and had passed English proficiency exams to be accepted to the English teaching program. Three participants were native English speakers who had immigrated to Israel as adults.

Participants from Germany were 21 student teachers of EFL (primary and secondary). They were either in their third or fourth year of study. 19 students were German natives, two students had a migrant background. The overall language competence is proficient, i.e. C1 of the Common European Framework of Reference for languages (CEFR). Apart from one student, none of them had been in contact with Israeli students before.

2.2. Telecollaboration project

The telecollaboration was integrated into the student teachers' SLA courses in both institutions. Implementation followed the design constructed by the Israeli researchers in an earlier project between Israeli and American students (Waldman & Harel, 2015). It included three stages: information exchange, comparison, and collaboration. Information exchange about personal details and aspects of home culture took place at the beginning of the process so the students could get to know each other. Over the following weeks, student teams comprising three Israeli and two German students worked collaboratively on a PBLT comparing and critically analyzing the ways EFL is taught in Israel and Germany. Finally, they co-constructed electronic posters showcasing their findings.

The first synchronous videoconference was carried out using Skype and a projector and screen. The participants discussed their career choice of becoming EFL teachers; the status of bilingualism and multiculturalism in their respective countries and educational systems, as well as student life. Between the first and the second synchronous videoconferences, the student teams worked on their projects communicating on a regular basis. They chose the digital tools themselves, both synchronous (Skype and WhatsApp) and asynchronous tools (e-mail and Google Docs). We encouraged their independence so that they would look for ways to solve problems as they encountered them. The main goal of their collaboration was to compare and evaluate teaching EFL in the Israeli and the German education system. The student teams decided amongst themselves which aspect of teaching EFL to focus on for the creation of an electronic poster which was presented in the second video conference. We deemed this project relevant to the participants to raise awareness of alternative methods of teaching EFL to those used in their own communities. Furthermore, it is likely that in today's global society, trainee-teachers will find themselves teaching abroad, hence, they should be aware of multiple pedagogies.

2.3. Data collection

In order to answer the research question, the students completed a pre- and post-collaboration survey, which we designed based on a number of the descriptors provided in O'Dowd (2015). The Cronbach's alpha for the survey was 0.84, indicating high levels of internal consistency. The survey questions reflected the construct of self-efficacy within the domain of telecollaboration. We asked the students to assess the degree with which they agreed with eighteen statements, ranked from disagree (1) to fully agree (5). Some of these statements targeted factors relating to capability e.g. "I can organize an online exchange between my pupils and other pupils". Other statements targeted beliefs about the value of telecollaboration in EFL classrooms, e.g. "Telecollaboration plays an important role in language learning". We think that belief in the positive value of telecollaboration is a motivating factor for the student teachers to achieve empowerment through perceived self-efficacy.

We analyzed the survey quantitatively based on group comparisons between the means in the pre- and post-survey.

3. Results

The findings from the quantitative analysis are presented below, see Table 1.

Table 1. Comparison of student responses in the pre- and post-collaboration survey

	Pre-survey			Post-Survey		
N	Mean	SD	Range	Mean	SD	Range
54	3.90	0.40	1-5	4.09	0.42	1-5

Table 1 shows the number of participating students (54), the mean, standard deviation and range of pre- and post-collaboration survey scores. A paired t-test showed a significant difference between the mean scores in the pre- and post-survey ($t(53)= -3.07$, $p<0.01$). In other words, the mean score in the post-survey was significantly higher than the mean score in the pre-survey. Perceived self-efficacy was higher among the students following the telecollaboration experiential learning.

4. Discussion and conclusion

Results show that the student teachers' telecollaboration experience was meaningful within the process of their teacher training. Following the telecollaboration experiential learning, the students' post-survey results revealed a higher sense of self-efficacy originating from their experience. The survey showed raised feelings of competence in designing, organizing, running and assessing an online exchange with their future pupils. Moreover, it showed willingness to cooperate with partners and capability in choosing appropriate digital tools. The initial results from this ongoing study support the notion that telecollaboration exchange deserves a place in pre-service EFL teacher education programs. By equipping future teachers with telecollaboration knowledge and skills, there is hope that there will be an eventual backwash effect and telecollaboration exchange will be applied to EFL curricula.

References

Bandura, A. (1997). *Self-efficacy: the exercise of control*. New York: Freeman.

Belz, J. (2003). Linguistic perspectives on the development of intercultural competence in telecollaboration. *Language Learning & Technology, 7*(2), 68-99. http://llt.msu.edu/vol7num2/belz/

Hanna, B., & De Nooy, J. (2009). *Learning language and culture via public internet discussion forums*. New York: Palgrave. http://dx.doi.org/10.1057/9780230235823

Kramsch, C. (2009). *The multilingual subject:what foreign language learners say about their experience and why it matters*. Oxford: Oxford University Press.

O'Dowd, R. (2015). Supporting in-service language educators in learning to telecollaborate. *Language Learning & Technology, 19*(1), 63-82.

Pendergast, D., Garvis, S., & Keogh, J. (2011). Pre-service student-teacher self-efficacy beliefs: an insight into the making of teachers. *Australian Journal of Teacher Education, 36*(12), 46-57. http://dx.doi.org/10.14221/ajte.2011v36n12.6

Tschannen-Moran, M., & Woolfolk Hoy, A. W. (2001). Teacher efficacy: capturing an elusive construct. *Teaching and Teacher Education, 17*(7), 783-805. http://dx.doi.org/10.1016/S0742-051X(01)00036-1

Waldman, T., & Harel, E. (2015). Participating in a technology enhanced internationalization project to promote students' foreign language motivation. In D. Schwarzer (Ed.), *Internationalizing teacher education: successes and challenges within domestic and international contexts*. Lexington Books: New Jersey.

21. Teacher competences for telecollaboration: the role of coaching

Sabela Melchor-Couto[1] and Kristi Jauregi[2]

Abstract

This paper explores the role of coaching in enhancing teachers' key competences for integrating Telecollaboration (TC) in their language course. A total of 23 secondary school teachers participated in this case study as part of the EU-funded project TILA. Quantitative and qualitative data were gathered via two surveys, the first one measuring coaching satisfaction and a second one tackling teacher competences. The results show that teachers highly value coaching to integrate complex pedagogical innovations in their teaching. Participants reported that coaching contributed to an improvement of key competences necessary to implement TC exchanges successfully.

Keywords: telecollaboration, teacher competences, coaching.

1. Introduction

The use of TC for language learning has increased considerably in recent years, however, it is still seen as an add-on activity (O'Dowd, 2011, p. 8). Teachers must be equipped with specific competences required for TC, which O'Dowd (2015) divides in organisational, pedagogical and digital competences and attitudes and beliefs. This contribution explores the use of 'coaching' to help

---

1. University of Roehampton, London, United Kingdom; s.melchor-couto@roehampton.ac.uk

2. Utrecht University, Utrecht, The Netherlands; k.jauregi@uu.nl

How to cite this chapter: Melchor-Couto, S., & Jauregi, K. (2016). Teacher competences for telecollaboration: the role of coaching. In S. Jager, M. Kurek & B. O'Rourke (Eds), *New directions in telecollaborative research and practice: selected papers from the second conference on telecollaboration in higher education* (pp. 185-192). Research-publishing.net. https://doi.org/10.14705/rpnet.2016.telecollab2016.506

teachers develop some of these key competences, which may ultimately lead to a sustained use of TC practices.

Coaching in education is a relatively new field of research (Van Nieuwerburgh, 2012, p. 7). It has been defined as "focused professional dialogue designed to aid the coachee in developing specific professional skills to enhance their teaching repertoire. [...] For teachers, it often supports experimentation with new classroom strategies" (Lofthouse, Leat, & Towler, 2010, p. 8). The value of coaching has been highlighed by recent research, which indicates that, when training is complemented with coaching, teachers are significantly more likely to adopt and maintain the skills developed and have greater self-efficacy beliefs regarding the new practices (Driscoll, Wang, Mashburn, & Pianta, 2011; Forman, Olin, Hoagwood, Crowe, & Saka, 2009; Ransford, Greenberg, Domitrovich, Small, & Jacobson, 2009; Wenz-Gross & Upshur, 2012). Conversely, when training is provided in isolation, teachers tend to abandon the practices learnt (Fixsen, Naoom, Blase, Friedman, & Wallace, 2005; Noell et al., 2005).

Coaching strategies focus on discussing with the coachee specific difficulties that may arise in teaching, planning and evaluating teaching activities jointly and reflecting on teaching practices in a critical but constructive way (McGrane & Lofthouse, 2010, p. 188). Taking these coaching principles as starting points, a number of secondary school language teachers were trained and intensively coached in the process of preparing, carrying out and evaluating TC exchanges in their language course.

2. Methodology

The participants of the study are 23 secondary school teachers who were involved in the TILA project (six French teachers, three Dutch, seven Spanish, three English and four German). All of them completed training on TC and were assigned to a coach that guided them in the design and implementation of TC activities in the classroom. An estimated 550 hours of coaching were provided in the form of weekly or biweekly remote meetings among the coach and the two collaborating teachers. Pedagogical and technical guidance was provided before, during and after TC sessions in terms of:

- goal-setting: including agreement on the number of TC sessions to be completed throughout the term, scheduling tasks and choosing topics among other aspects;

- session planning: consisting of designing task sequences, devising supporting materials like worksheets, discussing pedagogical and technical considerations, namely student pairings or material upload, identifying potential challenges and solutions;

- in-session coaching and support: involving provision of remote troubleshooting during TC sessions, such as problems with log-in or *ad hoc* adjustments like regrouping students due to absences;

- post-session reviewing: taking place after each task sequence. Both the coach and coachees could view the actual student interactions, which were automatically recorded. This was a useful basis for discussions on what worked and what could be improved, and perceived degrees of success.

Two surveys were designed to evaluate the coaching experience and gather information about the teacher competences developed through the coaching. The latter is based on O'Dowd's (2015) model of TC teacher competences. Both surveys were available in the teachers' languages and disseminated via SurveyMonkey. The surveys included closed items with 5-point Likert scales (1: lowest score; 5: maximum score) and open questions. Frequencies were calculated and answers to open-ended questions and comments were grouped according to topics.

3. Results

Most respondents valued highly the guidance offered for task design (five points: 70% of the participants), the support to solve technical problems (five points: 57%; four points: 26%). Positive feedback was also obtained in terms of the help provided to learn to use new platforms and with organisational issues, with a majority of five and four scores in both cases. Most teachers indicated that they feel prepared to integrate TC in their courses (five points: 30%; four points: 39%). The satisfaction with the coaching provided is extremely high, with 78% of the participants rating it with five points out of five; most participants state that coaching responded to their needs (five points: 35%; four points: 22%) (see Table 1).

Table 1. Coaching survey results

Item	Mean	StandardDeviation
Help setting up partnerships	4.5	0.8
Help with task design	4.5	1
Help with technical problems	4.3	1
Help with platforms	4.3	1
Help with organisational aspects	4.4	0.8
Confidence for TC	3.9	1
Satisfaction with coaching	4.7	0.8
Coaching responded to needs	3.9	1

The quantitative data detailed above are accompanied by open-ended comments. Participants value greatly the support provided by coaches in terms of the encouragement and ideas offered. Practical aspects such as the coach's role in keeping both parties to agreed deadlines were also mentioned. The coaches' availability and the timeliness of their responses feature highly in the comments gathered. In terms of task design, teachers highlight the importance of their coaches' input in creating and organising realistic tasks. Finally, the coach is also a valued guide when it comes to solving technical difficulties, something which is mentioned repeatedly.

With respect to teacher competences, the participants' perceived telecollaborative competence increased after the TC experience across all items, particularly digital competence. Teachers also expressed considerable progress in organisational aspects and, to a lesser extent, pedagogical competences and attitudes and beliefs.

An item-specific analysis (see Figure 1) reveals that the most noticeable changes in teachers' perceived ability are in items related to the following[3]:

- implementing an exchange successfully [organising synchronous interactions (C5, +1.83); designing an exchange effectively (A3, +2.17); adjusting to changing conditions (A7, +1.34)];

- communicating with partner-teachers [plans and expectations (A2, +1.59); negotiating the specific aspects of an exchange for both institutional contexts (A4b, +1.75];

- task design and task selection [identifying tasks that meet the curriculum's objectives (B1, +1.66); designing attractive tasks that lead to rich interaction (B4, +1.5)];

- working with students [creating effective partnerships (A5b, +1.75); explaining to students how to use tools (C3, +1.5)].

Figure 1. Items showing the most noticeable perceived improvement

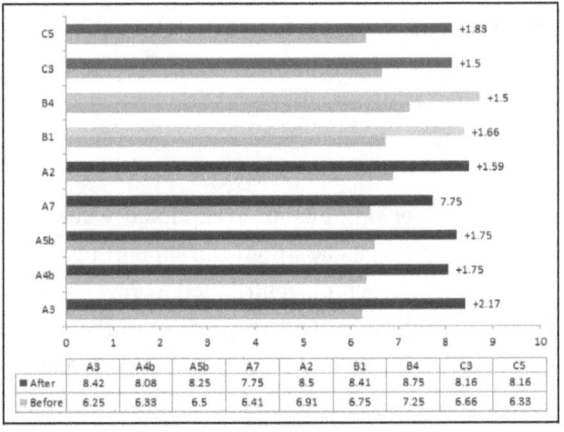

---

3. The descriptor codes used in O'Dowd's (2015) model of competences have been included here. A2 to A7 refer to organisational competences, B1-B4 to pedagogical, C3 and C5 to digital and D3 to attitudes and beliefs.

Minor perceived improvements were reported in items relating to their ability to support students (B9), matching students (A5a), integrating TC topics into regular classes (B8) and willingness to reach a compromise in how the TC is designed (D3) (Figure 2).

Figure 2. Least noticeable perceived improvement

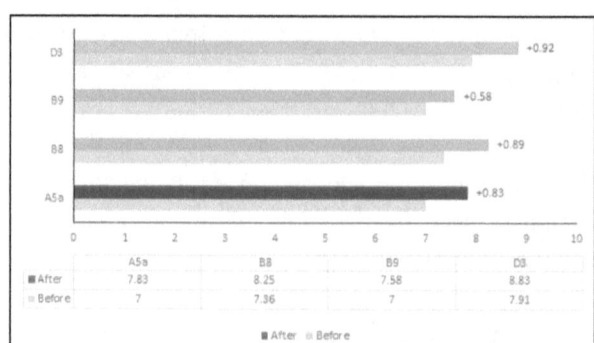

When asked about the role played by their coach in the development of their TC competences, the participants highlighted the assistance provided in organisational issues and task design. In general, teachers seemed to highly value the support provided.

4. Conclusions

These results show that coaching has an exceptional value when it comes to implementing TC in the language classroom and supporting teachers. According to the teachers' perceptions, coaching contributed to develop TC skills: teachers learned to (1) design an exchange effectively, adjust to changing conditions and difficulties, communicate with partner-teachers their plans and expectations and negotiate the specific aspects of an exchange, bearing in mind both institutional contexts; (2) design and select rich and attractive tasks that fit into the curriculum's objectives and that lead to rich interaction, and (3) work with the students to create effective partnerships and explaining how to use a given tool.

No studies have addressed, to our knowledge, the role that coaching plays in developing pedagogical, organisational and digital competences for TC. It is hoped that the conclusions obtained in this first attempt to do so will help to pave the way for future contributions in this thriving field of research.

References

Driscoll, K. C., Wang, L., Mashburn, A. J., & Pianta, R. C. (2011). Fostering supportive teacher–child relationships: intervention implementation in a state-funded preschool program. *Early Education and Development, 22*(4), 593-619. http://dx.doi.org/10.1080/10409289.2010.502015

Fixsen, D., Naoom, S., Blase, K., Friedman, R., & Wallace, F. (2005). *Implementation research: a synthesis of the literature*. Tampa: University of South Florida.

Forman, S. G., Olin, S., Hoagwood, K., Crowe, M., & Saka, N. (2009). Evidence-based intervention in schools: developers' views of implementation barriers and facilitators. *School Mental Health, 1*, 26-36. http://dx.doi.org/10.1007/s12310-008-9002-5

Lofthouse, R., Leat, D., & Towler, C. (2010). *Coaching for teaching and learning: a practical guide for schools*. Reading: CfBT Education Trust.

McGrane, J., & Lofthouse, R. (2010). *Developing outstanding teaching and learning: creating a culture of professional development to improve outcomes*. London: Optimus Education e-Books.

Noell, G. H., Witt, J. C., Slider, N. J., Connell, J. E., Gatti, S. L., Williams, K. L., et al. (2005). Treatment implementation following behavioral consultation in schools: a comparison of three follow-up strategies. *School Psychology Review, 34*, 87-106.

O'Dowd, R. (2011). Online foreign language interaction: moving from the periphery to the core of foreign language education? *Language Teaching, 44*(3), 368-380. http://dx.doi.org/10.1017/S0261444810000194

O'Dowd, R. (2015). Supporting in-service language educators in learning to telecollaborate. *Language Learning & Technology, 19*(1), 64-83.

Ransford, C. R., Greenberg, M. T., Domitrovich, C. E., Small, M., & Jacobson, L. (2009). The role of teachers' psychological experiences and perceptions of curriculum supports on the implementation of a social and emotional learning curriculum. *School Psychology Review, 38*, 510-532.

Van Nieuwerburgh, C. (Ed.). (2012). *Coaching in education: getting better results for students, educators and parents.* London: Karnac Books.

Wenz-Gross, M., & Upshur, C. (2012). Implementing a primary prevention social skills intervention in urban preschools: factors associated with quality and fidelity. *Early Education and Development, 23*(4), 427-450. http://dx.doi.org/10.1080/10409289.2011.589043

Section 4.
Telecollaboration in service of mobility

22. Preparing student mobility through telecollaboration

Marta Giralt[1] and Catherine Jeanneau[2]

Abstract

In recent years, going to a foreign country has become all the more significant for Higher Education (HE) students, as concepts such as internationalisation and intercultural competencies have gained a more prominent role in HE. For students to fully benefit from this experience, it is paramount to prepare them for their stay in a foreign country through reflection and analysis (Byram & Dervin, 2008). This paper focuses on a pre-mobility preparation programme: the I-Tell project (Intercultural Telecollaborative Learning). This initiative aims at raising intercultural awareness amongst students and promoting language practice through telecollaborative exchanges between students of Spanish in Ireland and students of English in Spain prior to their sojourn abroad. The data gathered from this initiative yield some interesting findings, especially in relation to linguistic and intercultural development. We will particularly highlight the findings pertaining to student preparation to their period abroad and show what students gained from partaking in this project.

Keywords: period abroad, intercultural awareness, telecollaboration, mobility programme.

1. University of Limerick, Limerick, Ireland; marta.giralt@ul.ie

2. University of Limerick, Limerick, Ireland; catherine.jeanneau@ul.ie

How to cite this chapter: Giralt, M., & Jeanneau, C. (2016). Preparing student mobility through telecollaboration. In S. Jager, M. Kurek & B. O'Rourke (Eds), *New directions in telecollaborative research and practice: selected papers from the second conference on telecollaboration in higher education* (pp. 195-200). Research-publishing.net. https://doi.org/10.14705/rpnet.2016.telecollab2016.507

Chapter 22

1. Introduction

Even though studying abroad is not a new phenomenon (Welch, 2008), student mobility has exploded in recent years (Dervin, 2011) and a higher emphasis in research has been placed on the period abroad (Byram & Dervin, 2008; Jackson, 2008).

In 1997, Coleman already highlighted that preparation was "all-important" (p. 15) before the period abroad and that "[p]reparation for the cultural dimension of discourse [could] obviate certain problems" (p. 2) but that in general, the preparatory tasks in this domain were nonexistent or inadequate as they were often limited to practical or linguistic advice. Recent research on mobility preparation has shed light on the importance of intercultural awareness (Borghetti, Beaven, & Pugliese, 2015; Holmes, Bavieri, & Ganassin, 2015).

The I-Tell project joins this trend as it aims at ensuring that students are prepared for their mobility period. It also explores the impact of this pre-departure intervention on students.

2. The I-Tell project

The goal of this project is to improve students' cultural, linguistic and digital competences before they go abroad. The main focus of this research was to investigate the impact of telecollaboration on students' preparation before their mobility period.

2.1. Participants

The participants consisted of a group of twelve students learning Spanish at the University of Limerick, Ireland and set to go to Spain on Erasmus or work placement. They were paired up with twelve students from the University of León, Spain. These latter students were learning English and were also preparing for their Erasmus placement either in the UK or in Ireland. The Irish students participated in the project on a semi-voluntary basis, i.e. as part of an option within a Spanish language module, while their Spanish partners received 2 ECTS credits for their participation.

2.2. Project description

For their project work, students had to conduct a series of telecollaborative tasks covering a range of intercultural topics during a period of eight weeks in the semester prior to their stay abroad. The participants were advised to have two weekly exchanges with their international partner using e-mail or video-conferencing. Each exchange had to be divided between the two languages, and students were recommended to use more than one communication mode (verbal, images, videos, hyperlinks). The Skype conversation should last at least 40 minutes.

3. Methodology

For this study, both quantitative and qualitative data were collected. The quantitative data were gathered using a feedback questionnaire which included a total of ten questions. Six of them were rating questions based on a five-point Likert scale. The remaining questions were multiple choice and yes or no questions. For each of the questions, students were invited to elaborate on their answers by leaving an additional comment. This allowed the researchers to explore different viewpoints.

The qualitative data were collected from participants' reflective portfolios completed at the end of the project and from focus group interviews.

4. Results

In the following part, the main findings of the study will be presented, focusing on the impact of the project on students' language learning, intercultural awareness and preparation for the period abroad.

4.1. Impact on language learning

In their feedback, students report that their grammar and writing/reading skills benefited from the exchanges. However, an analysis of the qualitative data reveals that they also increased their vocabulary (especially about university life). They highlight that they learnt new words and expressions in context and from peer native speakers. This seems important to them as it allowed them to develop their repertoire of colloquial expressions used by people their own age. As the exchanges between partners were not monitored, they felt free to use their own language, thus making the interactions more authentic: "*...and it's not like you were being watched by a teacher or someone, even though the teachers here are very friendly and all, they're in a position of authority*".

Moreover, most pairs engaged in peer-correction within all the tasks, even though this was just required for one of the tasks. They developed techniques to provide feedback to their partners (e.g. highlighting errors, sending back comments...). This led them to engage in reflection about their own learning (e.g. "*one thing that struck me is I had been using some words/expressions in the wrong context so it's great to have that corrected now*") and to further develop their learning and communication strategies (e.g. "*...antes de empezar este proyecto siempre intenté de traducir una palabra inglés al español*" ["*Before starting the project I always tried to translate each word from English into Spanish*"]).

4.2. Developing intercultural awareness

The data we analysed contain many instances of intercultural learning taking place within the exchanges as the tasks carried out by the pairs led them to discuss each other's culture. They compared aspects of their everyday life, such as daily routines, and discussed cultural events in their countries. More importantly, they developed their socio-pragmatic competence by sharing concrete information about their own culture to help their partner's integration, such as ways to address lecturers: "*I think it gives you good information you wouldn't find out otherwise (...) general things that you wouldn't do if you don't want to offend someone*". One student reports that she felt more "*street-smart*" after the project.

Witte (2014) argues that the intercultural competence develops in stages. Some evidence of these stages can be traced in the qualitative data collected. The discussions between the learners went from factual exchanges to deeper reflection on culture. In the first instance, differences were perceived as strange and the feeling of alienation dominated (*"Creo que su calendario es muy extraño en comparación a nuestro"* [*"I think that their calendar is very strange compared to ours"*]). They then became aware of the cultural differences and were able to anticipate their cultural shock (*"Ahora sé que llevará tiempo para adaptarse a las diferencias entre Irlanda y España"* [*"Now I am aware that it will take time to adapt to the differences between Ireland and Spain"*]) and discuss stereotypes: *"We talked about stereotypes of both of our countries and what's true/untrue"*.

4.3. Period abroad preparation

Data results show a positive impact of the project on students' preparation before their period abroad. Thanks to exchanges of information, students gained some guidance regarding the university system (class sizes and dynamics, academic calendar, university services) and cultural recommendations. The analysis of the interviews and the portfolios reveals that, during the exchanges, students also received emotional support from their partners as they shared their feelings, fears or worries about living abroad. Reflection about their time abroad made students aware of the adaptation time needed when living in a different country (*"Ha cambiado la manera abordaré mi viaje allí para Erasmus. Ahora sé que llevará tiempo para adaptarse a las diferencias entre Irlanda y España"* [*"It has changed the way I am going to face my trip there for Erasmus. Now I am aware that it will take time to get used to the differences between Ireland and Spain"*]) and the difficulties that could arise.

5. Conclusion

Overall, I-Tell was successful. Our students and their partners fully engaged with the project and showed a strong preference for working autonomously. Our initial outcomes were achieved: students had a relevant linguistic practice during the eight weeks the project lasted and the cultural dimension was a crucial part of the exchanges, developing students' intercultural awareness and cultural learning. Students also shared practical advice and provided emotional support, thus increasing the motivation for the period abroad and reducing anxiety. At the end of the project, most of the students involved reported that they were going to keep in touch with their partners, making the links between the two cultures longer lasting.

We were very satisfied with the results from this first stage of the project and we are now planning to extend the project to other languages (namely French, German and Japanese) as well as to offer the project to advanced and beginner students of Spanish in a regular basis. It will also be interesting to analyse whether the preliminary findings from this first stage are confirmed in subsequent iterations of this initiative.

References

Borghetti, C., Beaven, A., & Pugliese, R. (2015). A module-based approach to foster and document the intercultural process before and during the residence abroad. *Intercultural Education, 26*(1), 31-48. http://dx.doi.org/10.1080/14675986.2015.993515

Byram, M., & Dervin, F. (Eds.). (2008). *Student, staff and academic mobility in higher education*. Newcastle: Cambridge Scholars Publishing.

Coleman, J. (1997). Residence abroad within language study. *Language Teaching, 30*(1), 1-20.

Dervin, F. (2011). *Analysing the consequences of academic mobility and migration*. Newcastle: Cambridge Scholars Publishing.

Holmes, P., Bavieri, L., & Ganassin, S. (2015). Developing intercultural understanding for study abroad: students' and teachers' perspectives on pre-departure intercultural learning. *Intercultural Education, 26*(1), 16-30. http://dx.doi.org/10.1080/14675986.2015.993250

Jackson, J. (2008). *Language, identity and study abroad*. London: Equinox.

Welch, A. (2008). Myths and modes of mobility: the changing face of academic mobility in the global era. *Students, staff and academic mobility in higher education*, 292-313.

Witte, A. (2014). *Blending spaces. Mediating and assessing intercultural competence in the L2 classroom*. Boston/Berlin: De Gruyter.

23. What are the perceived effects of telecollaboration compared to other communication-scenarios with peers?

Elke Nissen[1]

Abstract

What are the perceived effects of Telecollaboration (TC), compared to other types of communication-scenarios with peers (i.e. local peers in small groups and Erasmus students abroad)? This is the question this exploratory study tackles within a blended language learning course. The analysis of students' perceptions paints a rather contrastive picture of telecollaboration. While it stays in the shadow of interaction with Erasmus students, it is complementary to local small-group work and does sustain learning.

Keywords: communication-scenario, telecollaboration, interaction with peers, social presence, blended learning.

1. Introduction

Interaction is of utmost importance within Blended Learning (BL) (Garrison & Vaughan, 2008; Osguthorpe & Graham, 2003), and contributes to the interweaving of face-to-face and distant learning modes. Interactions may not only embrace both modes, but also several communication-scenarios. Thus, in a course design integrating TC, two communication-scenarios are generally blended: one with distant peers and one with local peers (Guth, Helm, & O'Dowd, 2012). In a

---

1. Lidilem, University Grenoble-Alpes, Saint Martin d'Hères, France; elke.nissen@univ-grenoble-alpes.fr

How to cite this chapter: Nissen, E. (2016). What are the perceived effects of telecollaboration compared to other communication-scenarios with peers? In S. Jager, M. Kurek & B. O'Rourke (Eds), *New directions in telecollaborative research and practice: selected papers from the second conference on telecollaboration in higher education* (pp. 201-210). Research-publishing.net. https://doi.org/10.14705/rpnet.2016.telecollab2016.508

Blended Learning Course (BLC), a pedagogical scenario – or learning design – combines face-to-face classroom sessions and online activities in a coherent way: they target, together, the achievement of the course's learning objectives. A communication-scenario is part of the pedagogical scenario; it is defined here as interaction with specific types of interlocutors who play specific roles, and with a distinct set of goals (Nissen, 2014; Tricot & Plégat-Soutjis, 2003) it unfolds face-to-face, at a distance, or in both learning modes.

This exploratory study seeks to determine to what extent and regarding which aspects students perceive that telecollaboration with distant peers contribute to their learning in comparison to other communication-scenarios with peers (i.e. local peers and local Erasmus students) within the same course. The different types of issues the study examines concern *language learning*, *task accomplishment*, *intercultural issues*, and *relationship building*.

2. Methodology and learning design

2.1. Methodology

Data were collected within a blended language learning course that integrates three communication-scenarios with peers:

- local peers working in small groups of three, face-to-face and online;

- TC partners in an asynchronous distant mode;

- Erasmus students abroad, attending three face-to-face lessons.

All three were oriented toward the accomplishment of the course's successive tasks. The students (N=13) filled out a Questionnaire (Q) at the end of semester 1 2015/2016, and wrote a Reflective Essay (RE) on the different communication-scenarios within their course (N=9). Additionally, comparative data were gathered through the same questionnaire on:

- TC partners' perception of the same communication-scenarios (N=2);

- BLC students' perception of another TC project during semester 2 (N=5).

The RE were analysed by means of content analysis. Regarding every item, for each of the four issues and for each of the communication-scenarios, the arguments the students gave, and the number of students who gave that specific argument were counted. TC online interactions were counted separately in each of the forums and categorised regarding their content.

2.2. BLC learning design

Figure 1. BLC: learning design

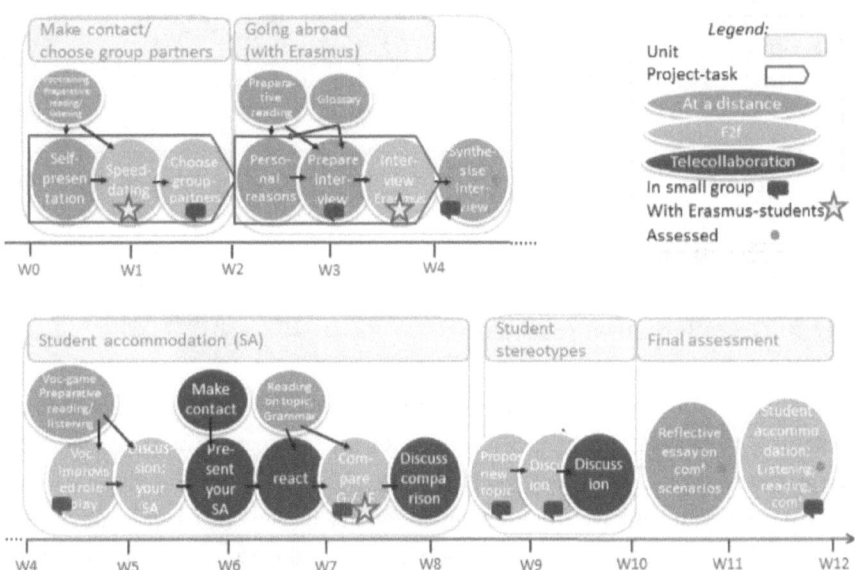

The context of this study is a 12-week (24h-hour) intermediate (B1/B2) BL German course for non-language specialists consisting of several units. In each unit, tasks (represented as bubbles in Figure 1) are logically linked to one another. The first unit aims at choosing partners for small-group work occurring later in the term; in the second, students interview German/Austrian Erasmus students. After presenting and comparing their accommodation with TC partners in Hannover in unit 3, students propose and choose the term's last topic (student stereotypes).

In the course design, focuses and objectives of the two communication-scenarios with Erasmus students and TC partners are rather identical (see Table 1). Work within small groups targets the same aspects, but puts greater emphasis on language. Here, discussions on intercultural aspects are always linked to the exchange with students in Hannover and/or with Erasmus students.

Table 1. Focuses of tasks, in decreasing order of importance

	Within small groups	With TC partners	With Erasmus students
1.	Language (help & correct each other, practice communication)	Intercultural issues	
2.	Intercultural issues	Language (input & practice communication)	
3.	Make contact (relationship building)	Make contact (relationship building)	

3. Results and discussion

3.1. Complementary issues

BLC students' declarations on their own objectives related to each communication-scenario (yes/no items in Q; see Figure 2) indicate that there is only little overlap between working in small groups with students of the same course on the one hand, and working with students from the target country on the other hand. Hence, the communication-scenarios with local and with external partners complement each other rather well. With peers of the same course, students aim at accomplishing the given task(s) as well as possible, and the help they declare they give and get serves this goal, partly "in order to get a good mark" (Q).

3.2. TC in the shadow of interaction with Erasmus students

In accordance with the tasks' objectives, BLC students state (questionnaires, reflective essays) that intercultural aspects are an important issue for them when interacting with TC partners as well as with Erasmus students. However, besides this item, communicating with TC partners appears as a pale copy of interaction with Erasmus students, regarding all the other valued goals in these two communication-scenarios with external partners: language learning, task accomplishment, and relationship building (see Figure 2).

Figure 2. Declared objectives

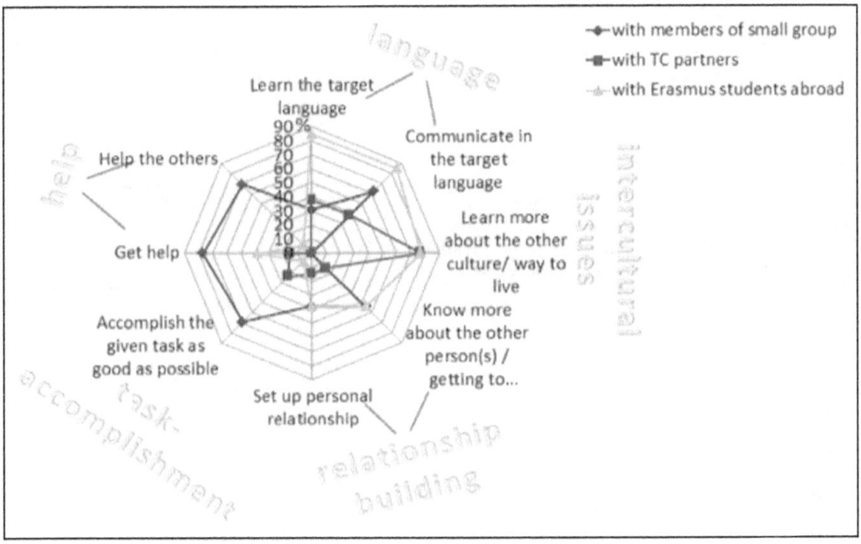

This contrasts with positive feedback on TC students gave within this course during the second term after another TC project, and from the TC partners in Germany.

Several reasons for this gap can be identified through the reflective essays and the online forum discussions.

1) The TC project was conducted exclusively asynchronously (via Moodle forums and Voicethread). This appeared, in the eyes of the students and in comparison to the more immediate contact with Erasmus students who attended 3 classroom sessions, as not interactive enough.

2) Interaction with Erasmus students mainly took place within the first part of the term, telecollaboration exclusively within the second. Still, students felt both scenarios were too similar objective-wise.

3) Only 3 German students participated in the TC exchange. Since course participation is not compulsory and enrolment takes place very shortly before the term starts, this was not foreseeable during the project planning phase. In addition, their level of participation was rather low (see Table 2), which discouraged several French students.

Table 2. Posts in TC online discussion forum

Discussion forum	Total number of messages	Messages from students in France	Messages from students in Germany	Type of message / production
Present yourself	15	10 3	1 1	Self-presentation Reaction
That's how I live. And you?	23	12 1 1 1	3 3 2 -	Simple link to Voicethread-presentation Reaction Attempt to draw comparison Summary of 3 groups' comparisons
Student stereotypes	7	5	1 1	Stereotype-statements Good-bye

4) One TC partner notes a discrepancy with the official aims of her course, which do not normally include much communication. This difference in classroom level (O'Dowd & Ritter, 2006) could have affected learner motivation and expectation.

5) Predominantly, BLC students did complete their TC tasks (self-presentation, accommodation-presentation on Voicethread, indication

of stereotypes). However, despite contrary instructions, they most often simply deposited their productions on the forums. Almost no one initiated, or responded to, any online exchange.

3.3. Importance of social presence

Table 3. Items linked to social presence

	Within small groups	With TC partners	With Erasmus students
Feeling of belonging to a group / community *(Likert scale 0-5; average)*	3.8	1.2	3.0
Feeling of being close to at least several partners *(Likert scale 0-5; average)*	3.4	1.4	2.4
Most interaction *(declarations in Q; 8% gave no answer)*	69%	0%	23%
Issue of relationship building *(yes/no items in Q)*	46%	15%	46%

What likely determined the students' feeling of belonging to a group/community is regularity and synchronicity of exchanges. Students state it was with BLC peers they interacted most – and this communication-scenario was principally synchronous. At the same time, it is this communication-scenario that best allows them to feel they belong to a group/community, and to feel close to several partners (see Table 3). As Garrison and Vaughan (2008, p. 9) argued, social presence is important for community building and creating a sense of belonging to a group. On the contrary, TC gets the lowest scores, including for relationship building.

Regarding interaction with Erasmus students, BLC students claim that good personal contact leads to better work. Compared to the highly valued communication-scenario with Erasmus students, communicating exclusively asynchronously and receiving a low number of messages results in perceiving a higher interpersonal distance and being less engaged in TC, which is in line with Moore's (1993) theory of transactional distance.

3.4. Learning within TC

However, the students perceive they learned rather well through interacting with TC partners; less than with Erasmus students, but more than with their BLC peers (see Figure 3).

Figure 3. Perception of learning through interaction

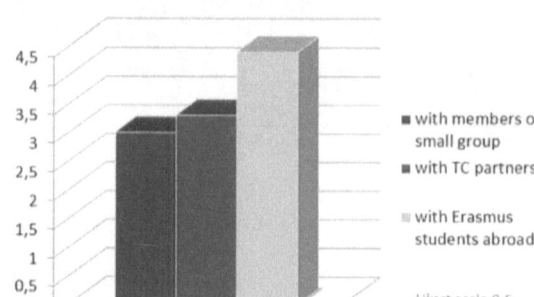

Table 4 shows BLC students consider exchange with TC partners mainly as an occasion to get language input, but also to increase intercultural awareness; with Erasmus students, the greatest outcome is intercultural issues. The communication-scenarios they value most for their learning are those with both external partners. Small groups are mainly dedicated to the completion of task completion (see 3.1) which prepare or use interaction with these external partners.

Table 4. Students' perception of what they learned (RE)

Within small groups	With TC partners	With Erasmus students
Task accomplishment (2)	Language (5)	Intercultural issues (8)
• How to work in groups	• Vocabulary (3)	• See how students live in the other country (3)
Language (1)	• Sentence structure (1)	• See why the students chose Grenoble (3)
• Through correction	• Communication training (1)	
	Intercultural issues (4)	• See different study systems (2)
	• Intercultural exchange (3)	Language (2)
	• Good to see why the partners learn French (1)	• Pronunciation and vocabulary

4. Conclusion

In this study, students value interaction with Erasmus students during face-to-face lessons much higher, mainly as far as language learning but also relationship building are concerned, than asynchronous online interaction with TC partners with low engagement on both sides. In addition, they perceive working within small groups of BLC peers principally as a way to complete course tasks, and getting/giving help in order to complete them. However, in their eyes, learning primarily occurs when interacting or at least exchanging information and getting input from students from the target country. This is why students nevertheless consider they learned quite a lot through TC.

This TC focuses on making contact and on exchanging information (O'Dowd & Ware, 2009), but has no proper collaborative dimension (i.e. jointly accomplishing a task). Still, learner engagement and social presence, which play a major role within more collaboratively oriented learning situations such as small learning groups (Pléty, 1998) and communities of inquiry (Garrison & Vaughan, 2008), appear to also be crucial in this TC.

References

Garrison, D. R., & Vaughan, N. D. (2008). *Blended learning in higher education. Framework, principles, and guidelines*. San Francisco: JosseyBass.

Guth, S., Helm, F., & O'Dowd, R. (2012). *University language classes collaborating online. A Report on the integration of telecollaborative networks in European universities*. http://intent-project.eu/sites/default/files/Telecollaboration_report_Final_Oct2012.pdf

Moore, M. G. (1993). Theory of transactional distance: the evolution of theory of distance education. In D. Keegan (Ed.), *Theoretical principles of distance education* (pp. 22-38). New York: Routledge.

Nissen, E. (2014). *Modéliser le fonctionnement de la formation hybride en langues à travers des recherches ingénieriques*. Habilitation à diriger des recherches, Université Grenoble-Alpes.

Osguthorpe, R.-T., & Graham, C. R. (2003). Blended learning environments. *The Quaterly Review of Distance Education, 4*(3), 227-233.

O'Dowd, R., & Ritter, M. (2006). Understanding and working with 'failed communication' in telecollaborative exchanges. *CALICO Journal, 23*(3), 623-642.

O'Dowd, R., & Ware, P. (2009) Critical issues in telecollaborative task design. *Computer Assisted Language Learning, 22*(2), 173-188. http://dx.doi.org/10.1080/09588220902778369

Pléty, R. (1998). *Comment apprendre et se former en groupe*. Paris: Retz.

Tricot, A., & Plégat-Soutjis, F. (2003). Pour une approche ergonomique de la conception d'un dispositif de formation à distance utilisant les TIC. *Sticef, 10*, n.p.

24. The "Bologna-München" Tandem – experiencing interculturality

Sandro De Martino[1]

Abstract

This case study describes the "Bologna-München" Tandem, a cross-border collaboration[2] which began in 2011. The aim of the collaboration is to give students studying Italian at the Ludwig-Maximilians-University in Munich and students studying German at the University of Bologna the opportunity to experience interculturality through interaction with native speakers. The interaction takes place in the classroom through lessons via Skype and during study trips. The "Bologna-München" Tandem combines telecollaboration and student mobility in order to promote a language and cultural exchange as well as an awareness of interculturality.

Keywords: interculturality, telecollaboration, student mobility, interaction.

1. Context "Bologna-München" Tandem

If we agree with Liddicoat and Scarino (2013) that "interculturality is not simply a manifestation of awareness and knowledge, it also necessitates acting" (p. 50), it follows that you have to ask how and with whom students can interact in foreign language classes. The "Bologna-München" Tandem was created with the aim of giving foreign language students in Bologna and Munich the opportunity

---

1. Università di Bologna, Bologna, Italy; sandro.demartino@unibo.it

2. The "Bologna-München" Tandem is organised in cooperation with Nicoletta Grandi, Italian language teacher at the Ludwig-Maximilians-University in Munich.

How to cite this chapter: De Martino, S. (2016). The "Bologna-München" Tandem – experiencing interculturality. In S. Jager, M. Kurek & B. O'Rourke (Eds), *New directions in telecollaborative research and practice: selected papers from the second conference on telecollaboration in higher education* (pp. 211-216). Research-publishing.net. https://doi.org/10.14705/rpnet.2016.telecollab2016.509

to experience interculturality through interaction with native speakers. The collaboration started in 2011 and is ongoing.

1.1. Participants

The "Bologna-München" Tandem is designed for students studying German in Bologna and Italian in Munich. The participants are both undergraduates and postgraduates and their language levels range from A1 to C1. The activities of the exchange project are integrated within our regular language courses[3]. It is important to point out that the attendance at the courses in Bologna and Munich is not mandatory. However, if students sign up for our courses, they are automatically involved in the exchange project.

Students have the same roles in the tandem: they are experts in their language as they are native speakers and at the same time they are foreign language learners. However, there is an important difference in the understanding and the perception of each other's country, in that a lot of the German students know the north of Italy quite well because they often spend time there on holiday. For them, Italy is a place they feel familiar with. On the other hand, most of the Italian students have never been to Germany and consequently feel no familiarity with the country.

1.2. Objectives

The initial aim was to bring our students into contact in order to start a bilingual dialogue and to open up the classroom to new and stimulating learning experiences. The initial focus was not on the improvement of intercultural communicative competence but it quickly became clear that the intercultural aspect emerges automatically once learners come into contact with native speakers of the language.

For this reason, the principal objectives of the exchange are now twofold. The first is to give our students the opportunity to experience interculturality

---

3. Usually three courses with about 60 students in Bologna and seven or eight courses with about 60 students in Munich. In case of beginner classes the number of students is about 100 in Bologna and up to 150 in Munich.

inside and outside the classroom by putting them into contexts of authentic communication with native speakers. Secondly, we want to sensitise our students to interculturality and to promote cultural awareness.

1.3. Project development

The cooperation started with lessons via Skype and a blog called "e-tandem Bologna-München". Six months after the start of the telecollaboration, ten students from Munich organised a private trip to Bologna in order to get to know their partners from the Skype sessions. The students from Munich took part in the German lessons in Bologna and the experience of the shared lessons of foreign language learners and native speakers gave a new dimension to the project.

The tandem was redesigned for the following year to integrate study trips into the project. So far eight study trips have been organised: four to Munich and four to Bologna. In 2013 we decided to focus only on the Skype sessions and student mobility and to abandon the blog. We wanted to focus on activities in the classroom as the blog activities were not integrated in our lessons and so were more difficult to monitor.

2. Experiencing interculturality

The "Bologna-München" Tandem provides the opportunity for acting through telecollaboration and during real-life encounters. As Liddicoat and Scarino (2013) argue, "exposure to interaction of itself does not necessarily equate with intercultural learning" (p. 111), reflective practice on the experience is an integral part of the learning process as well.

2.1. Telecollaboration

The Skype lessons are organised in one course in Bologna and Munich and take place in real time once a week. The telecollaborative activities are part of the curriculum of both courses. The students are paired randomly at the beginning of the exchange and they normally speak with the same partner throughout the course. Usually, 8 to 12 students participate in the Skype lessons. Skype conversations last 60 minutes and are bilingual – students speak half of the time in one language and then switch to the other one.

Skype sessions aim at improving students' ability to interact in the foreign language as well as at sharing experiences and knowledge about contemporary questions and issues which young people can easily relate to. The personalisation of the given topics is important as students are seen not as representatives of a culture or broadcasters of knowledge, but as individual interlocutors. The students' conversations are guided through established tasks. Following the conversation, reflective practice takes place through guided classroom discussion and learner diaries.

2.2. Student mobility

The aim of the one-week study trips is full immersion in the language and culture of the target country. The participation is voluntary and usually the students who attend the Skype lessons take part in the study trips. Students experience interculturality through contact with their hosts. This kind of accommodation not only gives an insight into the daily life of a student of the same age, but also forms the basis for authentic communication. Students can also have contact in real-life situations with other people such as family members, flatmates and friends.

The shared lessons are organised in all our classes and are held in German in Bologna and in Italian in Munich. They are integrated into the curriculum and allow all our students to have an intercultural experience in their classroom. One important part of the shared lessons are presentations by the guest students on pre-determined topics, for example presentations about Munich, the Ludwig-Maximilians-University or specific topics of interest. Learning, or rather acting, takes place inside and outside the classroom. Examples of shared learning experiences are guided tours organised by the students, or visits to museums or monuments.

3. Project evaluation

Student feedback emerges from the student reports as well as end-of-course questionnaires. When it comes to the Skype sessions, for most of the students in Bologna the conversations are their first contact with German native speakers. Students consider the telecollaboration a stimulating and important experience which allows them to test their German. Students focus primarily on the content of the conversation and the interaction itself, not on the correct form. The tandem situation is normally perceived as informal and this reduces inhibitions or fear of speaking. From a pedagogical view we can state that the successful interaction with equals contributes to the learners' personal development by making them more confident in the use of the language and consequently more self-assured and autonomous.

Time spent abroad does not necessarily guarantee contact with local students and may not lead to real interaction. In contrast, in the tandem situation, interaction is facilitated because students stay with their partners and all guided activities are designed to make students interact with one another. Due to the participation in the exchange activities, students open up to intercultural issues, e.g. the role of culture in communication or the perceptions different countries can have of each other. These issues are often not the focus of students' interest when studying a foreign language. Reflective practice on the intercultural experience broadens not only their view of the foreign culture, but also their own. Student feedback is very positive both in Bologna and in Munich. As the participation in the exchange activities is voluntary, only motivated students participate and their engagement contributes positively to the outcomes of the project. Negative aspects mentioned in the reports concern mainly technical problems during the Skype sessions.

4. Conclusion

The "Bologna-München" Tandem lives on the initiative and the enthusiasm of all its participants and is continuously evolving. Proof of this is the private trip which was organised by the students from Munich during the first year of the project. Due to this initiative, the project developed in a new direction.

The "Bologna-München" Tandem combines computer-mediated communication with student mobility and due to this concept it is different from many other telecollaboration projects[4]. Telecollaboration and student mobility complement each other because the online activities not only form the basis for the real-life encounter but also allow for the continuation of the contact after the study trip. On the basis of the experiences in Bologna and Munich, we can confirm that telecollaboration is effective in establishing relationships between learners. However, acting – as the basis for experiencing interculturality – requires not only interlocutors, but also freedom in terms of space and time to allow personal engagement. The real-life encounters give students space and time to interact and allow for a live intercultural experience.

The "Bologna-München" Tandem shows that language teaching can successfully overcome the challenges involved in going beyond national borders and in achieving authentic contact between language learners and native speakers, thereby allowing them to experience interculturality.

References

Guth, S., & Helm, F. (Eds.). (2010). *Telecollaboration 2.0: language, literacies and intercultural learning in the 21st century.* Bern: Peter Lang.

Guth, S., Helm, F., & O'Dowd, R. (2012). *University language classes collaborating online. Report on the integration of telecollaborative networks in European universities.* https://goo.gl/DYp8G6

Liddicoat, A. J., & Scarino, A. (2013). *Intercultural language teaching and learning.* Chichester: Wiley-Blackwell. http://dx.doi.org/10.1002/9781118482070

---

4. See for example the case studies in Guth and Helm (2010) and Guth, Helm, and O'Dowd (2012).

25. Comparing the development of transversal skills between virtual and physical exchanges

Bart van der Velden[1], Sophie Millner[2], and Casper van der Heijden[3]

Abstract

This paper aims to compare the impact on the development of transversal skills, such as self-esteem, of virtual and physical exchanges. This is done by comparing the Europe on the Edge programme to the results of the Erasmus Impact Study. In doing so it fills the need that has been expressed in the telecollaboration field to study the impact of online education programmes "outside of students' and educators' beliefs" (Helm, 2015, p. 212). We shall argue that it is indeed possible to compare physical and virtual exchanges by measuring the impact on so-called transversal skills.

Keywords: virtual exchange, transversal skills, Erasmus, impact study, curiosity, self-efficacy.

1. Introduction

With the rise of the internet we also see a rise in online education. At the same time we see that employers attach great value to international experiences (Brandenburg et al., 2014, p. 14). Virtual Exchanges (VE) intend to provide this

---

1. Sharing Perspectives Foundation, Amsterdam, The Netherlands; bart@sharingperspectivesfoundation.com

2. Sharing Perspectives Foundation, Amsterdam, The Netherlands; sophie@sharingperspectivesfoundation.com

3. Sharing Perspectives Foundation, Amsterdam, The Netherlands; casper@sharingperspectivesfoundation.com

How to cite this chapter: Van der Velden, B., Millner, S., & Van der Heijden, C. (2016). Comparing the development of transversal skills between virtual and physical exchanges. In S. Jager, M. Kurek & B. O'Rourke (Eds), *New directions in telecollaborative research and practice: selected papers from the second conference on telecollaboration in higher education* (pp. 217-224). Research-publishing.net. https://doi.org/10.14705/rpnet.2016.telecollab2016.510

international experience in an online setting. The question arises as to how well these virtual exchanges compare to physical ones.

The Virtual Exchange Coalition (VEC) defines VEs as technology-enabled, sustained, people-to-people education programmes (Virtual Exchange Coalition, n.d.). They differ from telecollaboration as the acquirement of foreign language is not the primary objective. We use the definition of the VEC, meaning that VEs are (1) technology-enabled, i.e. take place over the internet; (2) people-to-people, thus primarily focused on facilitated interaction between learners; and (3) sustained, meaning curriculum based over a set period of time. In this way they can be seen as the online equivalent of physical exchanges facilitated through the ERASMUS programme.

The stated goals of the VEC invite one to make a direct comparison between their impact and the impact of Physical Exchanges (PEs). One of the broadest studies to date on this subject is the Erasmus Impact Study (EIS) (Brandenburg et al., 2014). The EIS makes use of the Monitoring Exchange Mobility Outcomes (MEMO) tool. The MEMO-tool was developed to measure the effects of international mobility on the development of students' personality traits which are closely linked to employability and intercultural competence (CHE Consult, n.d., p. 3). These are classed as 'transversal skills'. The MEMO-tool consists of ten factors, but for the EIS only those factors pertaining to employability were kept: *confidence, curiosity, decisiveness, serenity, tolerance of ambiguity,* and *vigour* (Brandenburg et al., 2014, p. 15). It is against these transversal skills that we compare physical exchanges and virtual ones.

2. Methodology

This study looked at the impact of the Sharing Perspectives Foundation programme 'EUROPE ON THE EDGE', which ran in the fall semester of 2015. In the programme, students from ten different European countries met online in facilitated video conference sessions in subgroups of ten students for two hours per week over ten weeks to discuss current European socio-political issues. The setup of this impact study was developed by the Sharing Perspectives Foundation research team as part of the evaluation of the programme. The evaluation survey was presented to students at both the start and end of the programme.

The MEMO-tool does not provide sources for the way they measure personality traits, therefore the measures we use in this study are based on our interpretation of the definitions provided in the EIS. As such, *vigour*, or 'problem-solver' (Brandenburg et al., 2014, p. 26), had to be dropped, as no comparable psychometric scale was found. The other scales, their definitions, and the comparable psychometric measures we used are presented in Table 1.

Table 1. Definitions of personality measures in the EIS and comparable psychometric scales

Name EIS	Definition EIS	Comparable Scale	Definition
Tolerance of Ambiguity	Acceptance of other people's culture and attitudes and adaptability	Intolerance of ambiguity (Subscale of the Need for Closure Scale) (Webster & Kruglanski, 1994)	A range, from rejection to attraction, of reactions to stimuli perceived as unfamiliar, complex, dynamically uncertain or subject to multiple conflicting interpretations (McLain, 1993)
Curiosity	Openness to new experiences	Curiosity and exploration Inventory-II (Exploration Subscale) (Kashdan, Rose, & Fincham, 2004)	The orientation toward seeking novel and challenging objects, events and ideas with the aim of integrating these experiences and information. (Kashdan et al., 2004)
Confidence	Trust in own competence	Single-item Self-esteem scale (Robins, Hendin, & Trzesniewski, 2001)	A favorable or unfavorable attitude toward the self (Rosenberg, 1965, p. 15)
Serenity	Awareness of own strength and weaknesses	General self-efficacy scale (Schwarzer, 2014)	Beliefs in one's capabilities to mobilise the motivation, cognitive resources, and courses of action needed to meet given situational demands (Wood & Bandura, 1989)

| Decisiveness | Ability to make decisions | Decisiveness (Subscale of the need for closure scale) (Webster & Kruglanski, 1994) | Ability to reach decisions as quickly as possible (Kosic, 2004) |

In consideration of the length of the survey, some items were cut from the original psychometric scales. To determine which items to retain, factor loadings of previous studies with comparable samples were examined. Those questions with factor loadings above the mean of all factor loadings were retained. For an overview of the retained items see Table 2. All items were measured on a five point Likert scale.

Table 2. Items retained for the survey

Name EIS	Factor loadings from:	Mean factor loadings	Items retained
Tolerance of Ambiguity	Webster and Kruglanski (1994)	0.46	30, 36, 8, 31, and 14
Curiosity	Kashdan et al. (2004)	0.63	3 and 7
Confidence	Robins et al. (2001)	Not applicable	1
Serenity	Schwarzer (1999)	0.7	5, 4, 7, 9, and 10
Decisiveness	Webster and Kruglanski (1994)	0.62	22, 17, and 16

3. Results

Of the five different personality traits we measured, three had significant results: curiosity, self-efficacy, and tolerance of ambiguity (see Figure 1). Self-esteem did show an increase of the median (from 3.5 to 4 out of a five point scale), but no significant change. All items have an N of 52.

For self-efficacy, the paired t-test is significant at an alpha of 0.1 ($p=0.061$). The mean growth is 0.12 (5 point scale), or 3.11%. The growth found by EIS for Erasmus students was 0.17 out of a ten point scale.

A Wilcoxon signed rank test showed that our programme increased curiosity significantly (Z=-2.492, p=0.013). The mean score showed an increase of 0.19, or 4.4%. The effect is relatively large compared to the EIS with an increase of 0.12.

Tolerance of ambiguity is the only scale where we saw a significant decrease. For our sample, a paired t-test (p=0.034) showed a decrease of -0.23, or 11.6%.

Figure 1. Curiosity, self-efficacy, and tolerance of ambiguity

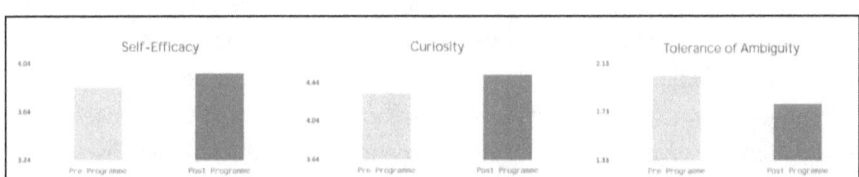

4. Discussion

The results show that over ten weeks our sample became more self-efficacious and curious. Although our results are significant, some points need to be addressed. The decrease in tolerance of ambiguity was surprising given the rise in curiosity and self-efficacy. The relationship between self-efficacy and tolerance of ambiguity is normally positive (Endres, Chowdhury, & Milner, 2009), as is the relationship between curiosity and tolerance of ambiguity (Litman, 2010). Questions to test tolerance of ambiguity included:

> "I feel uncomfortable when I don't understand the reason why an event occurred in my life".

> "When I'm confused about an important issue, I feel very upset".

One explanation for this exceptional result could be that the responses were influenced by the Paris attacks of November 2015. Reflecting on the attacks during the discussions, it was clear that students were upset by what happened and had trouble comprehending these events, so the influence of the attacks cannot fully be discounted. More research is needed to see if we can isolate the effect of the programme.

The relatively small scale and lack of control group in our study prohibits any strong interpretations, and the differences between our results and those of the EIS might be a consequence of different measurement techniques. However, our results indicate that overall VEs have the potential to impact students' development of transversal skills in a similar way as physical exchanges. This study has shown that the impact of VEs can be assessed independently of students' or educators' beliefs. The relatively large effects found, in comparison to the EIS, might be due to limitations in the current study, or could be a consequence of the high starting point of Erasmus students. If the latter is the case this is positive. A goal of VEs is to make exchange experiences accessible to those who lack resources to go on a PE. Therefore, if the students caught up to the level of Erasmus students this is promising for VEs.

5. Conclusion

We have seen that the programme under consideration had significant effect on transversal skills, and that the effects are comparable to those of the EIS. We set out to see if, and how, one could compare VEs and PEs. Although this study is small in scale, it has shown that comparing VEs to PEs is a valuable endeavour. Using the same survey, the next step is to expand the scale of this research to compare the development of transversal skills across a number of European VEs and PEs.

References

Brandenburg, U., Berghoff, S., Taboadela, O., Bischof, L., Gajowniczek, J., Gehlke, A., & Hachmeister, C. (2014). *The Erasmus impact study: effects of mobility on the skills and employability of students and the internationalisation of higher education institutions.* Luxembourg: European Union. https://doi.org/10.2766/75468

CHE Consult. (n.d.). *Memo tool: monitoring exchange mobility outcomes*. CHE Consult GmbH. https://www.che-consult.de/fileadmin/pdf/memo_tool_presentation.pdf

Endres, M., Chowdhury, S., & Milner, M. (2009). Ambiguity tolerance and accurate assessment of self-efficacy in a complex decision task. *Journal of Management & Organization, 15*(1), 31-46. https://doi.org/10.1017/S1833367200002868

Helm, F. (2015). The practices and challenges of telecollaboration in higher education in Europe. *Language Learning & Technology, 19*(2), 197-217

Kashdan, T., Rose, P., & Fincham, F. (2004). Curiosity and exploration: facilitating positive subjective experiences and personal growth opportunities. *Journal of Personality Assessment, 82*(3), 291-305. https://doi.org/10.1207/s15327752jpa8203_05

Kosic, A. (2004). Acculturation strategies, coping process and acculturative stress. *Scandinavian Journal of Psychology, 45*(4), 269-278. https://doi.org/10.1111/j.1467-9450.2004.00405.x

Litman, J. (2010). Relationships between measures of I- and D-type curiosity, ambiguity tolerance, and need for closure: an initial test of the wanting-liking model of information-seeking. *Personality and Individual Differences, 48*(4), 397-402. https://.doi.org/10.1016/j.paid.2009.11.005

McLain, D. (1993). The Mstat-I: a new measure of an individual's tolerance for ambiguity. *Educational and Psychological Measurement 53*(1),183-189. https://doi.org/10.1177/0013164493053001020

Robins, R., Hendin, H., & Trzesniewski, K. (2001). Measuring global self-esteem: construct validation of a single-item measure and the Rosenberg self-esteem scale. *Personality and Social Psychology Bulletin, 27*(2), 151-161. https://doi.org/10.1177/0146167201272002

Rosenberg, M. (1965). *Society and the adolescent self-image*. Princeton, NJ: Princeton University Press.

Schwarzer, R. (1999). *General perceived self-efficacy in 14 cultures*. http://userpage.fu-berlin.de/~gesund/publicat/ehps_cd/health/world14.htm

Schwarzer, R. (2014). *Everything you wanted to know about the general self-efficacy scale but were afraid to ask*. http://userpage.fu-berlin.de/~health/faq_gse.pdf

Virtual Exchange Coalition. (n.d.). http://virtualexchangecoalition.org/

Webster, D., & Kruglanski, A. (1994). Individual differences in need for cognitive closure. *Journal of Personality and Social Psychology, 67*(6), 1049-1062. https://doi.org/10.1037/0022-3514.67.6.1049

Chapter 25

Wood, R., & Bandura, A. (1989). Impact of conceptions of ability on self-regulatory mechanisms and complex decision making. *Journal of Personality and Social Psychology, 56*(3), 407-415. https://doi.org/10.1037/0022-3514.56.3.407

26. Making virtual exchange/telecollaboration mainstream – large scale exchanges

Eric Hagley[1]

Abstract

Language educators' goals include promoting cultural understanding and improving the language skills of their students. Virtual Exchange (VE) is a powerful means to do this. Students in English as a Foreign Language (EFL) classrooms often have few opportunities to communicate with other users of English. VE gives them virtual mobility, enabling them to participate in a global community, use English in real world communicative events and become more culturally acclimatized. Though there are many benefits to VE, it is often not easily accessible to teachers. This paper introduces a large scale VE that includes over 1500 students and 53 teachers from 21 institutions in six countries. The paper outlines benefits and drawbacks of this VE, some initial findings on student engagement and participation in the VE, in addition to information on how the project is planned to expand, making it accessible to a larger number of teachers and their students around the world.

Keywords: virtual exchange, telecollaboration, intercultural communication, language learning, EFL.

---

1. Muroran Institute of Technology, Muroran, Japan; hagley@mmm.muroran-it.ac.jp

How to cite this chapter: Hagley, E. (2016). Making virtual exchange/telecollaboration mainstream – large scale exchanges. In S. Jager, M. Kurek & B. O'Rourke (Eds), *New directions in telecollaborative research and practice: selected papers from the second conference on telecollaboration in higher education* (pp. 225-230). Research-publishing.net. https://doi.org/10.14705/rpnet.2016.telecollab2016.511

Chapter 26

1. Introduction

Many EFL classes, particularly in Asia and South America, have students from only one cultural background in them. Communication taking place in the classroom is between those same students, hence the immediacy of the Foreign Language (FL) is often lost. With the Internet came the possibility of VE. The Intent project group (2015) states VE is "technology-enabled, sustained, people to people education programs […] entailing the engagement of groups of students in online intercultural exchange, interaction and collaboration with peers from partner classes in geographically distant locations, under the guidance of educators and/or expert facilitators" (para. 2). In its different forms, it has been shown to have a number of positive effects (Chen & Yang, 2014; Kern & Warschauer, 2000; Pais Marden & Herrington, 2011).

Dual Language VE (DLVE), often called eTandem, is possibly the more commonly used but is limited by the number of students studying one of the languages. Single Language VE (SLVE), where one language is used as the lingua franca, particularly when the language used is English, has a potentially far greater number of students able to join and thus the capability of becoming mainstream in EFL communication classes around the world.

2. The SLVE platform

The SLVE described here has students interacting asynchronously in English as a lingua franca. The server on which it is based is maintained with financial assistance from a Japanese government Kaken grant. Exchanges are carried out over 8 week periods using Moodle. Two, three or four classes from different countries are combined. Teachers from each of the participating classes send the exchange administrator a CSV file with their students' information and this is uploaded into the system. Alternatively, students access the system via Learning Tools Interoperability (LTI). Online groups are formed containing approximately 25 students from each of the countries. Hence, each group would have between 40-50 (two countries) to 100 (four countries) students in it. Online communication then takes place using the Moodle forums. As groups are set to 'separate', multiple groups can be in the one VE participating in the same forums, but because they are 'separate', students only see the classmates they are paired with. In the present course there are 27 groups. Participation in the forums involves posting and replying using self created text, audio and video posts. Students can also add links and other multimedia to their posts. Almost all the students in this course are non-English majors at low-intermediate level.

Teachers are encouraged to monitor the forums and give feedback to students. They are also asked to keep in contact with their partner teacher and find out about their teaching and learning environments. Teachers are also offered resources to help their students reflect on their participation. There is no obligation to assign grades to students for their participation, but teachers are encouraged to do so. All teachers are included in a separate teachers' course where they exchange ideas and information.

3. Course content

The discussion topics are 'self introduction', 'about my place', 'events in our lives', 'future plans' and one open forum. Each forum is open for three to four weeks. These topics were decided by the teachers involved in the initial exchange. In the teachers' forum, ideas are being exchanged on how these may develop in the future. Admittedly, many of the criticisms that O'Dowd (2016) mentions apply here. The topics are limiting and the intercultural learning is not guaranteed just because the students are linked. Genres are also blurred. However, if students are beginners or of a low intermediate level, forum topics need to be simple. With only pre-intermediate language skills or less, students are limited in what they can do. It is impossible for beginner level language students to participate fully in topics of deeper meaning and pushing them to do so can result in miscommunication and possibly develop resentment toward their partner because of this. Hence, in these beginner level exchanges, the style is often one of "a written exchange but in the form of a spoken chat" (Ware & Kramsch, 2005, cited in O'Dowd, 2016, p. 285). Starting with a simple VE, teachers can prepare their students for more robust tasks. As the alternative is a mono-cultural classroom with no real world communication, VE is to be preferred.

Presently, teachers are encouraged to ensure students reflect on the interactions taking place and introduce concepts of intercultural learning. At this language level, perhaps true 'intercultural learning' does not take place but cultural acclimatization certainly does. Before climbers ascend a major peak they acclimatize themselves at lower levels. VE students, who have never had interaction with foreign culture, do not have the shock that often comes with physically entering another country. VE is a far more gentle introduction to foreign culture and can therefore be considered a form of cultural acclimatization.

4. Feedback

Student responses in surveys carried out to date have been, where the forums are active, overwhelmingly positive. Perhaps some of the positive feedback can be attributed to 'the illusion of commonality' (Ware & Kramsch, 2005, cited in O'Dowd, 2016, p. 277), but students are being exposed to other cultures that they would not be without the VE and this reduces students' initial fear of all things foreign. It is also a motivator for them to begin learning more deeply about other cultures.

There have been situations where students from a partnered class, for a variety of reasons, did not participate in the forums to the level expected. When students post but receive no replies, obviously their responses in follow up surveys will be less than positive. This is the number one issue that has plagued some of the group exchanges. Teacher interaction is key to reducing the angst felt by students not receiving replies. If students understand the problems in the other country, they are more understanding. In some cases, due to poor teacher to teacher communication, information was not passed onto students, leaving some with bitter feelings toward their partner class. With better teacher to teacher communication and more planning, these problems can be overcome.

5. Future of the VE

To ensure the problems outlined by O'Dowd (2016) above are taken into consideration, this VE will develop to allow students longer participation. There is a pilot continuers' course for some of the students that participated in previous VE. This will develop to include more robust tasks. We also plan to create two more levels – an intermediate and advanced level in which students will have the language skills to participate in collaborative tasks and carry out projects that will lead to real intercultural learning whilst developing their language skills further. It will be carried out on the International Virtual Exchange Project's site iveproject.org. Our goal is to have approximately 20,000 students participating in three levels by 2020. The project is open to more institutions joining until that point in time. The server configuration and courseware will then become creative commons so others who want to create a similar project can easily do so.

6. Conclusion

When used well, VE is a powerful method for language educators to improve their students' communication skills and cultural awareness. However, from a technical and practical perspective it is often difficult for teachers to do so, as they do not have the technical prowess or the contacts to find a partner class. The project detailed here is one simple way for teachers to join in a VE project and attain all the benefits therein. As VE becomes more mainstream, teachers will, more and more, want their students to use the language they are learning in real world communication. If cultural acclimatization can also occur as a precursor to cultural competence, then another major benefit has been achieved. The VE outlined here is one way of achieving those goals.

7. Acknowledgments

This research was partially supported by the Ministry of Education, Science, Sports and Culture in Japan, Grant-in-Aid for Scientific Research (C), 2014-2016 (25370613, Eric Hagley).

I am very grateful to all the teachers and students that are working so hard to make this exchange a success. Teachers wanting to join this project should email hagley@mmm.muroran-it.ac.jp, ideally from their school's email address.

References

Chen, J. J., & Yang, S. C. (2014). Fostering foreign language learning through technology-enhanced intercultural projects. *Language Learning & Technology, 18*(1), 57-75. http://llt.msu.edu/issues/february2014/chenyang.pdf

INTENT project group. (2015). *Position paper on virtual exchange*. http://uni-collaboration.eu/?q=node/996

Kern, R., & Warschauer, M. (2000). Theory and practice of network-based language teaching. In M. Warschauer & R. Kern (Eds), *Network-based language teaching: concepts and practice* (pp. 1-19). New York: Cambridge University Press. http://dx.doi.org/10.1017/cbo9781139524735.003

O'Dowd, R. (2016). Learning from the past and looking to the future of online intercultural exchange. In R. O'Dowd & T. Lewis (Eds.), *Online intercultural exchange: policy, pedagogy, practice*. London: Routledge.

Pais Marden, M., & Herrington, J. (2011). Supporting interaction and collaboration in the language classroom through computer mediated communication. In T. Theo Bastiaens & M. Ebner (Eds), *ED-MEDIA, World Conference on Educational Multimedia, Hypermedia and Telecommunications* (pp. 1161-1168). Chesapeake, VA: AACE.

Ware, P. D, & Kramsch, C. (2005). Toward an intercultural stance: teaching German and English through telecollaboration. *The Modern Language Journal, 89*(2), 190-205. http://dx.doi.org/10.1111/j.1540-4781.2005.00274.x

Section 5.

Telecollaboration for other disciplines and skills

27 Searching for telecollaboration in secondary geography education in Germany

Jelena Deutscher[1]

Abstract

The majority of studies on telecollaboration for educational purposes focus on language-related aspects. Therefore, a qualitative explorative research project was set up at the Ruhr-University Bochum, Germany, dealing with telecollaboration from the perspective of a non-language discipline; it is based on the approach of transferring telecollaboration to content subjects, more precisely to geography education in the context of Content and Language Integrated Learning (CLIL). In this paper, the proceedings and main findings of the preliminary study of the research project are presented. The aim of the preliminary study was to learn more about the extent to which telecollaboration existed in geography education in the whole of Germany and in particular in the federal state of North-Rhine Westphalia (NRW).

Keywords: telecollaboration, CLIL, geography education, content subject teaching and learning.

1. Introduction

Research on telecollaboration for educational purposes has produced a substantial amount of publications. The majority of these publications focus on language-related aspects (cf. Dooly & O'Dowd, 2012, pp. 7-8), especially

---

1. Ruhr-University Bochum, Bochum, Germany; Jelena.Deutscher@rub.de

How to cite this chapter: Deutscher, J. (2016). Searching for telecollaboration in secondary geography education in Germany. In S. Jager, M. Kurek & B. O'Rourke (Eds), *New directions in telecollaborative research and practice: selected papers from the second conference on telecollaboration in higher education* (pp. 233-238). Research-publishing.net. https://doi.org/10.14705/rpnet.2016.telecollab2016.512

on Computer-Assisted Language Learning (CALL) and on the development of Intercultural Communicative Competence (ICC) (cf. O'Dowd, 2013, pp. 123-126). Accordingly, the term telecollaboration often refers to "telecollaborative language learning" (cf. Dooly, 2008, p. 15). The strong connection between telecollaboration and language-related aspects surprises because telecollaboration offers opportunities which are also relevant to non-language subjects, i.e. content subjects. Most notable is its motivating effect achieved by putting students in touch with peers outside of their classroom. However, telecollaboration may also be defined without any connection to a specific subject area: It may be understood as a teaching method enabling students in distant locations to learn together, usually with the help of Information and Communication Technology (ICT) (cf. O'Dowd, 2013, p. 123).

The study presented in this paper was based on this broader understanding of telecollaboration. Its objective was to learn more about the extent to which telecollaboration existed in the teaching practices of the content subject geography in Germany. Geography was chosen because it is a space-related subject (DGfG, 2014, p. 5): by letting students at distant locations collaborate, the discussion of regional similarities or differences as well as the students' personal or local perspectives may be included into the teaching. Geography is also a subject which makes use of a great variety of media, e.g. charts or maps (DGfG, 2014, p. 6). As learners may select or create media to exchange topic-related information, telecollaboration offers a goal-oriented way for developing method skills. Furthermore, geography is a subject typical for Content and Language Integrated Learning (CLIL)[2] in Germany (KMK, 2013, p. 13). By integrating telecollaboration in geography education into CLIL settings – i.e. by adding the use of a target language – the amount of possible partners and consequently of geographical topics which can be dealt with is increased. Also, students may benefit from the authentic language-use resulting from the fact that the target language becomes the only means to exchange content-related information with their peers. For the study, English

---

2. It is important to differentiate between the acronyms CLIL and CBLL (Content-Based Language Learning). Although both approaches combine language and content learning, the pursued teaching aims are crucially different: whereas CBLL aims at developing language-related skills (Müller-Hartmann & Schocker-von Ditfurth, 2004, p. 152), CLIL aims at developing proficiencies in the content subject (cf. Eurydice, 2006, p. 7).

was chosen as a target language because it has the status of a world language and is most commonly used for CLIL in Germany.

2. Proceedings and findings

In the beginning of this study, only a small number of publications on telecollaboration in geography education could be found (e.g. Schuler, 2001). However, because of the above-mentioned opportunities offered by this method, it was assumed that at least some telecollaborations existed in the teaching practices in geography education. Consequently, an extensive search for telecollaborations was conducted.

In a first step, E-Twinning and PASCH – two of the largest web portals supporting telecollaborative activities in Germany and offering search engines for a partner- and/or project-search – were searched for telecollaborations in geography education in Germany. The search on these web portals proved to be inefficient partly due to the fact that the search engines did not support the search for telecollaborations in specific content subjects.

In a second step, ministries, educational institutions and educational and/or geographical societies in the 16 federal states of Germany were asked if they knew of the existence of telecollaborations, i.e. projects which fulfilled all of the following criteria: integration into the geography curriculum, collaboration between students in Germany and abroad, and communication with the help of digital media and English. Responses to this survey came from seven federal states, but no report on any such project was received.

In a third step, it was decided to search in more detail in one of the federal states. NRW was chosen as a research area because it has a high population density and the highest density of schools offering German-English CLIL-programmes in Germany (DIPF, 2006, p. 58). About 900 secondary geography teachers at about 550 schools were questioned if they had conducted – or were about to conduct – a project fulfilling all of the above-mentioned criteria. The response rate of this survey was approximately 20 percent and seven teachers reported on having conducted eleven such projects altogether. These seven teachers were interviewed and it was found that none of the projects fulfilled all of the criteria: in two projects there was no collaboration with partners abroad and in five projects the collaborations took place fully or partially as face-to-face meetings. While two of the projects were set in geography classes but dealt with topics which did not form part of the official geography curriculum, the other nine projects took place as extracurricular activities. The extracurricular projects can be characterized by either addressing topics of world-wide relevance such as sustainability or tourism or by being held open as regards content. Interestingly, three were funded by national or international educational organizations. The findings are presented in more detail in Deutscher (forthcoming).

The projects found were not of interest for this study because it was assumed that extracurricular projects usually address a small number of (intrinsically) motivated and – in the case of funded projects – select students. In order to reach a larger number of students, it was regarded as essential that telecollaborations are set in regular classes and are integrated into the curriculum.

3. Conclusion

The findings imply that – if at all – only a small number of telecollaborations in geography education existed in the teaching practices in NRW and in the whole of Germany. This lack of telecollaborations is a possible explanation for the small amount of publications dealing with this topic from the perspective of geography education. Although none of the eleven projects found fulfilled all of the criteria regarded as relevant, the findings show nevertheless that telecollaborations on geography-related topics are in fact realizable, especially in CLIL-settings, and may contribute to education in non-language subjects.

The study presented in this paper forms part of a qualitative explorative research project which was set up at the Ruhr-University Bochum and deals with the approach of transferring telecollaboration to secondary geography education.

The findings led to a still ongoing follow up study which explores subject-related characteristics of telecollaborations set in CLIL-geography classes in NRW. For the follow up study, secondary geography teachers were encouraged to set up a telecollaboration according to their needs and facilities available and which fulfilled the above-mentioned criteria. This resulted in ten telecollaborations with partners in different parts of the world (cf. Deutscher, forthcoming).

References

DGfG (Deutsche Gesellschaft für Geographie). (Ed.). (2014). *Bildungsstandards im Fach Geographie für den Mittleren Schulabschluss*. http://dgfg.geography-in-germany.de/wp-content/uploads/geographie_bildungsstandards.pdf

Deutscher, J. (forthcoming). *Telekollaboration im bilingualen Geographieunterricht* (Dissertation). Ruhr-Universität Bochum, Bochum.

DIPF (Deutsches Institut für Internationale Pädagogische Forschung). (2006). *Unterricht und Kompetenzerwerb in Deutsch und Englisch: Zentrale Befunde der Studie Deutsch Englisch Schülerleistungen International (DESI)*. http://www.dipf.de/de/forschung/projekte/pdf/biqua/desi-zentrale-befunde

Dooly, M. (2008). Introduction. In M. Dooly (Ed.), *Telecollaborative language learning. A guidebook to moderating intercultural communication online* (pp. 15-19). Bern: Lang.

Dooly, M., & O'Dowd, R. (2012). Series editors' preface. In M. Dooly & R. O'Dowd (Eds), *Telecollaboration in education (Vol. 3). Researching online foreign language interaction and exchange. Theories, methods and challenges* (pp. 7-8). Bern, New York: Lang.

Eurydice. (Ed.). (2006). *Content and language integrated learning (CLIL) at school in Europe*. Brussels: Eurydice.

KMK (Ständige Konferenz der Kultusminister der Länder in der Bundesrepublik Deutschland). (Ed.). (2013). *Konzepte für den bilingualen Unterricht – Erfahrungsbericht und Vorschläge zur Weiterentwicklung: Beschluss der Kultusministerkonferenz vom 17.10.2013*. http://www.kmk.org/fileadmin/Dateien/veroeffentlichungen_beschluesse/2013/201_10_17-Konzepte-_bilingualer-_Unterricht.pdf

Müller-Hartmann, A., & Schocker-von Ditfurth, M. (2004). *Introduction to English language teaching. Fremdsprachendidaktik inhalts- und lernerorientiert (Vol. 15)*. Stuttgart: Klett Sprachen.

O'Dowd, R. (2013). Telecollaboration and CALL. In M. Thomas, H. Reinders & M. Warschauer (Eds.), *Contemporary studies in linguistics. Contemporary computer-assisted language learning* (pp. 123-139). London, New York: Bloomsbury Academic.

Schuler, S. (2001). Global lernen – E-Mail-Projekte im Geographieunterricht. *Praxis Geographie, 11*(31), 23-28.

28 Communication strategies in a telecollaboration project with a focus on Latin American history

Susana S. Fernández[1]

Abstract

This paper will present and discuss the linguistic challenges that Argentinian university students of history and Danish university students of Spanish met during the course of a telecollaboration project based on synchronous communication in Skype. The purpose of this discussion is to identify linguistic pitfalls and the solutions adopted by both native and non-native participants in order to keep the conversations going in spite of misunderstandings, vocabulary limitations and other breaches in communication. The purpose of the discussion is to detect areas of strategic competence that need to be addressed in class, particularly for the benefit of the non-native speakers.

Keywords: telecollaboration, communication strategies, native/non-native communication, strategy training.

1. Introduction

The overall object of the telecollaboration project – for literature on telecollaboration and its role in language learning see e.g. O'Dowd (2007) – presented in this paper has been the acquisition of intercultural competence, with

---

1. Aarhus University, Aarhus, Denmark; romssf@cc.au.dk

How to cite this chapter: Fernández, S. S. (2016). Communication strategies in a telecollaboration project with a focus on Latin American history. In S. Jager, M. Kurek & B. O'Rourke (Eds), *New directions in telecollaborative research and practice: selected papers from the second conference on telecollaboration in higher education* (pp. 239-244). Research-publishing.net. https://doi.org/10.14705/rpnet.2016.telecollab2016.513

particular focus on the learning and teaching of Argentinian regional history, by a group of Argentinian pre-service history teachers and a group of Danish university students of Spanish (a number of them pre-service Spanish teachers). The project[2] and its results regarding the acquisition of intercultural awareness have been described in detail in Fernández and Pozzo (2015, in preparation). In the present discussion, the focus will be narrowed to linguistic aspects of this very particular kind of asymmetrical telecollaboration in Spanish, where Native Speakers (NS) of Spanish were coupled with Non-Native Speakers (NNS) of Spanish with a level no higher than B1 in most cases. Although the project included several forms of collaboration (e-mail communication, production and exchange of teaching materials and Skype conversations), the present paper focuses on the Communication Strategies (CS) applied by both groups in their Skype conversations.

The selected focus on CS relies on the conviction – reaffirmed in the language pedagogical literature (e.g. Cohen & Macaro, 2007; Griffiths, 2013) – that teaching learning strategies in the foreign language classroom (including CS, i.e. strategies that allow the learners to engage in communication despite the lack of sufficient linguistic resources) promotes both language learning and facilitates communication in the target language. As many telecollaboration projects nowadays include internet-mediated synchronous communication, the discussion presented in this paper aims at contributing to generally more successful exchanges by bringing attention to the necessary preparation work that should be done in order to exploit online communication to its full extent.

2. Methodology

In the present project, several data collection tools were employed (demographic questionnaires, e-mails, evaluation forms, reflection essays, interviews and audio recordings of Skype conversations), but only transcribed recordings of Skype

---

2. The telecollaboration project presented here is part of a broader research project, 'Construcción de espacios interculturales en la formación docente: competencia comunicativa intercultural, cultura regional y TIC', funded by the Secretariat of Science, Technology and Innovation of the province of Santa Fe, Argentina. The Linguistic Research Programme at Aarhus University has also contributed financially to the telecollaboration project.

conversations will be used in this paper in order to examine the use of CS. Out of 21 Skype conversations held by seven groups of students (each group consisting of around 4-5 Danish students and 1-2 Argentinian students), ten conversations have been retrieved[3], amounting a total of 25,860 words.

The analysis of this material, qualitative in nature, has the purpose of identifying

- different types of CS used by the NS and NNS groups of participants;

- aspects of CS use that need to be trained prior to a new edition of the project (potentially also applicable to other telecollaboration projects with synchronous communication between NS and NNS).

In order to identify CS, the threefold classification of functions provided by Jamshidnejad (2011) – "promoting meaning transfer in communication, promoting the accuracy of language in communication, keeping the interaction going" (p. 3762) – was adopted, and the individual strategies were labelled based on Dörnyei and Scott's (1997) classical taxonomy, with additions by Jamshidnejad (2011) and this researcher.

3. Results

As regards the NS group (the Argentinian participants), two groups of CS are salient: strategies for promoting meaning transfer and strategies for keeping the conversation going. Among the former, the material presents multiple examples of comprehension checks (*Do you understand?*[4]), self-rephrasing (*Are you at the faculty? At the* **university**?), self-repetition, syllable spelling *(dic-ta-tor-ship)*, definition and other-repair (i.e. correcting the interlocutor), all of which are to be expected, as the NNS interlocutors show clear problems of comprehension

---

[3]. In spite of careful instruction on how to record the conversations, the remaining 11 conversations did not get recorded due to technical problems or forgetfulness on the side of the participants.

[4]. Because of space constraints, only a few examples will be provided, directly in own translation into English from the original Spanish source.

and self-expression. The interesting fact about the NS group and its strategy use is that there are clear personal differences, with some participants being skillful in the use of strategies and extremely attentive to the needs of their NNS interlocutors and other participants being oblivious to this or even impatient.

The second group of strategies exhibited by the NS group, aimed at keeping the conversation going, includes three types of strategies: continuers (*Have you noted something that we can discuss?*), change of topic/introduction of a new topic (*And in Denmark? Tell us something about Denmark!* / *Another thing that we had planned to talk with you about is...*), and the most extreme one, ending the conversation because of lack of understanding (*Eh, we will do the following because we are not understanding each other: I will talk to the coordinator and we plan another encounter*). Probably because of their linguistic superiority, the NS group is clearly in charge of the development and direction of the conversation and in several cases it is clear that the very frequent strategy of changing topic has the result of keeping the conversation at a very superficial level.

As for the NNS (the Danish participants), apart from the expected strategies aiming at overcoming their lack of understanding[5] (asking for repetitions, confirmation requests, expressing non-understanding, using translation for understanding) or their lack of linguistic resources (word coinage, self-repair and retrieval), the most interesting group of strategies exhibited by this group can be labeled as 'L1-based intragroup strategies for keeping the conversation going'. They are all about engaging in interactions in Danish with other Danish members of the group while the Argentinian interlocutors, still online, remain out of the conversation. These strategies include co-construction, translating to each other for understanding, intragroup comprehension checks, intragroup other-repair, choosing the best L2 speaker in the group as unwilling spokesperson, and making different kinds of intragroup comments. Up to 17 consecutive turns of intragroup conversation in Danish have been counted in the material, which can be seen as a major interruption to the natural flow of conversation across the telecollaborating partners.

---

5. A couple of examples seem to fall into the category 'promoting accuracy' as some self-repairs by NNS do not seem to be motivated by problems in promoting meaning transfer.

4. Discussion and conclusion

Based on the communication problems observed in the material presented above, the following suggestions for CS training might help improve online synchronous communication in new editions of this or similar projects:

- making NS aware of possible NNS language challenges;

- scripting the conversations in bigger detail so that NNS are better prepared to both ask and answer questions;

- assigning different roles/tasks to different group members;

- training students to use CS in the target language so that NNS rely less on help from the intragroup;

- teaching students how to pose elaboration questions in order to avoid too rapid topic changes.

Although the two groups of interlocutors exhibited a number of CS that in different ways contributed to the completion of the communication task, it is clear from this brief analysis that not all these strategies are equally suited and not all participants are skillful enough at choosing the most adequate strategies at any given moment. Focusing on CS and on possible language challenges prior to the telecollaboration task could pave the way for a more fluent communication between native and non-native participants.

References

Cohen, A., & Macaro, E. (2007). *Language learner strategies*. Oxford: Oxford University Press.

Dörnyei, Z., & Scott, M. L. (1997). Communication strategies in a second language: definition and taxonomies. *Language Learning,* 47(1), 112-130. http://dx.doi.org/10.1111/0023-8333.51997005

Fernández S., & Pozzo M. I. (2015). La telecolaboración como herramienta para la enseñanza / aprendizaje de la historia regional argentina en Dinamarca: un proyecto de intervención didáctica. In M. I. Pozzo (Ed.), *Construcción de espacios interculturales en la formación docente: competencia comunicativa intercultural, cultura regional y TIC*. Rosario: Laborde Editor.

Fernández, S., & Pozzo, M. I. (in preparation). Intercultural competence in synchronous communication between native and non-native speakers of Spanish.

Griffiths, C. (2013). *The strategy factor in successful language learning*. Bristol: Multilingual Matters.

Jamshidnejad, A. (2011). Functional approach to communication strategies: an analysis of language learners' performance in interactional discourse. *Journal of Pragmatics, 43*(15), 3757-3769. http://dx.doi.org/10.1016/j.pragma.2011.09.017

O'Dowd, R. (2007). *Online intercultural exchange: an introduction for foreign language teachers*. Bristol: Multilingual Matters.

29 Students' perspective on Web 2.0-enhanced telecollaboration as added value in translator education

Mariusz Marczak[1]

Abstract

The development of soft skills, which are the most critical skills in the global job market (Abbas & Hum, 2013), is an essential goal of contemporary translator education (Mathias, 2013). A solution that permits students to simultaneously develop translation skills and soft skills is telecollaboration (Dooly & O'Dowd, 2012), i.e. the use of Computer-Mediated Communication (CMC) for collaborative project work. This paper investigates students' views of the usefulness of telecollaboration in translator education, particularly in relation to the development of soft skills. Initially the author introduces the notions of soft skills (Bartel, 2011; Mathias, 2013) and telecollaboration (Belz, 2003; Dooly & O'Dowd, 2013). Then he demonstrates how the latter links to the development of the former (Fleet, 2013; Keedwell, 2013). Finally, he reports the results of a survey study on students' perceptions of the value of CMC in translator education.

Keywords: translator education, telecollaboration, CMC, soft skills.

1. Jagiellonian University of Cracow, Cracow, Poland; mariusz.marczak@uj.edu.pl

How to cite this chapter: Marczak, M. (2016). Students' perspective on Web 2.0-enhanced telecollaboration as added value in translator education. In S. Jager, M. Kurek & B. O'Rourke (Eds), *New directions in telecollaborative research and practice: selected papers from the second conference on telecollaboration in higher education* (pp. 245-252). Research-publishing.net. https://doi.org/10.14705/rpnet.2016.telecollab2016.514

Chapter 29

1. Introduction

Three major factors affect contemporary translator education: professional reality, educational trends and the demands of the job market. Translation worldwide is a rapidly growing industry, with an estimated annual growth rate ranging from 6.2% (DePalma, Hegde, Pielmeier, & Stewart, 2014) to 10% (Pym, 2016). In effect, speedy, low-cost language service delivery and automated translation are in heavy demand (Choudhury & McConnell, 2013). Moreover, elaborate commissions require joint translation, where all the parties involved in the process collaborate effectively (Beninatto & DePalma, 2007), often from distant locations, and an adequate response to the challenges comes from mobile translation technologies (Choudhury & McConnell, 2013).

At the same time, following calls by scholars such as Prensky (2001, 2012) or Tapscott (2008), computer technology has been harnessed to foster education, and as Zappa (2012) prophesises, the trend is to continue until the 2040s. Consequently, it seems justifiable to shift translator education towards telecollaborative methodologies, involving the use of CMC, Web 2.0 tools and cloud computing technologies.

Telecollaboration entails sociocultural learning, i.e. interaction in social contexts scaffolded by the teacher and followed by critical reflection (Guth & Helm, 2010). It may be designed to involve the use of file-sharing media and work modes engaging students in synchronous/asynchronous and oral/written communication (Guth & Helm, 2010). Although telecollaboration is usually utilised with a view to developing intercultural competence (cf. Dooly, 2008; Dooly & O'Dowd, 2012), it may also foster the development of operational, cultural and critical literacies, which correspond to: practical computer and language skills; knowledge of the nature of communication and communication practices; and the ability to reflect on the values and power relations beyond the communication tools used (Lankshear & Knobel, 2006).

Telecollaboration may also further the development of soft skills, i.e. universal, transferrable skills which increase a person's employability, regardless of the domain. Although various taxonomies of soft skills have been proposed by researchers, e.g. Bartel (2011), Han (2011), Mathias (2013), and business or career advisory bodies, e.g. the Academic Career Advice Office at the University of Łódź, Poland (Szulc, n.d.) and the Committee for Economic Development from Arlington, VA, USA (Herk, 2015), a set of core skills can be identified, which includes: communication skills; teamwork skills; interpersonal skills; cultural awareness; flexibility, strategic planning and self-organisation skills; creativity; (analytical/critical) thinking skills; and leadership skills.

2. Method

A survey was conducted in order to answer three research questions:

- Do students perceive telecollaboration as a useful approach in translator education?

- In students' views, which soft skills were actually developed through the telecollaboration project in question?

- What implications do the findings have for course design?

The questionnaire was administered in January 2016 at the Pedagogical University of Cracow on a convenience sample of 18 student translators (N=18) in their first year of an MA programme. The subjects were surveyed online through a set of close-ended questions. Prior to the study, the students completed a telecollaboration project in which they worked in four groups of three, a group of four and a pair, and used online tools, e.g. *Facebook Messenger*, *TitanPad*, and *Google Live Docs*, to compile a term bank containing entries relating to the area of Computer Assisted Translation. The project work involved a number of actions, e.g. online search for reference texts, parallel text alignment, term extraction with Computer-Assisted Translation (CAT) tools (*memoQ* or *PlusTools*), data collection, database creation with CAT tools, and data transfer to a printable format through the *Mail Merge* functionality of *Microsoft Word*. The telecollaboration stage was preceded by face-to-face instruction in: special purpose languages, terminology and its role in translation as well as CAT/terminology tools.

3. Results

According to the results, all the students (100%) viewed telecollaboration as useful in translator education. As Figure 1 graphically illustrates, they also perceived telecollaboration as a work mode which facilitates the development of a wide range of soft skills – drawn from the afore-mentioned list proposed by Han (2011) – although students differed in their support for the idea with regard to particular skills.

Figure 1. Proportions of students believing that particular soft skills can be developed through telecollaboration, based on their experience of a telecollaborative translation project

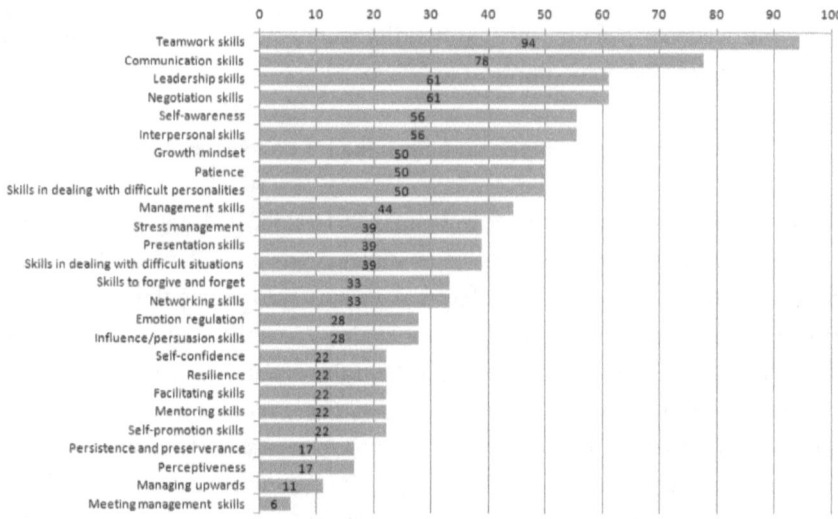

Given their experience, the largest proportions of students (over 50% of the sample) believed that telecollaboration helped develop teamwork skills (94%), communication skills (78%), leadership skills (61%), negotiation skills (56%) and self-awareness (56%).

50% of the students expressed the view that telecollaboration fostered the development of growth mindset – i.e. perceiving challenges as an opportunity to learn, grow, and change – patience, and the ability to deal with difficult personalities. Relatively large proportions of students (over 30%) were positive about the development of management skills, stress management skills, presentation skills, the ability to deal with difficult situations, skills to forgive and forget and networking skills. The smallest proportions of students (below 30%) were convinced about telecollaboration fostering the development of emotion regulation skills, influence/persuasion skills, self-confidence, resilience, facilitating skills, mentoring skills, self-promotion skills, persistence and perseverance, perceptiveness, managing upwards skills and meeting management skills. None of the students saw telecollaboration as a chance to develop savvy in office politics and selling skills.

4. Discussion

The most significant finding of the study is that the students unanimously approved of telecollaboration as an approach with which to facilitate translator education. The remainder of the data gathered indicates which soft skills telecollaboration may improve. In general, none of the soft skills listed in the survey were considered as those that cannot be developed through telecollaboration; however, the potential of telecollaboration for the development of specific soft skills was recognised by different proportions of students, which implies that the skills may be developed to varying degrees, depending on circumstances.

It is worth observing that although particular soft skills were not explicitly listed in the questionnaire, they were – as it were – disguised under different names, and the respondents also recognised that the skills can potentially be fostered by telecollaboration. For instance, skills in dealing with difficult situations and difficult personalities may be viewed as corresponding to flexibility and management skills; managing upwards skills may be perceived as relating to strategic planning, creativity and thinking skills; while skills in dealing with difficult situations, emotion regulation and stress management may be said to relate to cultural awareness.

5. Conclusions

The findings have a number of implications for translator education. Firstly, students admit that telecollaboration furthers the development of soft skills. However, course instructors should additionally make them aware of the value of soft skills in the professional world, which is likely to increase participation levels and overall student motivation in telecollaborative projects.

Secondly, as particular soft skills were developed to varying degrees in the telecollaboration project under investigation, it may be hypothesised that the degree to which that happens depends on a number factors, including: task design, learner roles, and online tool selection. That is why teachers must ensure that the tasks set are likely to foster the development of a broad range of soft skills.

Thirdly, the development of the soft skills that smaller proportions of students believed to have had a chance to work on, e.g. perceptiveness, might require additional stimulation, which might be achieved through critical reflection on the learning process, analysis of individual learning gains and identification of students' own strengths and weaknesses. Techniques to be used for that purpose could be those that involve the systematic recording of experiences, such as: diaries, logs or think-aloud protocols.

References

Abbas, A., & Hum, M. (2013). Integrating the English language teaching and learning process with soft skills. *International Conference on Education and Language 2013, UBL, Indonesia* (pp. 365-371).

Bartel, J. (2011). *Soft skills: what, why and how to teach them in ESL classes using Office Soft Skills*. A summary of the conference presentation at the TESL Toronto Spring Conference, May 2011. http://tesltoronto.org/wp-content/uploads/2011/05/BartelSoftSkillsSpring2011-.pdf

Belz, J. A. (2003). Linguistic perspectives in the development of intercultural competence in telecollaboration. *Language Learning & Technology, 7*(2). http://llt.msu.edu/vol7num3/belz/

Beninatto, R. S., & DePalma, D. A. (2007). *Collaborative translation. The end of localization taylorism and the beginning of postmodern translation*. Lowell, MA: Common Sense Advisory.

Choudhury, R., & McConnell, B. (2013). *Translation technology landscape report*. DeRijp: TAUS BV.

DePalma, D. A., Hegde, V., Pielmeier, H., & Stewart, R. G. (2014). *The language services market: 2014 annual review of the translation, localization, and interpreting services industry*. Cambridge, MA: Common Sense Advisory.

Dooly, M. (2008). *Telecollaborative language learning*. Bern: Peter Lang.

Dooly, M., & O'Dowd, R. (2012). *Researching online foreign language interaction and exchange: theories, methods and challenges*. Oxford: Peter Lang. http://dx.doi.org/10.3726/978-3-0351-0414-1

Fleet, L. (2013). A blended learning approach to soft skill training at Al Azhar University, Cairo. In B. Tomlinson & C. Whittaker (Eds.), *Blended learning in English language teaching: course design and implementation*. London: British Council.

Guth, S., & Helm, F. (2010). *Telecollaboration 2.0: language, literacies, and intercultural learning in the 21st century*. New York, NY: Peter Lang.

Han, L. (2011). *Soft skills list - 28 skills to working smart.* https://bemycareercoach.com/soft-skills/list-soft-skills.html

Herk, M. (2015). *The skills gap and the seven skill sets that employers want: building the ideal new hire*. Committee for Economic Development. https://www.ced.org/blog/entry/the-skills-gap-and-the-seven-skill-sets-that-employers-want-building-the-id

Keedwell, A. (2013). Blended learning for English for occupational purposes: no frills, soft skills, gaps filled. In B. Tomlinson & C. Whittaker (Eds.), *Blended learning in English language teaching: course design and implementation*. London: British Council.

Lankshear, C., & Knobel, M. (2006). *New literacies: everyday practices and classroom learning*. (2nd ed.). Maidenhead: Open University Press.

Mathias, A. J. (2013). *Introduction to soft skills*. http://elearning.vtu.ac.in/18/enotes/SK/SK.pdf

Prensky, M. (2001). Digital natives, digital immigrants. *On the Horizon 9(*5), 1-6. http://dx.doi.org/10.1108/10748120110424816

Prensky, M. (2012). *From digital natives to digital wisdom: hopeful essays for 21st century education*. California: Corwin. http://dx.doi.org/10.4135/9781483387765

Pym, A. (2016). *Teaching what you don't know: the challenge of future technologies*. An unpublished plenary paper delivered at a conference entitled *Inspirations for Translation Pedagogy. 1st CTER Congress* on 14th March, 2016 in Cracow, Poland.

Szulc, W. (n.d.). *Kompetencje miękkie Jak je rozwinąć i wykorzystać na rynku pracy?* Łódź: Akademickie Biuro Karier Zawowodych Uniwersytetu Łódzkiego.

Tapscott, D. (2008). *Grown up digital: how the net generation is changing your world*. New York: McGraw-Hill.

Zappa, M. (2012). *Envisioning the future of educational technology*. http://www.envisioning.io/education/

30 Intercultural communication for professional development: creative approaches in higher education

Linda Joy Mesh[1]

Abstract

This study examines the development of telecollaborative exchange activities within blended language courses that are aimed at preparing post-graduate students for an intercultural workplace by developing valuable transversal competencies and intercultural awareness, which enable one to better adapt to changing work situations. A description is given of the collaborative activities completed by students at the University of Siena, Italy, and the University of Maastricht, Netherlands. The relevance of intercultural communication exchanges for meeting the needs of students who are searching for career opportunities or research collaboration abroad is also highlighted. The study concludes with a discussion of how activities and applications can be used to increase motivation and critical thinking skills as students work together collaboratively.

Keywords: intercultural communication, tandem, workplace skills, language learning.

---

1. University of Siena, Siena, Italy; linda.mesh@unisi.it

How to cite this chapter: Mesh, L. J. (2016). Intercultural communication for professional development: creative approaches in higher education. In S. Jager, M. Kurek & B. O'Rourke (Eds), *New directions in telecollaborative research and practice: selected papers from the second conference on telecollaboration in higher education* (pp. 253-259). Research-publishing.net. https://doi.org/10.14705/rpnet.2016.telecollab2016.515

Chapter 30

1. Introduction – intercultural competencies and workplace skills

This study aims to present how telecollaborative exchange activities have been integrated in language courses for students learning English at the University of Siena, Italy, and students learning Italian at the University of Maastricht, Netherlands.

The teachers involved in this project adopted a blended learning approach, including an average of 50 per cent of course hours in the classroom and an online component of 50 per cent of the total course hours, composed of guided forum activities, wikis and the optional use of social applications to provide communicative opportunities for interaction in the second language.

The English courses in Siena are part of an innovative project, *USiena Open – Constructing Competences for the Future*, funded by the Italian Ministry of Instruction, University and Research (MUIR), which aims to provide outgoing orientation to students to facilitate entrance into the workplace by developing transversal competencies. These skills include the ability, digital competence and initiative to manage one's learning throughout life, as well as being able to communicate effectively in foreign languages, in cross-cultural situations and interpersonal relationships. Therefore, the objective of the language courses that are part of this project is to provide opportunities for improving transversal competencies through guided activities based on mobile and social applications.

The effect that mobile devices have had on developments in communicative language teaching has provided new opportunities, as well as the reconceptualisation of materials and methodologies. A learner-centred perspective suggests that "mobile devices can support self-directed forms of language learning and greater learner autonomy" (Kukulska-Hulme, 2013, p. 5), which is supported by a growing body of evidence to that effect. With this in mind, the intercultural exchange in this study includes several collaborative applications compatible with mobile devices.

2. Project description

Maastricht, Netherlands, and Siena, Italy, are both relatively small European cities that are steeped in historical and cultural relevance, although they are located in very different areas of Europe. Intercultural exchanges, which may be carried out through internet technologies, can provide interesting 'windows' through which students who are studying languages in distant universities can exchange viewpoints and enhance their language-learning experiences. The groups that have participated in this project are students who are studying Italian at the Maastricht University Language Centre and students who are studying English at the University of Siena Language Centre. Therefore, a tandem approach lends itself naturally to the organisation of the activities, providing mutual interest and linguistic appeal.

3. Intercultural exchange

This section will describe the characteristics of the groups of students in Siena and Maastricht, as well as briefly illustrate the various aspects of the intercultural exchange activities.

3.1. Siena

The students from the University of Siena Language Centre are studying for second cycle degrees (Master's degrees) and Ph.Ds and have attained an upper-intermediate level B2 in English. The students, who are from many different regions of Italy, are taking one of two blended courses in *Moodle*, with a combination of face-to-face lessons and online activities, offered at levels B2+ and C1 as part of the project *USiena Open,* mentioned above. Since the participants are concluding their university studies, they are strongly motivated to look for employment or research opportunities abroad. Therefore, they feel a need to develop effective intercultural communication skills. As part of the blended courses, students are asked to participate in guided online forum discussions that are closely integrated with the classroom lessons. The teacher facilitates the online activities, providing feedback and assessment of the skills-based projects that are completed. For the students in Siena, participation in the tandem exchange is obligatory.

3.2. Maastricht

The students from Maastricht University Language Centre are studying for a variety of degrees taught in English as a lingua franca, and are primarily enrolled in the European Studies programme. Although most of the students are German and Dutch, there are also many students from Eastern Europe, Italy and Saudi Arabia, who are taking blended Italian courses at intermediate levels. Some are preparing for an Erasmus exchange program in Italy, while others began studying Italian in Maastricht, then went to Italy for their Erasmus experience. When they returned, they enrolled in a higher-level course because of their studies abroad.

Figure 1. Wikispace home page for the Siena-Maastricht intercultural tandem exchange

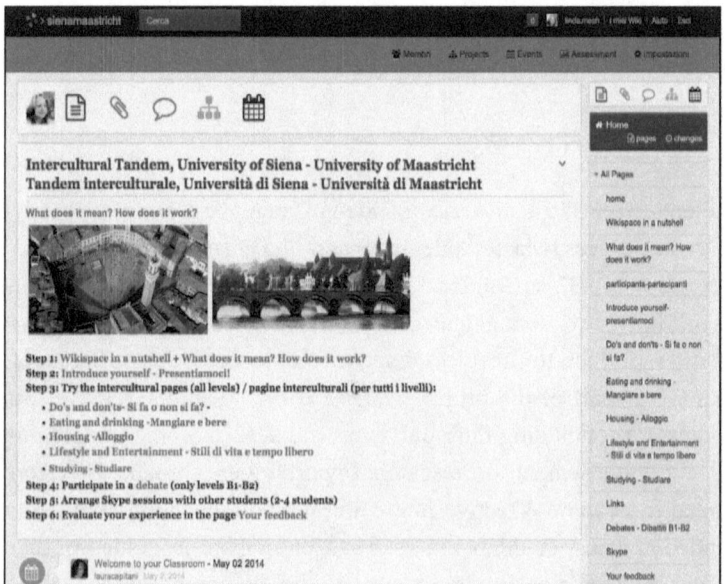

The learning environment used for communication and interaction between the students is *Wikispaces Classroom* (Figure 1). The wikispace provides not only course information, but is used primarily for exchanging opinions and ideas for collaborative assignments.

3.3. Collaborative exchange – 'Getting to know you' (part 1)

The first part of the tandem exchange involves an ice-breaking activity in which students from Siena introduce themselves in English as their target language, whereas those in Maastricht participate in Italian by describing aspects of everyday life, cultural aspects and their activities as students. The purpose of this activity is to provide a space for virtual storytelling in which students can develop personal narratives, an important skill for developing effective interpersonal communication at both personal and professional levels. The students decide how to write the wiki and are encouraged to offer each other language support. A mobile application is used in this part, *Fotobabble.com,* for posting photographs with audio clips.

3.4. Collaborative exchange – discussion of intercultural issues (part 2)

During the second part of the telecollaboration activities, students are given a more challenging activity that increases motivation between the two groups. First, a topic of mutual interest is selected by the students from a suggested list of options; for example, in this case the topic of immigration and migration was chosen. The students from Maastricht and Siena were asked to read two articles in Italian and two in English, which were chosen to present various points of view. Then students expressed their opinions by writing individual compositions in the wikispace in their target language. Some also chose to create digital posters illustrating their opinions by using the application checkthis. com. On the basis of the written discussion that was generated (27 short compositions), the students in Maastricht conducted a classroom debate on the topic in Italian. Two student moderators summarised the opinions found in the wikispace and stimulated the debate in class. As a result, the students were able to carry on a long discussion in Italian with good competence in both language and content. A similar in-class debate in English was held in Siena. The students were given the task of managing the discussion, hence improving motivation and critical thinking skills, which can be further developed as life-long abilities (Aguilar, 2010).

3.5. Reflection and evaluation

At the end of parts 1 and 2, students were asked to write a series of reflective diary entries about their feelings and experiences, reflecting on the learning that took place and any changes they noticed in communication abilities, their perspectives of cultural issues as well as any approaches needed for effective communication across cultures. The design of the activities used in the intercultural exchange is evaluated at the end of each course by using Byram's (1997) model of intercultural communicative competence.

4. Conclusions

The result of the entire collaboration has certainly been positive regarding both the improvement of intercultural competences, the first objective of the project, and the more advanced development of both writing and speaking abilities that are directly related to skill-based applications. Moreover, because mobile and social technologies are a part of students' lives, the careful integration of selected applications enhanced the learning process. The opportunity to develop cross-cultural exchanges in which aspects of the learning process can be handed over to the students promotes ownership and helps to foster learner autonomy.

Finally, we have demonstrated that language competences that are developed in conjunction with intercultural exchange activities can provide opportunities for students to develop a range of transversal skills that may aid their transition into the global workplace.

References

Aguilar, M. J. C. (2010). Intercultural communicative competence as a tool for autonomous learning. *Revista Canaria de Estudios Ingleses, 61*, 87-98.

Byram, M. (1997). *Teaching and assessing intercultural communicative competence.* Clevedon, UK: Multilingual Matters.

Kukulska-Hulme, A. (2013). *Re-skilling language learners for a mobile world.* Monterey, CA: The International Research Foundation for English Language Education. http://www.tirfonline.org/wp-content/uploads/2013/11/TIRF_MALL_Papers_Kukulska-Hulme.pdf

31 Illustrating challenges and practicing competencies for global technology-assisted collaboration: lessons from a real-time north-south teaching collaboration

Stephen Capobianco[1], Nadia Rubaii[2], and Sebastian Líppez-De Castro[3]

Abstract

In this paper, we outline the structure, goals, and lessons from our international teaching and learning collaboration in the spring 2015 semester. We took two public affairs courses with students in a U.S. and a Colombian university and combined them into a single hybrid course with the use of technology. The main goals of the course were to expose students to issues regarding governance in the twenty-first century in a technological, globalized and diverse world, and to recognize and work on their own competencies to be successful public affairs practitioners in such a world. We document four lessons learned from the experience which can help to improve practice and assist others who wish to engage in a virtual teaching and learning collaboration. We encourage other professors to engage in this type of technology-facilitated international exchange if they incorporate these lessons and can align desired competencies and learning objectives.

Keywords: telecollaboration, digital fluency, teamwork, public affairs education.

---

1. Binghamton University, SUNY, Binghamton, New York, U.S.A.; scapobia@binghamton.edu

2. Binghamton University, SUNY, Binghamton, New York, U.S.A.; nadia.rubaii@binghamton.edu

3. Binghamton University, SUNY, Binghamton, New York, U.S.A., and Pontificia Universidad Javeriana, Bogotá, Colombia; slippez1@binghamton.edu, slippez@javeriana.edu.co

How to cite this chapter: Capobianco, S., Rubaii, N., & Líppez-De Castro, S. (2016). Illustrating challenges and practicing competencies for global technology-assisted collaboration: lessons from a real-time north-south teaching collaboration. In S. Jager, M. Kurek & B. O'Rourke (Eds), *New directions in telecollaborative research and practice: selected papers from the second conference on telecollaboration in higher education* (pp. 261-266). Research-publishing.net. https://doi.org/10.14705/rpnet.2016.telecollab2016.516

© 2016 Stephen Capobianco, Nadia Rubaii, and Sebastian Líppez-De Castro (CC BY-NC-ND 4.0)   261

Chapter 31

1. Introduction

This paper highlights four broad and transferable lessons learned based on an experience of a fully-integrated synchronous class at two universities in different countries which was designed to achieve three overarching goals: (1) to demonstrate the challenges and opportunities for public governance derived from globalization, collaboration, diversity and technology, (2) to model competencies for students in these areas, and (3) to provide students with opportunities to practice and develop their own competencies in these areas concurrently (see Rubaii, Capobianco, & Líppez-De Castro, 2016).

The combined course offered in the spring 2015 semester paired first semester pre-service Master of Public Administration (MPA) students at Binghamton University in New York with advanced professional undergraduates of Political Science undertaking a concentration in public management at Pontificia Universidad Javeriana (PUJ) in Bogotá, Colombia.

The course consisted of 42 students, 23 in Binghamton and 19 in Bogotá. Among the 31 female and 11 male students, the modal age category was 20-29, with the majority holding citizenship in their country of study, although two Binghamton students were from other countries (Kenya and South Korea).

The language of instruction was English, although all three instructors (one full-time faculty member at each institution and a doctoral student completing his co-teaching experience) were fluent in Spanish as well.

In order to maintain an integrated experience, we developed a common syllabus with identical learning objectives, topics, readings, assignments, the same weights placed on graded components, and a common class schedule. The syllabus and other course materials were available for everyone in a single class website created in www.coursesites.com by Blackboard. Although the learning objectives and desired competencies for the two classes were congruent, this high level of coordination required considerable time and attention in advance of the class (see Table 1).

Table 1. Learning outcomes

Learning Outcomes
Be able to distinguish between classic Weberian models of bureaucracy and models of new public management and new public service, identify the fundamental ideas and core values of each school of thought, and apply those theories to specific issues facing local governments in Colombia and the United States.
Understand how the pressures of globalization are affecting public administration in various contexts and influence the role of the contemporary state (broadly defined).
Be able to identify and evaluate the relative effectiveness of various uses of technology and how public service values are reflected in policies and practices regarding technology.
Be able to identify and evaluate the relative effectiveness of various responses to diversity and how public service values are reflected in policies and practices regarding diversity.
Be able to articulate how core values of democracy, participation, accountability, sustainability, and transparency might look different in different contexts.
Develop an understanding of the theory and practice of inter-organizational collaborations and intercultural competence for the individuals and organizations engaged in public service.

The class design was supported by the Binghamton University's Center for Learning and Teaching (CLT) and followed the collaborative online international learning model (Rubin & Guth, 2015; Strickland, Adamson, McInally, Tiittanen, & Metcalfe, 2013). It was scheduled for three hours utilizing CISCO WebEx technology to allow everyone in both classrooms to see and hear each other, as well as to share files in different formats. The three hours were split to allow for initial separate instructional time, longer joint instructional time, and for the students to work on their semester-long team projects. For these projects, we set up a rotating schedule for teams to use eight different free online technologies that not only allowed them to meet and discuss their assignment, but also to expand their digital literacy. All teams were required to research and present a comparative analysis of an issue facing both U.S. and Colombian communities and to place their research in the context of the course material on governance challenges and pressures of globalization. Students also had individual assignments like completing the Intercultural Effectiveness Scale (IES)[4] survey and submitting a written reflective essay on what they learned and how they

---

4. http://www.kozaigroup.com/intercultural-effectiveness-scale-ies/

intended to use those results. Below we highlight the four most important lessons we learned with the goal of providing useful guidance to other faculty interested in pursuing similar collaborations.

2. Lessons learned and reflections

2.1. Lesson 1: select partners carefully and start planning early

High levels of trust, respect, and openness among the individual instructor partners is critical. Before undertaking this project, the three co-instructors had professional relationships spanning several years and taking many forms which provided a foundation for resolving problems as they arose. As instructors, we held weekly debriefing meetings, using the same WebEx technology used in our classes, to determine how to respond to issues such as team dynamics and assessment of student work.

A full year of planning was necessary to make decisions regarding course objectives, assignments, grading criteria, technology, etc. To emphasize that fully shared instructional approach, we developed a common grading rubric for each assignment and then rotated responsibility for grading. In terms of technology, we had to spend a significant amount of time working with the CLT to settle on WebEx as our collaborative platform, to identify the eight free communication tools we required our students to use, and to identify the single course management system (Coursesites) we used.

2.2. Lesson 2: prioritize process and provide time

In retrospect, we note that one of our biggest mistakes was to add the layer of international collaboration on top of the usual expectations rather than in lieu of some. We did not take into account in our course design how much work would be required for students to engage in the collaboration effectively, to reflect on the experience, and to take advantage of the opportunity to learn more from their international partners than what was required by the class. Even though 34 of the 42 students (81%) had strong positive or generally positive perceptions of the course as received on their mid-semester course evaluations, we took note of some problems and concerns. The most frequently mentioned impediments to learning were technological difficulties and insufficient time. In response to this, we cut some readings from the last classes and allowed for additional time for team meetings in the two weeks leading to the presentations and made ourselves available during that time to provide advice.

2.3. Lesson 3: provide students with more choice

In response to mid-semester evaluations, we dropped the obligatory rotation of team meeting technologies as students reported it was hindering the progress of some groups. In their course evaluations, students scored making the group presentations and watching other groups' presentation relatively high, with overall average scores greater than 4.0 on a 5-point scale of contributing to learning, but they rated using a variety of technologies for group work and group work during class time lower with average ratings of 3.34 and 3.52, respectively. We would not repeat the requirement that students rotate team meeting technologies because too much time was spent on figuring out the technologies at each meeting rather than addressing substantive issues. In the future, we would give the students more freedom in deciding what technology to use or provide a smaller list of alternatives.

2.4. Lesson 4: deliberately model the competencies you want students to develop

In keeping with our goal of modeling desired competencies, as we encountered problems and challenges during the semester – whether with technology or in making decisions about anything else – we deliberately shared with the students the nature of the problems, the options we had considered, the processes we used to reach a decision, the decision itself, and our rationale. We also had to demonstrate digital fluency in the technological tools and assist students when they encountered difficulties communicating. Of the 10 groups, two had issues that rose to the level of requiring faculty intervention and assistance.

Although we explained it at the beginning of the semester, we found it necessary to repeatedly remind and reinforce that students had three co-equal instructors. We required that all assignments and all email communication be sent to all three of us. It was also important that we regularly remind students that the frustrations they were experiencing with international collaborations or technology were contributing to the course learning objectives and would serve them well in the long term.

3. Conclusion

Technology-facilitated international collaborations have the potential to provide learning experiences which model and allow for the practice of skills that will be increasingly important in the future. Our experience illustrates that these collaborative efforts are not without challenges and that they probably are best suited for instances in which the telecollaboration experience directly corresponds to the learning objectives of the course and when the faculty have established relationships of trust upon which to build.

References

Rubaii, N., Capobianco, S., & Líppez-De Castro, S. (2016). *Promoting team work. Intercultural competencies, and digital fluency: lessons from a real-time north-south teaching collaboration.* Poster presentation at the Binghamton University research fair. http://binghamton.edu/ims/images/research-day-2016-rubaii-etal.pdf?

Rubin, J., & Guth, S. (2015). Collaborative online international learning: an emerging format for internationalizing curricula. In A. Schultheis Moore & S. Simon (Eds), *Globally networked teaching in the humanities* (pp. 15-27). New York: Routledge.

Strickland, K., Adamson, E., McInally, W., Tiittanen, H., & Metcalfe, S. (2013). Developing global citizenship online: an authentic alternative to overseas clinical placement. *Nurse Education Today, 33*(10), 1160-1165. http://dx.doi.org/10.1016/j.nedt.2012.11.016

32 Telecollaboration as a tool for building intercultural and interreligious understanding: the Sousse-Villanova programme

Jonathan Mason[1]

Abstract

The Paris and San Bernardino attacks in autumn 2015, along with various retaliatory incidents, and Donald Trump's suggestion that Muslims should be banned from entering the US, have reminded us again of the deep misunderstandings and resentments that often exist between the Muslim and Western worlds. In order to improve intercultural and interreligious understanding, students at the University of Sousse, Tunisia, took part in an online exchange programme with students from Villanova University in Pennsylvania, USA. Using student diaries and end of course reflection exercises, this study investigated both the benefits and limits that the exchange had in developing understanding, as well as the impact the process had on the outcomes. The findings showed numerous positive developments in intercultural and interreligious understanding, but also limits to the depth of discussion, particularly concerning conflict situations. The diaries also revealed some cases of limited communication, which undermined some of the benefits of the exchange.

Keywords: interreligious understanding, Muslim-Western dialogue, telecollaborative exchange.

---

1. University of Sousse, Sousse, Tunisia; jonathanmason1967@gmail.com

How to cite this chapter: Mason, J. (2016). Telecollaboration as a tool for building intercultural and interreligious understanding: the Sousse-Villanova programme. In S. Jager, M. Kurek & B. O'Rourke (Eds), *New directions in telecollaborative research and practice: selected papers from the second conference on telecollaboration in higher education* (pp. 267-273). Research-publishing.net. https://doi.org/10.14705/rpnet.2016.telecollab2016.517

Chapter 32

1. Introduction

In his landmark book, *Orientalism*, Said (2003) documented how the *Occident*'s distorted view of the *Orient* has deep historical roots. Similarly, Holliday (2011) suggested that "there seems to be a wiring, deep in the discourses of Western civilization [...] which makes the Othering of the non-West inescapable" (p. 93). However, in his preface, Said (2003) commented that an "easy anti-Americanism that shows little understanding of what the US is really like as a society" (p. xxi) had also been spreading in the Arab world. Historical misconceptions have been exacerbated by more recent conflicts in Iraq and Palestine, resulting in significant prejudices and misunderstandings among both Tunisian and American students.

It was with these prejudices and misunderstandings in mind that an online 'intercultural dialogue' exchange programme was developed between Cultural Studies Masters students at the Faculty of Arts and Humanities, University of Sousse, Tunisia, and undergraduate students from Villanova University in Pennsylvania, US, taking a course in 'US Foreign Relations'. It was hoped that a process of intercultural dialogue, "an open and respectful exchange of views between individuals [...] with different ethnic, cultural, religious and linguistic backgrounds and heritage" (Council of Europe, 2008, p. 10), in which the "other" was transformed from "it" to "you" (Buber, 1983, cited in Phipps, 2014, p. 117), might contribute positively to overcoming misunderstanding. This dialogue was not only intercultural, but also interreligious, given the close association between Muslim culture and religion in the minds of both groups of participants.

Although a growing body of research into intercultural learning from telecollaboration is developing, very little organised telecollaboration has taken place in Tunisia, and the author has been unable to find any other published material about Tunisian projects. Consequently, in the second year of this programme, which took place between February and April 2015, involving ten students at each institute, data was collected to investigate two main research questions:

- How did the telecollaborative exchange improve intercultural/ interreligious understanding?

- How did the process of the exchange influence the outcomes?

2. Methodology

2.1. Programme outline

The programme was based on the 'Cultura' model of telecollaboration (Furstenberg, Levet, English, & Maillet, 2001; Garcia & Crapotta, 2007; c.f. http://cultura.mit.edu/). Before starting the exchange, the students were given some instruction on phenomenology and interviewing, and were encouraged to ask questions and seek understanding, rather than to try to win arguments. After pairing the students, they shared short personal biographies with their online partners, and completed an introductory intercultural questionnaire (prepared by the researcher), including word association and sentence completion exercises. Responses to this were then shared with all participants so that students could discuss them. They were then free to explore further cultural, religious and foreign policy issues of their choice with their partners through email, Facebook and Skype. Although the initial interaction followed a standardised format, the development of the online relationship was very open, and deliberately 'low control' to give students flexibility.

2.2. Data collection and analysis

Students at both Sousse and Villanova completed an assignment at the end of the exchange, reflecting on their experience. Students in Sousse were also asked to keep a diary during the exchange, as diaries not only help students to reflect on their learning, but also "shed light on the learning process and factors influencing it" (Helm, 2009, p. 93). A thematic content analysis was then undertaken on both the reflection assignments and diaries of the Tunisian students.

3. Findings

Due to limited space, only a very brief selection of findings will be presented.

3.1. Positive outcomes

3.1.1. Overcoming religious misunderstanding

All the students discussed perspectives on Islam with their partners, and a number reported specifically on positive outcomes. For example Lilia[2] wrote:

> "I liked this experience because it gave me the opportunity to represent my country, Arabs and my religion i.e. Islam. I'm really happy because I was able to prove wrong some of the preconceived ideas related to Arabs and to Muslims" (Reflection).

Also, Miriam commented how her expectation that her American partner would be ignorant about Islam was unfounded:

> "She was familiar with some issues concerning the Middle East, Arabs and Islam. Her ideas are not mere reproduction of common stereotypes" (Diary, 06/03/2015).

3.1.2. Overcoming anti-American prejudice

Many students reported on the positive experience of building relationship with their American partners. Mona also commented on how she had reassessed some prejudices she had held:

> "I started the program with the assumption that Americans are racist, ignorant and arrogant. This was reinforced by the students' answers in the questionnaire... However, at the end of the programme, I went back

---

2. All names are pseudonyms.

to their answers… they're not all the same and I should have taken into consideration all the answers, not the ones that I could use to reinforce my view" (Reflection).

3.1.3. Showing sympathy concerning the fight against terrorism

During the program, a terrorist attack, claimed by Islamic State, took place at the Bardo National Museum in Tunis, in which 22 people died. Given the prior expectation that Americans often see Arabs and Muslims as terrorists (Miriam, Reflection), the Tunisian students were encouraged by the messages of sympathy they received from their American partners. For example, Maissa commented:

> "Aby also showed compassion towards the terrorist attacks of Bardo and tried to comfort me by explaining that terrorism is spread all over the world and is not only limited to Tunisia" (Reflection).

3.2. Limits to dialogue

Although some students were able to discuss a wide range of controversial issues, some reported 'no-go' areas. For example, Karim commented:

> "I disagree with CJ on many points [politics, democracy, capitalism (World Social Forum) and foreign policy] that's why I avoided deeply discussing Middle-East issues like the Palestinian cause and America's war on Iraq under Bush Jr." (Reflection).

Nour remarked "I've learnt that you should not put pressure on the interviewee" (Diary, n.d.), explaining that she felt her partner was just saying "I agree" without thinking (Diary, n.d.), and that when she probed deeper he would avoid the question.

3.3. The negative impact of differing communication expectations

Although students generally commented positively about the overall exchange process, one problem that was mentioned by about half of the Tunisian students in their diaries was the slow and limited initial response from their partners. Lilia's experience illustrates this:

> "Still nothing new about her" (Diary, 26/02/2015).
>
> "I noticed that she had seen my text but ignored it... She shattered all my positive expectations of Americans being hardworkers and as people who keep their promises" (Diary, 12/03/2015).
>
> "She apologized... she always gives me fake promises" (Diary, 01/04/2015).

As can be seen, this issue had a negative impact on intercultural attitudes, although all the students who had problems communicating had at least some fruitful discussion with their assigned partners by the end of the program.

4. Discussion

It is clear from the Tunisian students' feedback that this telecollaboration project played a positive role in developing aspects of intercultural and interreligious understanding. Feedback from the American students was similar. However, as Phipps (2014) argues, there are limits to the effectiveness of 'Intercultural Dialogue', particularly in conflict situations. Although not *in* a conflict situation, some of the students did not feel they could deeply discuss important conflict situations with their partners. Also, the poor telecollaborative experience that some students faced had a negative impact on intercultural attitudes.

5. Conclusion

Findings from this project suggest that developing further projects between Tunisian and American, British or European students could have a positive impact on intercultural and interreligious understanding for both parties.

However, dialogue on more controversial issues may need to be managed more closely in order to go deeper, and expectations for the exchange need to be clear in order to avoid unnecessary disappointments.

References

Buber, M. (1983). *Ich und Du*. Stuttgart: Reclam.

Council of Europe. (2008). White paper on intercultural dialogue: "Living together as equals with dignity". http://www.coe.int/t/dg4/intercultural/source/white%20paper_final_revised_en.pdf

Furstenberg, G., Levet, S., English, K., & Maillet, K. (2001). Giving a virtual voice to the silent language of culture: the Cultura project. *Language Learning & Technology, 5*(1), 55-102. http://llt.msu.edu/vol5num1/furstenberg/default.pdf

Garcia, J. S., & Crapotta, J. (2007). Models of telecollaboration (2): Cultura. In R. O'Dowd (Ed.), *Online intercultural exchange: an introduction for foreign language teachers* (pp. 62-84). Clevedon: Multilingual Matters.

Helm, F. (2009). Language and culture in an online context: what can learner diaries tell us about intercultural competence? *Language and Intercultural Communication, 9*(2), 91-104. http://dx.doi.org/10.1080/14708470802140260

Holliday, A. (2011). *Intercultural communication and ideology*. London: SAGE Publications

Phipps, A. (2014). 'They are bombing now': 'intercultural dialogue' in times of conflict. *Language and Intercultural Communication, 14*(1), 108-124. http://dx.doi.org/10.1080/14708477.2013.866127

Said, E. (2003, first published 1978). *Orientalism*. London: Penguin Books.

Section 6.
Analysing interaction in telecollaborative exchanges

33 Vicious cycles of turn negotiation in video-mediated telecollaboration: interactional sociolinguistics perspective

Yuka Akiyama[1]

Abstract

To examine how participants' different eTandem experiences could be attributed to the way they co-constructed turns, this study analyzed turn negotiation practices of one dyad who engaged in video-mediated interaction between Japan and America. This dyad was chosen for analysis because they expressed the greatest frustration and required a pedagogical intervention. It was found that silence, which was used by the Japanese learner of English as a Foreign Language (EFL) as a contextualization cue for linguistic help, triggered the American student's hyperexplanation to get the Japanese partner involved in conversation. Such a high-involvement strategy, however, only resulted in producing fewer opportunities for the Japanese partner to contribute to the conversation (i.e. vicious cycle). I conclude that 'missed communication' (Ware, 2005) in an autonomous, long-term eTandem project may entrench attribution of negative personal traits unless appropriate scaffolding/intervention is provided.

Keywords: conversational style strategies, contextualization cues, listener responses, silence, recipient design, complementary schismogenesis.

---

1. Georgetown University, Washington DC, United States; ya125@georgetown.edu

How to cite this chapter: Akiyama, Y. (2016). Vicious vs. virtuous cycles of turn negotiation in video-mediated telecollaboration: interactional sociolinguistics perspective. In S. Jager, M. Kurek & B. O'Rourke (Eds), *New directions in telecollaborative research and practice: selected papers from the second conference on telecollaboration in higher education* (pp. 277-282). Research-publishing.net. https://doi.org/10.14705/rpnet.2016.telecollab2016.518

1. Introduction

While numerous benefits of telecollaboration have been reported, the field is also characterized by its willingness to document failure, investigating "conflict as object of research" rather than regarding it as "accidental finding of research" (Lamy & Goodfellow, 2010, p. 3). For instance, previous studies on telecollaboration revealed that tensions might arise due to dissimilar styles of negotiation between two groups of learners (Ware, 2005). These studies revealed that differences in interactional norms and expectations might result in failed communication because "an emotional reaction [to cultural differences in communication styles] is often the major factor responsible for a deterioration of rapport and for the mutual attribution of negative personal traits which, in turn, effectively prevent any recognition of real differences in cultural values and norms" (House, 2010, p. 147).

Interactional sociolinguistics is a branch of discourse analysis with a long history of research analyzing communication between different cultural groups. Previous studies have identified conversational styles (Tannen, 2005), listenership behaviors (Erickson, 1986), and contextualization cues (Gumperz, 1977) that are culturally shaped and impact conversational participants' turn-taking practices. For instance, although Japanese people have the reputation for using frequent *aizuchi* (listener responses) to demonstrate active listenership, they are also known for using silence to achieve communicative goals. Without knowing how Japanese speakers use silence in accordance with *aizuchi*, Japanese speakers' silence may give a wrong impression that they are reticent and passive. Adopting an interactional competence view of language learning, the current study examined the turn negotiation practices of one dyad whose interactional outcomes were considered least successful.

2. Method

The participants in the current study were a dyad, Edwin and Hiroyuki. Their data were drawn from 30 dyads who participated in the current eTandem project between English learners in Japan and Japanese learners in the U.S. This focal dyad was considered least successful based on the following three criteria: (a) degree of satisfaction, (b) discontinuity beyond the curricular requirement, and (c) the necessity of the coordinator's intervention. These two participants' initial proficiency, intercultural competence, and motivation, as measured via a questionnaire, were similar to the group average. These participants engaged in nine weekly English-Japanese tandem sessions via *Google Hangout*. For each week, participants engaged in an open-ended information exchange task called visual-based conversation.

The English part of Session 2 was selected for analysis because it was considered the peak of missed communication; it was before the coordinator intervened with the unsuccessful dyad. After watching the whole video of Session 2, a conversation segment that was considered most representative of the session was selected. Silences lasting longer than one second were also indicated in parentheses.

3. Results

In the following conversation (Table 1), Edwin and Hiroyuki are talking about a party scene in the U.S. Hiroyuki asks Edwin questions regarding how American college students party. The dyad faces challenges in how to negotiate turns because (a) Edwin misinterprets Hiroyuki's silence as a lack of engagement, when in fact, Hiroyuki uses silence to seek linguistic help, (b) Hiroyuki's lack of listener responses leads to Edwin's hyper-involvement strategy of hyperexplanation, and (c) both prospective and retrospective recipient design starts to malfunction.

Table 1. Conversation between Edwin and Hiroyuki

	Edwin	Hiroyuki
1	Like um (1.49) the thing about the partying that I don't like as much is that (1.12) it's not very personal.	
2		(2.83)

Chapter 33

3	You just you you go inside the the house (1.16)? You (1.35) you um (2.28) like you you you drink a little bit. [um] and for us it's it's not yet legal? so I think it's more exciting because of that?	[Ah huh]
4		(3.76)
5	Um and then I mean (1.22) I guess you just hit on people.	
6		(1.72)
7	Do you do you do you know what "hit on" means?	
8		(2.60) hidon?
9	HIT ON?	
10		(1.81) No no.
11	Ok ok cuz it it doesn't mean like it's not like like that (punching gesture) It's like.	
12		Un=

This conversation demonstrates an extreme case of complementary schismogenesis where the American participant resorted to even more high-involvement strategies because he was not comfortable with silence, while the Japanese participant, who is used to receiving knowledge rather than questioning the authoritative figure (i.e. native speaker of English) (Nakane, 2006), used more silences to indicate comprehension difficulties, hoping that the American participant would use *sasshi* (guesswork) and offer help. In other words, while Hiroyuki resorted to silence as a rapport management strategy to avoid potentially face-threatening interactions, it was interpreted as an impolite conversational move that places "high inferential demands on the addressee" (Sifianou, 1997, p. 73). As such, Edwin, not knowing what to do with the silence, resorted to his first language high-involvement strategy, hoping that his partner would show more engagement. However, his using faster pacing, less wait time, and limited turn nomination, led to hyperexplanation, which only resulted in depriving Hiroyuki of the time to process Edwin's utterances and indicate comprehension difficulties. Also, Hiroyuki's use of silence reduced Edwin's chance to adjust his recipient design based on Hiroyuki's linguistic output. Hiroyuki's use of more frequent clarification requests, for instance, might have allowed Edwin to assess Hiroyuki's knowledge schema (Tannen & Wallat, 1987) and establish better recipient design. That is, frequent silences and lack of collaborative turn negotiation prevented the dyad from sharing their respective underlying conversational rules and establishing effective recipient design. In the end, this vicious cycle only aggravated the lack of co-construction of talk.

4. Conclusion

Ultimately, we may wonder how the two geographically distant groups of eTandem participants should engage in intercultural negotiation of turns. Should they follow the conversational rules of the target language community (e.g. adopting Japanese conversational rules during Japanese interaction and English rules during English interaction)? Or should they take a balanced approach, adopting a hybrid form of conversational rules that apply to both languages (e.g. mutually agreed-upon rules that integrate both English and Japanese rules)? Whether participants decide to choose one way or the other, practitioners should support learners by providing ample opportunities for the scaffolded exploration of situated turn negotiation practices, so they can maximize the institutional nature of telecollaborative arrangement.

References

Erickson, F. (1986). Listening and speaking. In D. Tannen & J. Alatis (Eds.), *Languages and linguistics: the interdependence of theory, data, and application* (pp. 294-319). Washington, DC: Georgetown University Press.

Gumperz, J. (1977). Sociocultural knowledge in conversational inference. *Linguistics and Anthropology, 76*, 785-98.

House, J. (2010). Impoliteness in Germany: intercultural encounters in everyday and institutional talk. *Intercultural Pragmatics, 7*(4), 561-595. https://doi.org/10.1515/iprg.2010.026

Lamy, M. N., & Goodfellow, R. (2010). Telecollaboration and learning 2.0. In S. Guth & F. Helm (Eds.), *Telecollaboration 2.0: language, literacies and intercultural learning in the 21st century* (pp. 107-138). Bern: Peter Lang.

Nakane, I. (2006). Silence and politeness in intercultural communication in university seminars. *Journal of Pragmatics, 38*(11), 1811-1835. https://doi.org/10.1016/j.pragma.2006.01.005

Sifianou, M. (1997). Silence and politeness. In A. Jaworski (Ed.), *Silence: Interdisciplinary perspectives* (pp. 63-84). Berlin: Mouton de Gruyter.

Tannen, D. (2005). *Conversational style: analyzing talk among friends*. Oxford: Oxford University Press.

Tannen, D., & Wallat, C. (1987). Interactive frames and knowledge schemas in interaction: examples from a medical examination/interview. *Social Psychology Quarterly, 50*(2), 205-216. https://doi.org/10.2307/2786752

Ware, P. (2005). Missed communication in online communication: tensions in a German-American telecollaboration. *Language Learning & Technology, 9*(2), 64-89.

34. A corpus-based study of the use of pronouns in the asynchronous discussion forums in the online intercultural exchange MexCo

Marina Orsini-Jones[1], Zoe Gazeley-Eke[2], and Hannah Leinster[3]

Abstract

This paper reports on research carried out on data extracted from *MexCo* (Mexico-Coventry), an ongoing Online Intercultural Exchange (OIE) in its fifth implementation cycle at the time of writing (May 2016). Based on a set of collaborative intercultural tasks that participants engage with through a tailor-made *Moodle* area, *MexCo* aims to embed internationalisation into the curriculum of the two institutions involved in order to promote global citizenship competences among both students and staff. This study reports on the corpus-based linguistic analysis of the written asynchronous exchanges in two of the discussion forums in *MexCo* in academic year 2014-2015. The analysis was carried out by an 'expert student' in collaboration with staff with a focus on the use of pronouns, and three key differences were observed regarding the use of the first person plural pronoun 'we'.

Keywords: MexCo, online intercultural exchange, corpus analysis, expert student.

1. Coventry University, School of Humanities, Coventry, United Kingdom; m.orsini@coventry.ac.uk

2. Coventry University, School of Humanities, Coventry, United Kingdom; ab2931@coventry.ac.uk

3. Coventry, United Kingdom; hannah.vicparker@gmail.com

How to cite this chapter: Orsini-Jones, M., Gazeley-Eke, Z., & Leinster, H. (2016). A corpus-based study of the use of pronouns in the asynchronous discussion forums in the online intercultural exchange MexCo. In S. Jager, M. Kurek & B. O'Rourke (Eds), *New directions in telecollaborative research and practice: selected papers from the second conference on telecollaboration in higher education* (pp. 283-290). Research-publishing.net. https://doi.org/10.14705/rpnet.2016.telecollab2016.519

Chapter 34

1. Introduction

The *MexCo* project, which started in 2010, has evolved from a project aimed at tandem language learning to an OIE that is integrated into the English and Languages curriculum of the two institutions involved: Coventry University (CU), UK and the Universidad de Monterrey (UDEM), Mexico. Its main aims are to support students and staff involved in it to develop:

- intercultural awareness;

- intercultural communicative competence (Byram, 1997; Helm & Guth, 2010, p. 74);

- multimodal digital multiliteracies when using English as a shared means of communication online. This requires an awareness of the concept of 'cyberpragmatics' (Yus, 2011), meaning how "information is produced and interpreted within the Internet environment" (Yus, 2011, p. 7).

Due to misunderstandings that had occurred in previous cycles of the exchange (Orsini-Jones et al., 2015), it was decided to utilise corpus linguistics tools and discourse analysis to investigate the use of pronouns in the online asynchronous discussion forums from the 2014-15 cycle of project *MexCo*. Data on student engagement, extracted using the *Moodle* analytics tools, also support the discussion of the results of the corpus investigations. One of the expected outcomes was to be able to devise data-driven tasks/materials to teach intercultural communicative competence and cyberpragmatics for academic purposes to the participants involved in future cycles of the project.

This OIE is supported by online content in a tailor-made and collaboratively designed *Moodle* course, which includes (Orsini-Jones, 2015):

- video lectures on intercultural awareness and features of effective online communication and global citizenship competences;

- intercultural scenarios, situation reactions, word associations, surveys and quizzes (inspired by the MIT project *Cultura*, Furstenberg, Levet, English, & Maillet, 2001);

- asynchronous discussion forums where students co-construct knowledge by, for example, carrying out comparative analyses of stereotypes in Mexican and British media;

- e-tutorials and Computer-Mediated Communication (CMC) exercises created by 'expert students' about politeness strategies and how to promote productive cultural discussion (these were based on real exchanges from previous cycles);

- multimedia intercultural group learning objects created by all participating CU students with the e-portfolio *Mahara*.

A distinctive feature of this project is that the online exchanges are analysed by staff in collaboration with 'Expert Students' (ESs) (Orsini-Jones, 2015, p. 50). The 'ESs' are students who have participated in previous online intercultural exchanges, hired as research assistants and student mentors in following cycles, and support staff with their investigations.

2. Method

2.1. Overview of the research

The broad aim of this research study was to investigate the asynchronous forum interactions in the *MexCo* project and involved extracting data from *MexCo* to create a custom-made corpus using the *Sketch Engine* corpus tool to identify interesting intercultural linguistic features in the exchanges. Another aim was to devise Data-Driven Learning (DDL) (Johns, 1991) tasks/materials to raise the awareness of intercultural communicative competence and cyberpragmatics (Yus, 2011) of future cohorts of participants in *MexCo*.

The study is based on the academic year 2014-2015, when participants consisted of 111 Mexican students, 1 Venezuelan and 1 Brazilian from UDEM, and a mix of nationalities from CU (97 British, 5 Chinese, 3 Polish, 2 Lithuanian, 1 Swiss, 1 Greek, 1 Latvian, 1 Czech and 1 Finnish). The corpus tool *Sketch Engine* was used, looking at the use of pronouns in the 'Video Introductions Forum' and in the 'Film Representations Forum'.

The main question that this study intended to answer was:

> What does the application of corpus linguistics techniques reveal about the use of pronouns in the MexCo forum interactions?

The specific corpus linguistics techniques used to address this research question were the Key Word in Context (KWIC) concordance and the frequency list generator on *Sketch Engine*. Each occurrence of 'we' was then qualitatively analysed to see how it was used. It was also considered important to look separately at British and non-British students, of which there were 97 and 14 respectively and Mexican and non-Mexican students, of whom there were 111 and 2 respectively, to investigate whether this variable may have impacted on the students' use of 'we'.

The extracted .html files were recognised by the corpus software and uploaded to create an online database of 101 files constituting a total of 48,558 words (59,457 tokens). The corpus was then automatically part-of-speech tagged using the Penn Treebank tag set (Sketch Engine, 2016) to facilitate corpus queries. In addition to nationality and gender data, information about number of forum posts, the dates of these and the number of times each participant viewed the 'Video Introductions' and 'Film Representations' forums were gathered for each student. These data were obtained using the *Moodle* analytics tools.

3. Discussion

The most interesting finding was that 'we' performed three main functions in the corpus:

- Function 1: to refer to people in general, for example 'I think we need to be careful with stereotypes', or all students in the project or all students within paired groups, for example 'I hope we can all learn from each other'.

- Function 2: to refer to just the students in one group, for example 'We hope you like our video'.

- Function 3: to refer to people of a national, city, or university group (people in Britain or Mexico, CU or UDEM), for example 'We [people in Mexico] have good weather most of the year' and 'We [students at Coventry] have loads of places to eat at uni'.

CU students tended to use 'we' more often to refer to just students in their own CU study group, that is function 2 (Figure 1 and Figure 2). UDEM students, on the other hand, were more likely to use it to refer to people of a nationality, city, or university group (people in Britain or Mexico, CU or UDEM), that is function 3 (Figure 3). Various reasons for these differences were considered including the possibility that the more multi-national CU group exhibited a less pronounced national identity than did the UDEM students, who were mostly mono-cultural.

Figure 1.   Highest percentage of function 1 in the corpus – CU non-British

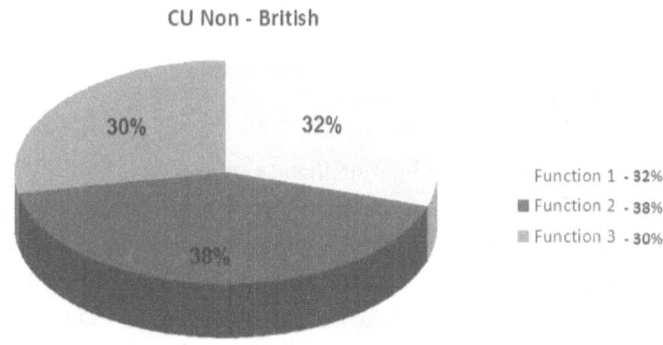

Figure 2. Highest percentage of function 2 in the corpus – CU British

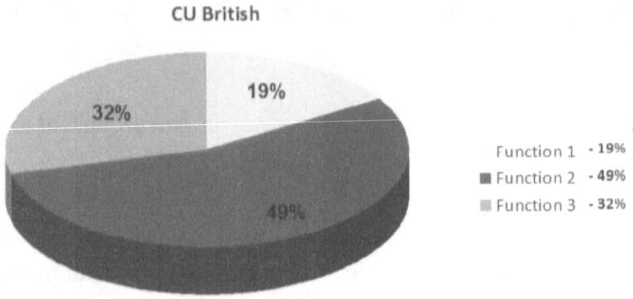

Figure 3. Highest percentage of function 3 in the corpus – UDEM Mexican

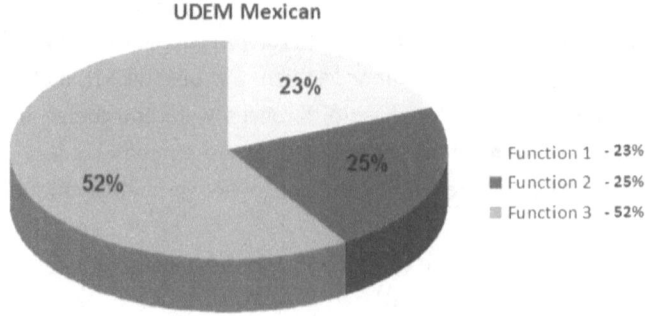

4. Conclusions

The project has shed interesting light on the use of pronouns by the participants in the exchanges that will require further investigation in terms of its CMC implications. In particular, the intercultural assumptions and associations betrayed by the use of 'we' by the two different groups and the different functional usage associated with it. DDL activities are being designed to help students to recognise that pronouns may have different referents by using contextual clues in the sample sentences extracted from the exchanges, thereby developing their "illocutionary competence" which involves identifying and producing intended meaning (Ishihara & Cohen, 2010, p. 5). Other tasks are also being designed to encourage students to discuss how the lack of contextual clues can affect communication in online exchanges (Yus, 2011, p. 275).

There are, however, three limitations to the research study presented here. Firstly, the '*MexCo* Forum Discussion Corpus' was not compared to a reference corpus, meaning that log likelihood calculations could not be made. Secondly, the triangulation of data was limited and, thirdly, only the pronoun 'we' was considered in detail. Further work on the use of pronouns in the corpus could, for example, focus on 'you'. A further suggestion for future research in the *MexCo* project is extending the work on *Moodle* analytics begun here to other academic years.

References

Byram, M. (1997). *Teaching and assessing intercultural communicative competence*. Clevedon: Multilingual Matters.

Furstenberg, G., Levet, S., English, K., & Maillet, K. (2001). Giving a virtual voice to the silent language of culture: the CULTURA project. *Language Learning and Technology, 5*(1), 55-102.

Helm, F., & Guth, S. (2010). The multifarious goals of telecollaboration 2.0: theoretical and practical implications. In S. Guth & F. Helm (Eds), *Telecollaboration 2.0* (pp. 69-106). Bern: Peter Lang.

Ishihara, N., & Cohen, A. D. (2010). *Teaching and learning pragmatics*. Harlow: Pearson.

Johns, T. (1991). Should you be persuaded: two examples of data-driven learning. *English Language Research Journal, 4*, 1-16.

Orsini-Jones, M. (2015). A reflective e-learning journey from the dawn of CALL to web 2.0 intercultural communicative competence (ICC). In K. Borthwick, E. Corradini, & A. Dickens (Eds), *10 years of the LLAS elearning symposium: case studies in good practice* (pp. 43-56). Dublin: Research-publishing.net. http://dx.doi.org/10.14705/rpnet.2015.000266

Orsini-Jones, M., Lloyd, E., Gazeley, Z., Vera López, B., Pibworth, L., & Bescond, G. (2015). Student-driven intercultural awareness raising with MexCo: agency, autonomy and threshold concepts in a telecollaborative project between the UK and Mexico. In N. Tcherepashenets (Ed.), *Globalizing on-line: telecollaboration, internationalization and social justice* (pp. 199-239). New York: Peter Lang.

Sketch Engine. (2016). *CQL corpus querying*. https://www.sketchengine.co.uk/corpus-querying/

Yus, F. (2011). *Cyberpragmatics: internet-mediated communication in context*. Amsterdam/Philadelphia: John Benjamins. http://dx.doi.org/10.1075/pbns.213

35. Cooperative autonomy in online lingua franca exchanges: a case study on foreign language education in secondary schools

Petra Hoffstaedter[1] and Kurt Kohn[2]

Abstract

We report on a case study on pedagogical affordances of intercultural telecollaboration for authentic communication practice and competence development in the local foreign language. Focus is on spoken and written conversations involving pairs of secondary school pupils of different linguacultural backgrounds. Particular attention is given to three task design features: multimodal home access to telecollaboration, lingua franca use of the target language, and soft intercultural topics addressing pupils' everyday concerns and experiences. Performance analyses of recorded conversations and reflective interviews reveal significant pedagogical advantages of the chosen task design features. The online lingua franca conversations are marked by a high degree of cooperative autonomy with an emphasis on creating common ground, negotiating a shared line of argumentation, ensuring a supportive and consensual atmosphere, and solving communication problems on the fly.

Keywords: learner autonomy, communicative language teaching, cooperative autonomy, intercultural telecollaboration, lingua franca pedagogy.

1. Steinbeis Transfer Center Language Learning Media, Konstanz, Germany; petra.hoffstaedter@gmail.com

2. University of Tübingen, Tübingen, Germany; kurt.kohn@uni-tuebingen.de

How to cite this chapter: Hoffstaedter, P., & Kohn, K. (2016). Cooperative autonomy in online lingua franca exchanges: a case study on foreign language education in secondary schools. In S. Jager, M. Kurek & B. O'Rourke (Eds), *New directions in telecollaborative research and practice: selected papers from the second conference on telecollaboration in higher education* (pp. 291-296). Research-publishing.net. https://doi.org/10.14705/rpnet.2016.telecollab2016.520

Chapter 35

1. Introduction

Learning a foreign language crucially involves developing communicative competence for intercultural encounters. Considering this objective and orientation, the traditional foreign language classroom is faced with the serious challenge of providing learners with opportunities for authentic communication. To enable secondary school pupils to engage in communicative interactions with peers from other countries and cultures, the EU project *TILA: Telecollaboration for Intercultural Language Acquisition* (Jan 2013 - June 2015) explores the pedagogical affordances of online exchanges for intercultural foreign language learning in secondary schools (www.tilaproject.eu)[3]. For more information on intercultural telecollaboration see O'Dowd (2012). The environments used in TILA include 3D virtual worlds (OpenSim), videoconferencing platforms (BigBlueButton, Skype) as well as chats and forums in Moodle. TILA's pedagogical approach is characterised by small group or pair interactions implemented in tandem or lingua franca constellations and embedded in blended learning task ensembles. In a lingua franca constellation, pupils communicate in their common non-native target language (Kohn, 2015). Because of a widespread preference for native speaker target models, most TILA teachers initially opted for tandem constellations. Gradually, however, lingua franca constellations became more accepted and teachers appreciated their pedagogical validity.

2. Case study approach

Our case study is part of the TILA research activities (http://bit.ly/1XuaI1I) and focuses on telecollaborative conditions that are expected to facilitate authentic intercultural communication in the foreign language outside of and complementary to regular classroom settings (Kohn & Hoffstaedter, 2015). Special attention is given to cooperative autonomy as a key to successful intercultural communication

---

3. The EU project TILA has been funded with support from the European Commission. This publication reflects the views only of the authors, and the Commission cannot be held responsible for any use which may be made of the information contained therein.

and learning. The exchanges under investigation involve pairs of pupils in spoken (video communication, virtual world) or written (text chat) interactions and are crucially characterised by three task design features:

- multimodal home access to the respective telecollaboration tools;

- lingua franca use of English and German as target languages;

- soft intercultural topics addressing pupils' everyday concerns and experiences.

Performance data from 8 oral conversations (36 min. and 4025 words on average) and 3 written conversations (53 min. and 670 words on average) are complemented by reflective feedback interviews with selected pupils. The analyses help to better understand the pedagogical effects of the chosen task design features; they also provide insights into manifestations of collaborative autonomy.

3. Task design features

Multimodal home access helps to avoid frequent shortcomings of computer labs in schools regarding poor communicative privacy and network overload. Pupils also feel on their own turf and act more naturally than in school. The different telecollaborative options are used according to preference or availability and allow for pedagogical scaffolding.

The **lingua franca condition** makes pupils feel in the same boat with their peers, which enables them to lower their communication apprehension, focus on the communicative task, and develop non-native speaker confidence. They communicate spontaneously, negotiate meaning, solve communication problems, and learn from each other.

Soft intercultural topics about everyday issues are well suited for enabling non-native speakers to engage in authentic conversations based on everyday knowledge, beliefs, and attitudes. Focus is on the roots of intercultural communicative competence in ordinary communication. Soft intercultural topics provide a safe ground for developing communicative attitudes and skills needed for intercultural topics that require special expertise or are emotionally loaded. In addition to the assigned conversation tasks, pupils also introduce their own personal topics, particularly in spoken communication. This is arguably an indicator of increased authenticity and a move beyond school towards real-life communication.

4. Cooperative autonomy

Pupils' conversations show evidence of cooperative autonomy in three respects: third space development, exercise of empathy, and handling of communication problems.

In our study, **third space development** (Kramsch, 2009) concerns an emphasis on creating a common ground of knowledge and attitudes. Pupils repeatedly use phrases for confirming, agreeing and disagreeing, or adding their own views, e.g. "Yes, I think so too", "Yeah, but I don't think…", or "Yeah, but scientists have found…". An English chat conversation between a German (A) and a Spanish pupil (B) illustrates steps in cooperative argument development:

>A: Do you think… social media are a blessing or a curse?

>B: In my opinion it's blessing because… but it's also a curse because…

>B: What do you think?

>A Yes, I have exactly the same opinion. It's very useful but you can… become addicted

>B: Yes and if you post a picture…

>A: Yes

> B: Yes there is no more privacy because...
>
> A: Yes and so much information about people are safed on the internet...
>
> A: I meant saved.

All in all, pupils' interactional strategies are predominantly supportive and consensual rather than confrontational, which is a key quality of their unfolding intercultural competence. In particular in oral conversations, students show a **high degree of social presence by exercising empathy**. When his German partner is unable to express what he wants to say, the Spanish pupil shows empathy ("Doesn't matter") and uses a face saving strategy: "I know we are beginners (laughs) of English, we haven't got such a level to speak about everything we want". Empathy is also combined with encouragement:

> A: I mean, I haven't idea for this but the only thing I can say is I wish you a luck... I hope you win.
>
> A: Just think maybe we are not the best but trying to do our best. This is what you must be thinking.

Other examples from oral conversations between pairs of Spanish and German pupils illustrate how **communication problems** are addressed on the fly and in highly cooperative and efficient ways, always drawing on the pupils' ordinary communication skills. A raising intonation ("Blessing or – ?") is, for instance, used to signal a lexical comprehension problem, which in turn elicits a reply in which the unknown word is repeated ("A curse") along with a paraphrasing meaning explication ("like if it is good for us, or if it is bad"). Examples of co-construction of meaning can be found as well: pupil A explicitly states a lexical production problem, pupil B offers a lexical option with rising intonation to request confirmation ("Annoying?"), A does not understand, and B repeats the word in a full sentence ("They are annoying") combining it with a clarifying paraphrase.

Chapter 35

In our lingua franca conversations, the pupils' attention is on ensuring successful communication: they want to be understood and convey their message. Focus on form plays a role too, but clearly serves the communicative purpose.

5. Conclusion

Our TILA case study demonstrates that an intercultural telecollaboration approach combining a multimodal home access with a pedagogical lingua franca constellation and soft intercultural topics is highly suitable for enabling pupils to develop their intercultural foreign language competence through authentic communication outside classroom constraints. Beneficial pedagogical effects show in pupils' focus on empathy and support and in the strategic skills they use for third space development and handling communication problems. All this helps them develop their sense and ability for cooperative autonomy and activate their ordinary communicative competence for intercultural communication.

References

Kohn, K. (2015). A pedagogical space for English as a lingua franca in the English classroom. In Y. Bayyurt & S. Akcan (Eds), *Current perspectives on pedagogy for ELF* (pp. 51-67). Berlin: De Gruyter Mouton.

Kohn, K., & Hoffstaedter, P. (2015). Flipping intercultural communication practice: opportunities and challenges for the foreign language classroom. In J. Colpaert, A. Aerts, M. Oberhofer, & M. Gutiérez-Colón Plana (Eds), *Task design & CALL. Proceedings of the seventeenth international CALL conference, 6-8 July 2015* (pp. 338-345). Antwerpen: Universiteit Antwerpen.

Kramsch, C. (2009). Third culture and language education. In V. Cook (Ed.), *Language teaching and learning* (pp. 233-254). London: Continuum.

O'Dowd, R. (2012). Intercultural communicative competence through telecollaboration. In J. Jackson (Ed.), *The Routledge handbook of language and intercultural communication* (pp. 342-358). Abingdon: Routledge.

36. Emerging affordances in telecollaborative multimodal interactions

Aparajita Dey-Plissonneau[1] and Françoise Blin[2]

Abstract

Drawing on Gibson's (1977) theory of affordances, Computer-Assisted Language Learning (CALL) affordances are a combination of technological, social, educational, and linguistic affordances (Blin, 2016). This paper reports on a preliminary study that sought to identify the emergence of affordances during an online video conferencing session between teacher trainees specialising in French as a Foreign Language and learners of French from an Irish university. We use Cultural Historical and Activity Theory (CHAT) (Engeström, 1987) as our epistemological framework to explore CALL affordances as they emerged in two tutor-learner triads. Deviations from the lesson plan are identified and some of the factors that promote or hinder the emergence of affordances for second language development in similar environments are highlighted.

Keywords: affordance, cultural historical activity theory, CHAT, video conferencing, language learning.

---

1. Dublin City University, Dublin, Ireland; aparajita.deyplissonneau2@mail.dcu.ie

2. Dublin City University, Dublin, Ireland; francoise.blin@dcu.ie

How to cite this chapter: Dey-Plissonneau, A., & Blin, F. (2016). Emerging affordances in telecollaborative multimodal interactions. In S. Jager, M. Kurek & B. O'Rourke (Eds), *New directions in telecollaborative research and practice: selected papers from the second conference on telecollaboration in higher education* (pp. 297-304). Research-publishing.net. https://doi.org/10.14705/rpnet.2016.telecollab2016.521

Chapter 36

1. Introduction

An affordance is an action possibility that is offered by an object or an environment to an organism in the environment "for good or ill" (Gibson, 1977, p. 68). It is a relational property which depends not only on the action possibilities offered by the objective features of a tool or environment, but also on the actor's perception and action capabilities. Introduced in Human Computer Interaction (HCI) by Norman (1988), the concept of affordance has since then been subjected to diverse interpretations in HCI and CALL research that have moved far beyond Gibson's (1977) original account (Blin, 2016).

Following Bærentsen and Trettvik (2002), this paper adopts an activity theoretical framework to study the emergence and realisation of affordances in the context of pedagogical interactions via a videoconferencing platform between tutor-trainees and language learners. According to this view, the features of a CALL environment only become affordances when they are related to the users' needs and activity. Furthermore, technological affordances are seen as interacting, on different timescales (Blin, 2016), with educational affordances, defined as "the relationships between the properties of an educational intervention and the characteristics of the learner that enable certain kinds of learning to take place" (Lee, 2009, p. 151), and linguistic affordances, which are relations of possibility between language users "that can be acted upon to make further linguistic actions possible" (Van Lier, 2004, p. 95).

From an ecological and activity theoretical perspective on CALL and language development (Blin, 2016), educational affordances are engineered through, for example, the design of lesson plans, learning activities or tasks, and resources, while others emerge in moment-to-moment interactions between learners or between learners and teachers, which respond to emerging contradictions (Engeström & Sannino, 2010) and are made possible by the enactment of technological affordances (e.g. use of text chat, webcam, etc.).

This paper reports on a preliminary study of videoconferencing for L2 development that sought to investigate the following research questions:

- What are the affordances that are offered by the environment?

- What are the affordances that have emerged during the online interactions?

- What triggered the emergence of these affordances?

2. Methodology

2.1. Context

As part of the online language teaching project *Le Français en Première Ligne*, Masters students of French as a foreign language from the University of Lyon 2 (France) tutored online learners of French from Dublin City University (Ireland). Six 45 minute weekly sessions were conducted via the videoconferencing platform VISU. These sessions were recorded, anonymised, transcribed, annotated and incorporated into a rich multimodal corpus (ISMAEL) which comprises a broad range of artefacts produced online and offline by both groups during the course of the project (lesson plans, multimodal feedback, reflective accounts etc.) and semi-structured interviews. This study will analyse

- the fifth session's lesson plan;

- debriefing sessions (tutors' post-session reflections);

- online instantiations of session 5 of two tutor-tutee triads.

Figure 1 represents the tutor-tutee activity system for session 5 wherein students and tutors interacted using 'tools and artefacts' as indicated below. The interaction design required students to formulate questions to study the market needs and accordingly advise the tutors to set up a food truck business plan (object). Session 5 was chosen because by this time both tutors and students had become well-acquainted with the videoconferencing interface and technical problems.

Chapter 36

Figure 1. Activity system for session 5

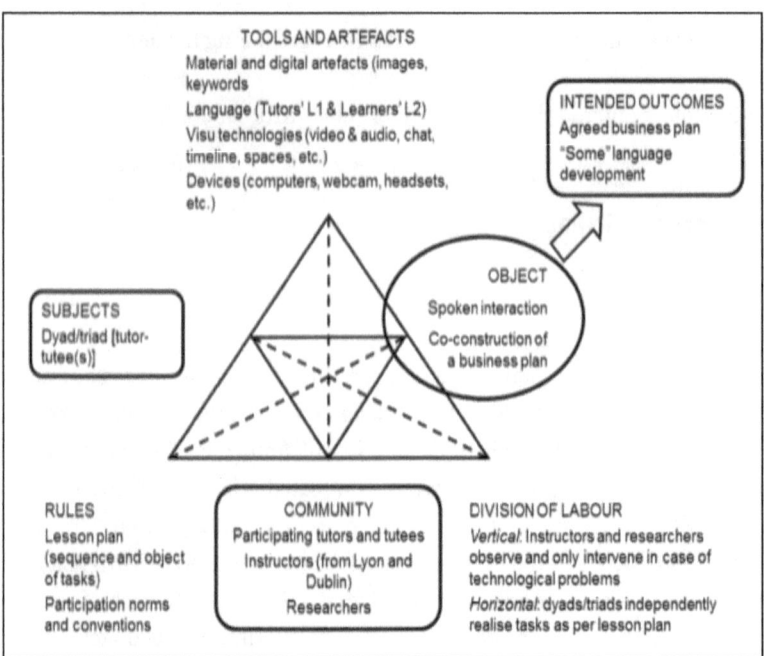

2.2. Data

The fourth activity of the fifth session (micro level interaction) was chosen for analysis because tutors faced problems with the proposed activity of eliciting questions from students. Two tutors, Adèle and Melissa's (chosen arbitrarily) activity systems were analysed closely.

Transcripts of the recorded debriefing sessions, the fifth lesson plan, and the corresponding online instantiations of the two tutors Adèle and Melissa were uploaded on the qualitative analysis software atlas.ti. The debriefing sessions and lesson plans were coded inductively to identify disturbances perceived by tutors in the environment. The online interactions of the two tutors were then coded deductively based on the coding scheme that emerged from the debriefing sessions and the lesson plan.

3. Analysis

3.1. Micro interaction 1

The interaction below took place between Melissa and her students Ana and Alejandra. Melissa had already announced the food truck context and had asked her students to ask questions about the target market. Ana's mic was not working properly so she used chat to send the first question: "what do you want to sell and to whom?" Melissa completely overlooked the text chat sent by Ana (this happens before the extract presented below in Figure 2) and starts sharing key words (line 1) enacting a technological 'multimedia affordance'. She reiterated three times "your objective is to ask questions" hammering an 'interactional communication' while overlooking Ana's written question.

Figure 2. Design for learning for tutor Melissa and students Ana and Alejandra

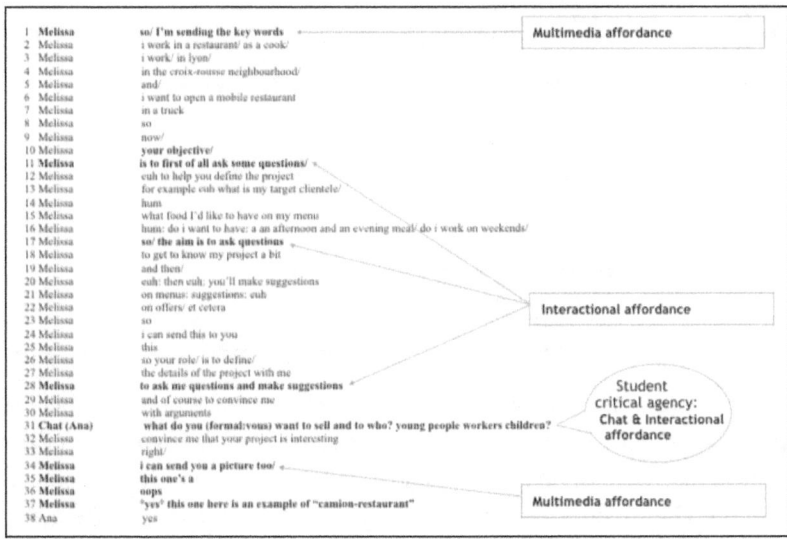

Furthermore, to help the students come up with questions, Melissa gave out questions herself (lines 13-16). This echoes the problem voiced by tutors in the debriefing session that they ended up asking the questions themselves. Ana

Chapter 36

resent her unanswered question a couple of seconds later (line 31), affording interactional communication. The negotiation of meaning seems to be disrupted due to a lack of perception of the written mode (chat affordance) by the tutor. Instead of picking up the interactional affordance that was triggered by Ana via chat, Melissa shared a picture of the food truck as indicated in the lesson plan.

3.2. Micro interaction 2

The interaction below (Figure 3) represents the same eliciting questions activity between Adèle and her 2 students Alannah and Caitriona.

Figure 3. Design for learning for tutor Adèle and students Alannah and Catriona

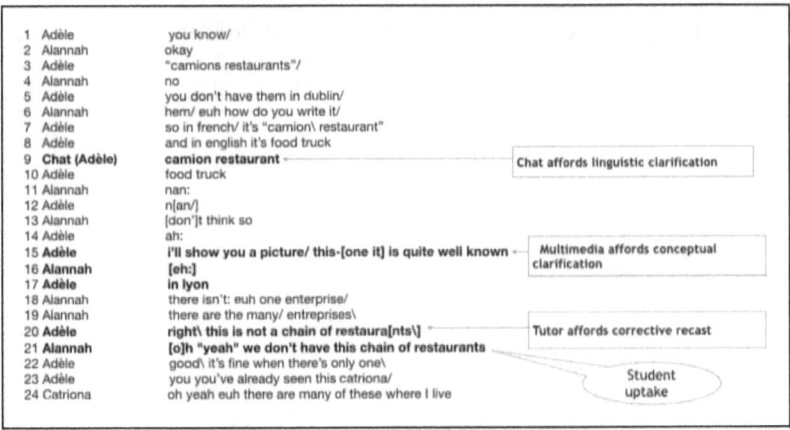

Adèle perceived that one of the students did not understand the concept of 'camion restaurant'. This focus shift triggered two technological affordances, 'chat' and 'sharing of image' which afforded Adèle to fill this perceived linguistic, cultural and conceptual gap. In line 18, Alannah gets the meaning and tries to convey that she thought Adèle was talking about a specific food truck chain. Adèle perceived Alannah's linguistic error and afforded corrective feedback using recast as the tutor replaces the expression "many enterprises" by the contextually accurate "chain of restaurants" (lines 20-21). This is followed by instantaneous 'uptake' (line 21) as Alannah repeats the corrected expression.

4. Discussion and conclusion

The same tools and artefacts gave way to different instantiations. Disturbances such as sound problems for Melissa and focus shift for Adèle afforded new opportunities for mediated actions. Thus, Ana used chat to communicate her question that triggered technological and linguistic affordances that are not directly perceived by tutor Melissa. Adèle on the other hand uses chat and shares an image to address the linguistic, cultural and conceptual gaps for Alannah.

In doing so, the tutor-learner triads displayed different degrees of deviation from the designed script. Melissa seems preoccupied by the designed lesson plan that indicated sharing of key words and images. She fails to perceive the emergent signifiers in the environment as Ana resorts to the written mode to formulate her question. It must be noted that Melissa had no teaching experience at the time and tends to show a greater reliance on the script. Adèle with three years face-to-face teaching experience, flouts the eliciting questions activity and mediates the designed technological and educational affordances to suit the students' needs.

We conclude that communicational or technological disturbances, focus shifts and/or change of object in activity afford new perception-action relations or affordances in the ecological learning system that are triggered by tutor or tutee agency. The realisation of these affordances allows some emerging contradictions to be resolved, but perhaps not always in expansive ways.

References

Bærentsen, K. B., & Trettvik, J. (2002). An activity theory approach to affordance. In *Proceedings of the second Nordic conference on Human-computer interaction* (pp. 51-60). New York: ACM. http://dx.doi.org/10.1145/572020.572028

Blin, F. (2016). The theory of affordances. In M.-J. Hamel & C. Caws (Eds), *Language-learner computer interactions: theory, methodology and CALL applications* (pp. 41-64). John Benjamins Publishing Company. http://dx.doi.org/10.1075/lsse.2.03bli

Engeström, Y. (1987). *Learning by expanding: an activity-theoretical approach to developmental research*. Orienta-Konsultit Oy.

Engeström, Y., & Sannino, A. (2010). Studies of expansive learning: foundations, findings and future challenges. *Educational Research Review, 5*(1), 1-24. http://dx.doi.org/10.1016/j.edurev.2009.12.002

Gibson, J. J. (1977). The theory of affordances. In R. Shaw & J. Bransford (Eds), *Perceiving, acting and knowing* (pp. 67-82). Hillsdale, NJ: Erlbaum.

Lee, M. (2009). How can 3d virtual worlds be used to support collaborative learning? An analysis of cases from the literature. *Je-LKS, 5*(1), 149-158.

Norman, D. (1988). *The design of everyday things*. New York: Basic books.

Van Lier, L. (2004). The ecology of language learning: practice to theory, theory to practice. *Procedia - Social and Behavioral Sciences, 3*, 2-6. http://dx.doi.org/10.1016/j.sbspro.2010.07.005

37. Telecollaboration in online communities for L2 learning

Maria Luisa Malerba[1] and Christine Appel[2]

Abstract

This paper reports on a PhD study about informal second language learning in online communities (Livemocha and Busuu). In these communities learners autonomously seek opportunities for telecollaboration with Native Speakers (NSs) in the absence of teachers and pedagogical tasks, and in an informal context. This paper focuses on learning and social resources of these communities as a support for tandem activities. The methodology adopted had an interpretative framework and consisted of six phases. Results showed that these online environments have a potential for learners to engage in naturalistic repair trajectories. The conclusions that can be drawn from this study are that, despite today's flourishing of social media and new technologies, tandem language learning still presents the same challenges and more investigation is required on the adequate support learners need.

Keywords: online communities, telecollaboration, tandem, learner autonomy, reciprocity.

---

1. Open University of Catalonia, Barcelona, Spain; m.marialuisa@gmail.com

2. Open University of Catalonia, Barcelona, Spain; mappel@uoc.edu

How to cite this chapter: Malerba, M. L., & Appel, C. (2016). Telecollaboration in online communities for L2 learning. In S. Jager, M. Kurek & B. O'Rourke (Eds), *New directions in telecollaborative research and practice: selected papers from the second conference on telecollaboration in higher education* (pp. 305-312). Research-publishing.net. https://doi.org/10.14705/rpnet.2016.telecollab2016.522

1. Introduction

Tandem language learning refers to a language exchange in which two learners who are native speakers of each other's target language work together. For a successful tandem partnership, the principles of reciprocity and autonomy need to be observed (Little & Brammerts, 1996), that is, both learners need to benefit equally and take ownership of their language learning. Tandem exchanges have taken place over time in a number of different formats, from face-to-face, letter writing, e-mail, to videoconferencing initiatives. With the arrival of the Internet, the potential for encounters with tandem partners increased exponentially, each new technology opening up a new range of possibilities.

In the realm of online communities designed specifically for Second Language (L2) learning, the literature has shed light on their affordances and constraints from technical and pedagogical points of view, and has stressed that online communities could play an important role if integrated in formal learning and in telecollaborative practices (Brick, 2011; Chotel, 2012; Chotel & Mangenot, 2011; Harrison & Thomas, 2009; Lloyd, 2012; Gonzales, 2012).

This paper presents partial results of a PhD thesis (Malerba, 2015a) on L2 learning in the online communities of *Livemocha* and *Busuu*, addressing the pedagogical needs of online learners and highlighting the importance of the design of learning environments for tandem language in out-of-class informal and semi-formal contexts.

2. Methodology

This study applies Engeström's (1987) model of Activity Theory (AT) to online communities for language learning to explain the division of labour and the social roles and norms among learners. This methodology, gradually narrowing the scope, consisted of six phases, and the results of each phase fed into the design of the following one.

- Contextualisation and identification of *Livemocha* and *Busuu* online communities.

- Participant observation of learners' learning experience in these online communities.

- Administration of an online survey to find out about learners' language learning experience.

- Semi-structured interviews to elicit more information about learners' subjective experience and perceptions of these communities.

- Identification of case studies and a micro-analysis of their online interactions to identify the ways in which they create opportunities for L2 use.

- Recall interviews to trace knowledge of the participants' learning experience over time.

In this way, throughout the different phases, a progressively deeper understanding of the behaviours enacted by learners in these communities was developed.

3. Results

Three learner profiles emerged from the analysis (Malerba, 2015b).

- The course taker, who is merely engaged with the learning affordances (didactic units and exercise corrections) of the communities and who has limited social exchanges with peers.

- The social networker, who is fully engaged with the social affordances (the chat tool) of the communities.

- The social course taker, who is a hybrid between the two previous profiles and who is the most likely to take the most out of the experience in the communities.

Under the lens of AT, the three profiles can be analysed as such (see Figure 1, Figure 2, and Figure 3).

Figure 1. The learning activity of the 'course taker' adapted from Engeström's (1987) model

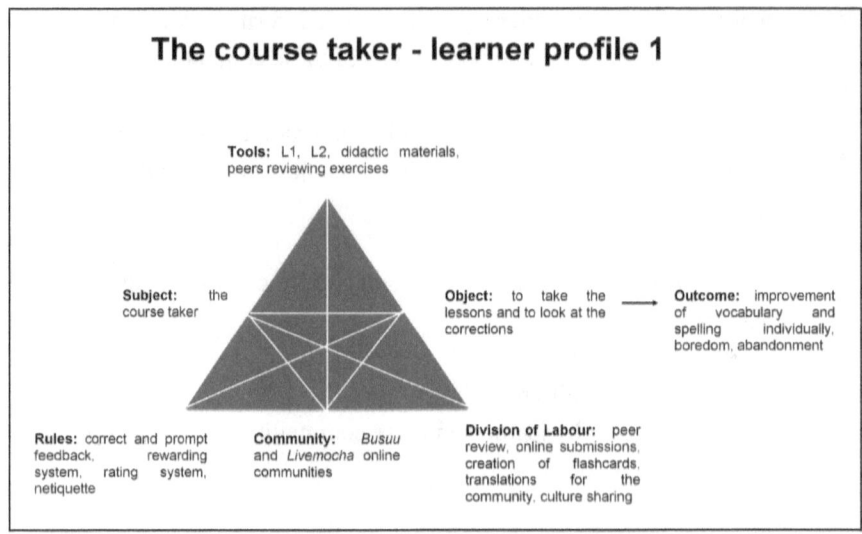

As Figure 1 shows, the learning content (*tools*) mediates the relationship between the course taker (*subject*) and his learning and sharing (*object*), which is the main aim of online communities. Moreover, in the case of the course taker, the relationship between learners (*subject*) and the completion of the didactic affordances (*object*) is mediated by a set of norms (*rules*) that are quite explicit and have been established in the community. In the case of the course taker, the collaborative practices (*division of labour*) are generated mainly by the peer review system. But, according to the perceptions of the learners interviewed, the lack and/or poor quality of peer feedback caused demotivation among learners.

Figure 2. The learning activity of the 'social networker' adapted from Engeström's (1987) model

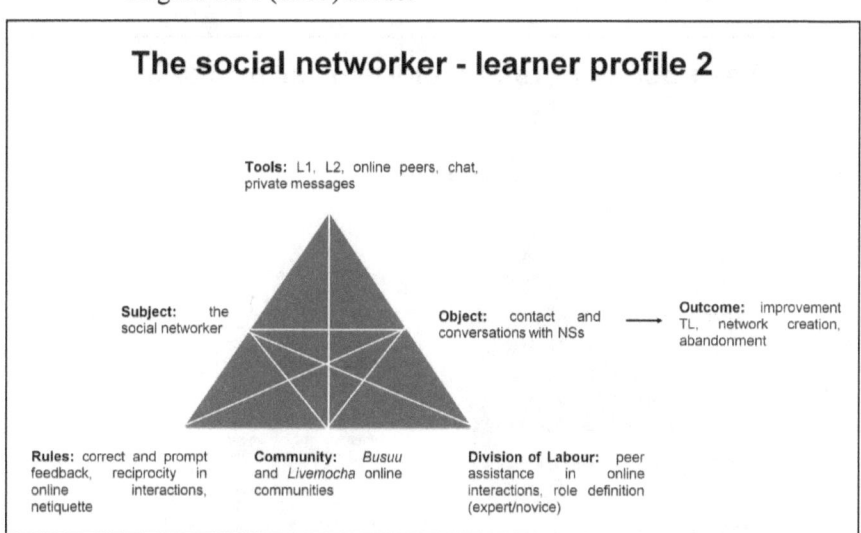

In the case of the social networker (Figure 2), the relationship between the online platforms (*community*) and the contact with NSs (*object*) is mediated by the exchanges and the opportunities for interactions (*division of labour*) among the participants occurring in the chat tool. For the social networker, the division of labour occurs mainly in the online chat tool and in a minority of cases through private messages (asynchronous tool) (*tools*). The norms (*rules*) of the social networker coincide with the norms of tandem language learning, are learned during the interactions and are constantly shaped according to the language partner.

As Figure 3 suggests, the social course taker's (*subject*) relationship with the platforms (*community*) is mediated by the social affordances (*tools*/chat), the didactic affordances (*tools*/learning materials), the L1 (or L2 in which he is proficient), and by the TL itself. The aim (*object*) of this learner is both the contact with NSs and reinforcing the knowledge of the TL through the learning units in collaboration with the peers encountered in the community. The norms (*rules*) combine the norms of the course taker and the norms of the social networker.

Chapter 37

Figure 3. The learning activity of the 'social course taker' adapted from Engeström's (1987) model

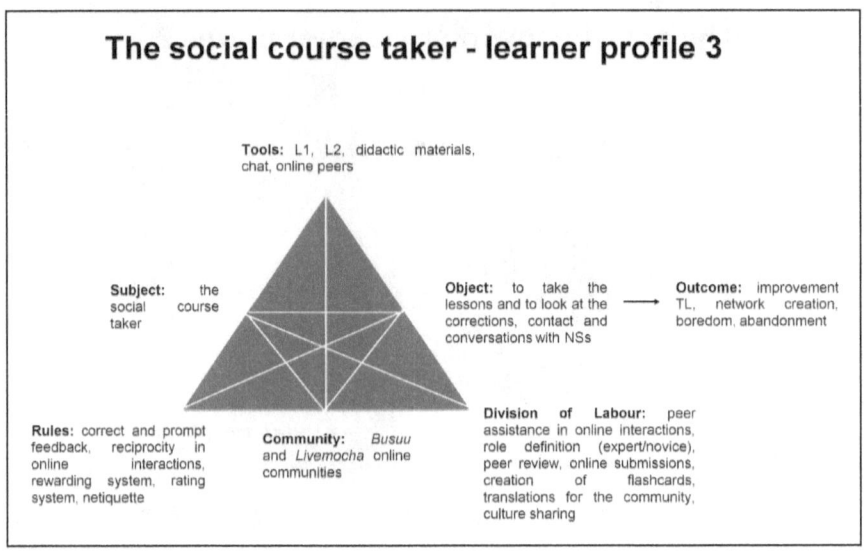

4. Discussion

Drawing on the analysis, some tensions and contradictions arose. First of all, there is no synergy between the learning and the social affordances of the communities. The design of the didactic units, rather than favouring contact and collaboration with NSs, isolates learners and engages them in repetitive behaviourist-like exercises. Another contradiction regards the presence of learners with different objectives and rules. When learners from different profiles meet, tensions cannot be avoided.

5. Conclusion

This leads us to the conclusion that social and learning affordances in online communities should work in synergy towards a common objective. Therefore, a task-based language teaching approach would be key for the success of tandem partnerships in these communities.

Comparing Appel's (1999) study on tandem language learning through emails, with Malerba's (2015a) study on tandem in online communities, it is evident that even though technology has developed and the environments have changed, we are still finding the same positive outcomes as well as the same challenges to cope with. New approaches and different supports for an effective tandem experience, both in terms of sustainability as well as learning gains, are still needed. A new recent attempt towards this direction is represented by the TandemMOOC initiative (Appel & Pujolà, 2015), which is a hybrid between social and course environments.

References

Appel, M. C. (1999). Tandem learning by email: some basic principles and a case study. *CLCS Occasional Paper, 54.* Dublin: Trinity College. Centre for Language and Communication Studies.
Appel, M. C., & Pujolà, J. T. (2015). Tandem MOOC: a new approach to LMOOC course and task design. In *Task Design & CALL. XVIIth International CALL Research Conference, Tarragona, 6-8 July 2015.*
Brick, B. (2011). Social networking sites and language learning. *International Journal of Virtual and Personal Learning Environments, 2*(3), 18-31. http://dx.doi.org/10.4018/jvple.2011070102
Chotel, L. (2012). *Interactivité et interactions sur un site d'apprentissage et de réseautage en langues : analyse systémique de l'activité de trois apprenants.* Unpublished Master's thesis, Université Stendhal - Grenoble III.
Chotel, L., Mangenot, F. (2011). Autoformation et sites d'apprentissage et de réseautage en langues. *Proceedings of the EPAL 2011 conference, University Stendhal Grenoble II, France.*
Engeström, Y. (1987). *Learning by expanding. An activity theoretical approach to developmental research.* Helsinki: Orienta-Konsultit.
Gonzales, A. (2012). *Interlanguage pragmatic development in native speaker/nonnative speaker participatory online environments.* Unpublished Ph.D. thesis, University of New Mexico.

Harrison, R., & Thomas, M. (2009). Identity in online communities: social networking sites and language learning. *International Journal of Emerging Technologies and Society, 7*(2), 109-124.

Little, D., & Brammerts, H. (Eds.). (1996). A guide to language learning in tandem via the Internet. *CLCS Occasional Paper, 46*. Dublin: Trinity College, Centre for Language and Communication Studies.

Lloyd, E. (2012). Language learners' "Willingness to Communicate" through Livemocha.com. *Alsic, 15*(1).

Malerba, M. L. (2015a). *Social networking in second language learning. Informal online interactions*. Unpublished Ph.D. thesis, Universitat Oberta de Catalunya.

Malerba, M. L. (2015b). Learners behaviours and autonomy in Livemocha and Busuu online communities. In *EDEN 2015 Annual Conference. Expanding Learning Scenarios* (pp. 1-6).

38 Fostering students' engagement with topical issues through different modes of online exchange

Marie-Thérèse Batardière[1] and Francesca Helm[2]

Abstract

This paper reports on two distinct models of telecollaboration – the Soliya Connect Program, a synchronous Computer Mediated Communication (CMC) project, and the Intercultural Franco-Irish Exchange, an asynchronous CMC project – which seek to provide students with a learning space to promote a more politically engaged and reflective pedagogy (Kramsch, 2014). Using Herring's (2007) faceted classification for computer-mediated discourse, it specifies the models' inherent features and draws attention to a number of differentiating characteristics of the two projects. The analysis of qualitative data collected through students' diaries and feedback questionnaires shows that both modes of online dialogue encouraged students to engage with peers and content and enabled them to achieve intended learning outcomes.

Keywords: computer-mediated discourse, telecollaboration models, faceted classification scheme, interactions.

---

1. University of Limerick, Limerick, Ireland; marie-therese.batardiere@ul.ie

2. University of Padova, Padova, Italy; francesca.helm@unipd.it

How to cite this chapter: Batardière, M.-T., & Helm, F. (2016). Fostering students' engagement with topical issues through different modes of online exchange. In S. Jager, M. Kurek & B. O'Rourke (Eds), *New directions in telecollaborative research and practice: selected papers from the second conference on telecollaboration in higher education* (pp. 313-319). Research-publishing.net. https://doi.org/10.14705/rpnet.2016.telecollab2016.523

1. Introduction

In a recent issue of the Modern Language Journal dedicated to foreign language teaching in an era of globalization, Claire Kramsch (2014) discusses how globalization has altered the contexts and conditions under which Foreign Languages (FLs) are taught, learned, and used. One of the points Kramsch (2014) makes in her introduction is that "[w]hile it is not the role of FL teachers to impose on their students their views on events, it is FL teachers' responsibility to expose students to various perspectives (even controversial ones) and to help them discuss the points of view adopted by speakers, writers, and bloggers on these events" (p. 307). Online intercultural exchange can help us achieve this by facilitating learner interaction with peers who have different views on often sensitive key issues.

The two distinct virtual exchange programmes explored in this study are the Soliya Connect Program (SCP; www.soliya.net) a synchronous CMC project which has been described as a 'dialogical' model of telecollaboration, and the University of Limerick project (ULP; http://www.uni-collaboration.eu/?q=node/429), an asynchronous model which could be labelled as a 'traditional' model of telecollaboration. In spite of the frequently evoked dichotomy (or what some call 'apparent incompatibility') of spoken versus written mode of discourse, these two collaborative projects follow a common approach (i.e. give students access to an online platform for an authentic and meaningful dialogue with peers) and set similar educational learning goals (i.e. promote intercultural dialogue, develop critical thinking and encourage reflection). This prompted the present researchers' interest in examining the two programmes more closely. They are also active practitioners, involved in the implementation and/or running of their respective project for nearly 10 years.

2. Methodology

Herring (2007) proposes a descriptive framework drawn from Hymes's (1974) etic approach to spoken discourse classification (also known as Hymes (1974) SPEAKING taxonomy). This classification scheme for Computer Mediated

Discourse (CMD) analysis introduces two types of influence that can affect communication: 'Medium' (i.e. technological factors such as synchronicity, message transmission, size of message, etc.) and 'Situation' (i.e. social factors such as information about participants, their relationships to one another, their purposes for communicating, etc.). Herring (2007) explains that this division does not necessarily imply that the computer medium itself is a determining factor in online language use and that technological and social factors may or may not interact but, recognises in agreement with Androutsopoulos (2006) "the interplay of *particular* technological and social/contextual factors in the shaping of computer-mediated language practices" (p. 421, emphasis added), hence the need to separate the two types of factors for a better understanding of their specific impact on CMD (Herring, 2007). Each set of factors comprises an open-ended list of categories or 'facets' (see Appendix). Additional categories can be included if these have an impact on online discourse (Herring, 2007). To proceed with a systematic comparison of the two projects, ULP and SCP, Herring's (2007) classification scheme seemed the most appropriate tool as it was intended to bring to light CMC features that directly influence language use in online interactions.

3. A comparative description

It is beyond the scope of this article to present in detail a classification of the two models of CMD, so attention will be drawn to their inherent features which contrast most. The main difference between the two projects regards synchronicity, with spoken and synchronous communication in the SCP which is thus expected to differ significantly from that in the asynchronous, written ULP due to access to "simultaneous feedback" (Herring, 2003, p. 618). However other affordances, such as 'persistence of transcript' and 'availability of quoting previous message' on the ULP forum come into play to compensate for the absence of this feature. One medium factor has been added to Herring's (2007) original classification: *Platform*. The familiarity (and easy access) to the online forum platform for the ULP group compared to the novelty of the SCP real-time video-conference (with occasionally poor internet connection) is likely to have an effect on students' CMD. Interestingly, while the 'channels of communication' on the SCP are predominantly spoken, participants welcome the support of text chat (drafted by the group facilitator). Conversely, participants in the ULP often add audio-visual material – related to the discussion topic – to their written posts.

Turning to the second set, the situation factors, the two CMC modes exhibit opposite characteristics in most categories except 'purpose' (of communication) and also to an extent, 'topic of discussion'. Starting with the facet 'participation structure', the divergence is quite marked: in the SCP small group (or 'many to many') exchanges can at times result in imbalanced participation compared to the one to one, symmetrical and fairly even exchange in the ULP; besides, for the SCP, the video-conference sessions are limited to two hours weekly while the ULP participants can rely on a 24 hour open access data and forum.

Looking at another dimension, 'norms of organisation', both models took a prescriptive approach to 'task and activities' to a stronger (SCP) or lesser (ULP) degree. 'Task sequencing' was perceived as essential in the two models to create a safe space for true dialogue to take place as both projects address challenging 'topics' involving controversial social issues (ULP) or sensitive cultural issues (SCP). The striking difference is the presence of a trained facilitator in the SCP interactions who is expected to lead the dialogue sessions, ensure all participants can be heard, and foster depth of discussion. In contrast, the ULP is organised in dyads with no teacher presence/intervention, each partner being an expert on his or her own country/culture. Another potentially significant situational factor has been added: *Design* (of curriculum/task). In the SCP, students from universities throughout the Middle East, North Africa, United States, and Europe follow a shared preset 'online curriculum' associated with the project, whereas the ULP fits in a teacher-designed fourth year course. This may have an impact initially on participants' attitude towards the online task in the SCP, as adjusting to unfamiliar settings as well as new curriculum can be a bit overwhelming for some.

4. Discussion and conclusion

This brief comparative description of the two CMC models has shown that while technical affordances influence students' language use, they have to be examined in relation to the situational factors, as these also shape the interaction in the online exchange. It would be easy to assume that the projects' differences found in the two sets of factors will have some bearing on students' level of engagement and will somehow accentuate the initial synchronicity divide between the two CMC models.

Yet reflecting on their online learning experience, some of the participants made very similar, almost interchangeable comments, particularly as regards their motivation to post a message or participate in sessions regularly. The following comments obtained from learner diaries and questionnaires exemplify this:

> "The *discussions* and the *interaction* were so rich that it almost seemed that 2hrs a week was not enough to cover what we had to give [SCP]; It was a very *interactive* experience. I looked forward to hearing from my partner and having an interesting *conversation* with her [ULP]" (emphasis added).

It is also worth mentioning that students in both projects made reference to project goals such as greater awareness and/or accepting their own as well as others' perspectives:

> "If we didn't agree we just made room to an open minded conversation, accepting all arguments [ULP]; It's important to put ourselves in another person's shoes in order to really understand them [SCP]".

Though we distinguish between written and spoken, synchronous and asynchronous CMC modes, these distinctions become increasingly blurred as CMC has become multimodal with audio-video conferencing including text, and text-based forums including hyperlinks to video. Furthermore, sustained engagement in synchronous audio-video sessions over a period of weeks can take on the form of an extended conversation, in a similar way to an asynchronous forum threaded discussion lasting up to 8 weeks. Notwithstanding the limitations of this study, provisional findings would appear to lend support to Herring's (2011) assertion that CMC is 'conversation'.

References

Androutsopoulos, J. (Ed.). (2006). Introduction: sociolinguistics and computer-mediated communication. *Journal of Sociolinguistics, 10*(4), 419-438.

Herring, S. (2003). Computer-mediated discourse. In D. Schiffrin, D. Tannen & H. Hamilton (Eds), *The handbook of discourse analysis* (pp. 612-634). Oxford: Blackwell.

Herring, S. (2007). A faceted classification scheme for computer-mediated discourse. *Language@Internet, 4*(1), 1-37. http://www.languageatinternet.org/articles/2007/761

Herring, S. (2011). Computer-mediated conversation, part II: introduction and overview. *Language@Internet, 8*(2). http://www.languageatinternet.org/articles/2011/Herring

Hymes, D. H. (1974). Foundations in sociolinguistics: an ethnographic approach. Philadephia: University of Pennsylvania Press.

Kramsch, C. (2014). Teaching foreign languages in an era of globalization. Introduction. *The Modern Language Journal, 98*(1), 296-311. https://doi.org/10.1111/j.1540-4781.2014.12057.x

Appendix

Medium and Situation factors from Herring's faceted classification scheme for computer-mediated discourse. http://www.languageatinternet.org/articles/2007/761

Table 1. Medium factors (Herring, 2007)

M1	Synchronicity
M2	Message transmission (1-way vs 2-way)
M3	Persistence of transcript
M4	Size of message buffer
M5	Channels of communication

M6	Anonymous messaging
M7	Private messaging
M8	Filtering
M9	Quoting
M10	Message format

Table 2. Situation factors (Herring, 2007)

S1	Participation structure	One-to-one, one-to-many, many-to-many Public/private Degree of anonymity/pseudonymity Group size; number of active participants Amount, rate, and balance of participation
S2	Participant characteristics	Demographics: gender, age, occupation, etc. Proficiency: with language/computers/CMC Experience: with addressee/group/topic Role/status: in 'real life'; of online personae Pre-existing sociocultural knowledge and interactional norms Attitudes, beliefs, ideologies, and motivations
S3	Purpose	Of group, e.g. professional, social, fantasy/ role-playing, aesthetic, experimental Goal of interaction, e.g. get information, negotiate consensus, develop professional/social relationships, impress/entertain others, have fun
S4	Topic or Theme	Of group, e.g. politics, linguistics, feminism, soap operas, sex, science fiction, South Asian culture, medieval times, pubs Of exchanges, e.g. the war in Iraq, pro-drop languages, the project budget, gay sex, vacation plans, personal information about participation, meta-discourse about CMC
S5	Tone	Serious/playful Formal/casual Contentious/friendly Cooperative/sarcastic, etc.
S6	Activity	E.g. debate, job announcement, information exchange, phatic exchange, problem solving, exchange of insults, joking exchange, game, theatrical performance, flirtation, virtual sex
S7	Norms	Of organization Of social appropriateness Of language
S8	Code	Language, language variety Font/writing system

39 A conversation analysis approach to researching eTandems – the challenges of data collection

Julia Renner[1]

Abstract

This article deals with the challenges of data collection from a Conversation Analysis (CA) perspective to researching synchronous, audio-visual eTandems. Conversation analysis is a research tradition that developed out of ethnomethodology and is concerned with the question of how social interaction in naturally occurring situations is organized. In the course of the first cycle of data collection for my PhD research, which was carried out within the L3 TASK project[2], four methodological issues ('multimodality', 'completeness', 'authenticity' and 'task-based vs. off-task conversation') that result from the particular requirements of CA to data collection were identified. In the following article these challenges and possible solutions are brought to light.

Keywords: synchronous audio-visual communication, eTandem language learning, conversation analysis, data collection.

---

1. University of Vienna, Vienna, Austria; julia.renner@univie.ac.at

2. http://www.l3task.eu

How to cite this chapter: Renner, J. (2016). A conversation analysis approach to researching eTandems – the challenges of data collection. In S. Jager, M. Kurek & B. O'Rourke (Eds), *New directions in telecollaborative research and practice: selected papers from the second conference on telecollaboration in higher education* (pp. 321-326). Research-publishing.net. https://doi.org/10.14705/rpnet.2016.telecollab2016.524

Chapter 39

1. Connecting CA to eTandem language learning research

Tandem learning refers to "language-based communication between two learners who are native speakers of different languages and who are learning each other's language as L2" (Cziko, 2004, pp. 26-27). Originally, language tandems were carried out in face-to-face settings, where the participants share the same physical space. Due to technological advancements, eTandems have increasingly been able to overcome spatial distance. Research in the field of synchronous, audio-visual eTandem language learning has been concerned with various aspects such as learner attitudes (El-Hariri & Jung, 2015; Tian & Wang, 2010), task design (El-Hariri, 2016) and interactional dimensions (e.g. Akiyama, 2014). However, detailed analyses of eTandem conversations from a CA perspective remain scarce. CA is an open, inductive approach that aims to understand how people manage spoken discourse. Because of its exploratory, hypothesis-generating nature, it is well suited to gather insight into new forms of social interaction, such as eTandem conversations. While the mechanisms of everyday conversation and various types of institutional communication have been thoroughly studied from a CA perspective, eTandem conversations as a hybrid of natural everyday communication and communication for the purpose of language learning (Bechtel, 2003) are yet to be explored. From the perspective of language teaching and learning, research CA may:

> "document in a way that, for example, main-stream SLA studies cannot, what students are doing when they are engaged in a learning activity, and what they are doing at a later stage when they have [...] learned to become accomplished users of certain linguistic resources in interaction" (Gardner, 2013, p. 609).

2. The project: L3 TASK

L3 TASK is a project funded by the European Commission that promotes language learning by means of synchronous, audio-visual eTandems. The participants of this project are university students majoring in either (Mandarin) Chinese, Spanish or German, who are proficient speakers of one of the other two languages. The main objective of the project was to foster oral communication. The present article refers to the experience of data collection of Chinese-German eTandems. Each eTandem consisted of one student from the University of Vienna (Austria) and one student from Xiangtan University (People's Republic of China). The students from the University of Vienna were majoring in Chinese Studies, the students from Xiangtan University were majoring in German Studies. The students at both universities participated in the project outside their regular language courses, but were offered a supplementary tandem course with monthly meet-ups. In addition, the participants were given a variety of tasks to facilitate communication. In weekly sessions, the students communicated via the online program ooVoo. It was mainly chosen for the purpose of data collection as audio/video chat sessions can be easily recorded with it. The eTandems were asked to record three or four conversations over a period of one semester (October–January 2014/15).

3. Challenges of data collection

3.1. Multimodality

Observations from the first cycle of data collection showed that eTandem conversations were not only limited to oral communication. Instead, participants made use of different modes to orchestrate meaning. Text-chat mode was used in three particular instances: to overcome comprehension problems, during technical difficulties, and to explain new vocabulary. During data analysis, we were able to identify situations that lead to a switch from audio/video chat to text chat, whereas what was actually communicated through the text chat could not be observed. Individual reports revealed that not only text, but also images were sent through the text chat. For a CA approach, it is crucial to get a complete picture of the conversation that is as detailed as possible. This is especially a challenge for telecollaboration practice that allows for the simultaneous use of different modes. Although it is of course not reasonable nor even possible to try to capture everything that happens on and off screen, the experience from the first cycle of data collection showed how important it is to consider all the possible modes participants may use to make meaning on the one hand and to stay open about making adaptations to the ways of data collection on the other.

3.2. Completeness

We are naturally tempted to only focus on the 'core' of a conversation, however, openings and closings build the frame of a conversation where the relationship between the speakers, the setting, and the purpose of the conversation is negotiated. From a CA point of view, a conversation cannot be sufficiently analyzed if we do not know how the speakers themselves interpret the situation (Deppermann, 2008, p. 27). It is therefore essential to document the entire conversation, even if conversation openings and closings are not the particular research focus. Observations of individual cases from the first data collection showed that conversations might start out in the text-chat, while then switching to video-chat for the main part of the session. If the participants are assigned to document the eTandem sessions themselves, which was the case in our project, it is crucial to stress the importance of 'complete' data, including conversation openings and closings.

3.3. Authenticity

Authenticity is a controversial topic in the field of CA. CA originally dealt with naturally occurring everyday conversation. Due to ethical, but also practical reasons, it is nowadays common to work with improvised, re-enacted scenes. From a CA perspective, rehearsed or prepared talk-in-interaction is not eligible for research purposes. The aim of the project was to promote authentic, realistic communication by means of eTandems. However, despite extensive explanations, certain participants were not comfortable being recorded. Although the eTandems were not part of a language course and the students were assured that the recordings were not being assessed, some participants who still felt irritated were more comfortable if they had rehearsed the conversations before. A solution to that particular problem is to thoroughly inform the participants about the research purpose and then let them simply volunteer for recordings, instead of deciding on a mandatory number.

3.4. The role of 'tasks'

Certain participants were worried that they were only allowed to speak about the proposed topic and that off-task conversations are of no interest, especially when recording a session. This might be true for research that is concerned with specific task-related research questions, but it is counterproductive for a CA based research. If tasks are given to the participants, it seems to be important to discuss the role of a task beforehand.

4. Conclusion

CA poses specific demands to its data and the process of data generation. This is especially a challenge if the participants of a study are the ones who carry out the recordings themselves. While for some research it is crucial to conceal the research purpose, the experience from the first cycle of data collection showed that this is the exact opposite for a CA based approach in a telecollaboration context. On one hand, participants who do not only serve as research objects, but are actively engaged in the process of data collection need to be aware of CA-specific demands to data collection, such as 'completeness', 'authenticity' and the 'role of tasks'. On the other, researchers need to consider the different modes participants use to make meaning in order to get a grasp of what really is happening on screen.

References

Akiyama, Y. (2014). Using Skype to focus on form in Japanese telecollaboration: lexical categories as a new task variable. In L. Shuai & P. Swanson (Eds), *Engaging language learners through technology integration: theory, application and outcomes* (pp. 181-209). Hershey / Pennsylvania: IGI Global. http://dx.doi.org/10.4018/978-1-4666-6174-5.ch009

Bechtel, M. (2003). *Interkulturelles Lernen beim Sprachenlernen im Tandem – eine diskursanalytische Untersuchung*. Tübingen: Narr Verlag.

Cziko, G. (2004). Electronic tandem language learning (eTandem). A third approach to second language learning for the 21st century. *CALICO Journal, 22*(1), 25-39.

Deppermann, A. (2008). *Gespräche analysieren - eine Einführung*. Wiesbaden: Verlag für Sozialwissenschaften. http://dx.doi.org/10.1007/978-3-531-91973-7

El-Hariri, Y. (2016). Learner perspectives on task design for oral–visual eTandem language learning. *Innovation in Language Learning and Teaching, 10*(1), 49-72. http://dx.doi.org/10.1080/17501229.2016.1138578

El-Hariri, Y., & Jung, N. (2015). Distanzen überwinden. Über das Potenzial audio-visueller e-Tandems für den Deutschunterricht von Erwachsenen in Kolumbien. *Zeitschrift für interkulturellen Fremdsprachenunterricht, 20*(1), 106-139.

Gardner, R. (2013). Conversation analysis in the classroom. In J. Sidnell & T. Stivers (Eds), *Handbook of conversation analysis* (pp. 593-612). Malden, Massachusetts: Wiley-Blackwell.

Tian, J., & Wang, Y. (2010). Taking language learning outside the classroom: learners' perspectives of eTandem language learning via skype. *Innovation in Language Learning and Teaching, 4*(3), 181-197. http://dx.doi.org/10.1080/17501229.2010.513443

40 DOTI: Databank of Oral Teletandem Interactions

Solange Aranha[1] and Paola Leone[2]

Abstract

This contribution aims at (1) discussing the characteristics of collecting, filing and storing data to have a databank of oral interactions between university students whose main objective is the learning of a second language through teletandem; and (2) defining the steps for further collections and storage. Our data are Skype sessions of foreign language learners who interact via Voice Over Internet Protocol (VOIP) with a proficient partner in the language they are learning. Our databank aims at (1) giving value to teletandem as a situated learning context, (2) substantiating the research carried out in the field, and (3) offering other researchers the possibility to access data to confirm or refute published research. We first define a schema for interpreting teletandem sessions according to the Interaction Space (IS) Model as defined by Chanier and colleagues (2014). Subsequently, we discuss metadata concerning contexts (e.g. description of the university and of the language courses) and learning scenarios (e.g. objectives, materials).

Keywords: teletandem, databank, oral communication, language learning, interaction space model, computer mediated communication.

---

1. Universidade Estadual Paulista - São José Do Rio Preto, Brasil FAPESP # 2015/02048-6; solangea@ibilce.unesp.br

2. Università del Salento, Lecce, Italy; paola.leone@unisalento.it

How to cite this chapter: Aranha, S., & Leone, P. (2016). DOTI: Databank of Oral Teletandem Interactions. In S. Jager, M. Kurek & B. O'Rourke (Eds), *New directions in telecollaborative research and practice: selected papers from the second conference on telecollaboration in higher education* (pp. 327-332). Research-publishing.net. https://doi.org/10.14705/rpnet.2016.telecollab2016.525

Chapter 40

1. Introduction

Teletandem (Vassallo & Telles, 2006) is a form of computer mediated interaction by which two students, proficient in two different languages, interact via VoIP technology and/or via text chat. This telecollaborative practice respects the principles proposed by Brammerts (1996): autonomy, separation of languages and reciprocity. Teletandem is nowadays a teaching/learning context which has been institutionalized in different universities around the world and has become a relevant research field in applied linguistics. Over the years, researchers have been collecting, transcribing and analyzing data in different ways according to the needs of their studies (c.f. www.teletandembrasil.org).

As part of a shared project between UNESP and University of Salento, we are now aiming at building a databank with common characteristics (same methodology of collection and transcription) which may be useful for researchers in planning their tasks within telecollaboration activities, in understanding how telecollaboration works and may be optimized, and in developing linguistic research within telecollaboration environments, among others. Our first step is to apply to teletandem data the IS model (Chanier et al., 2014), by which some researchers are trying to characterize different Computer-Mediated Communication (CMC) genres (mostly written, such as Facebook). IS is defined as "an abstract concept, located in **time** [...] where interactions between **a set of participants** occur within an **online location**" (Chanier et al., 2014, p. 5).

Considering that teletandem is organized around various tasks in which a language instructor and a class group are involved, the concept of Learning Scenario (LS) becomes relevant, since it describes different task sequences (Mangenot, 2008; Foucher, 2010). LS helps us determine the characteristics that underlie teletandem practice. In this paper, we show how these concepts (IS and LS) are applied to our data and how they can contribute to define Data of Oral Teletandem Interactions (DOTI) metadata which are mostly created for interrogating the databank.

2. Methodology

At UNESP and at University of Salento, teletandem is not a stand alone practice but it comes together with other tasks, carried out both via Information and Communication Technologies (ICT) and in the classroom. Each teletandem session takes about one hour and occurs once a week. At UNESP, Brazilian students, whose mother tongue is Portuguese, interact with American students, proficient in English. At UNISALENTO, Italian students interact with British students.

Both contexts – UNESP and Unisalento (and partner institutions) – have students from different courses who are learning the language and practising it via teletandem sessions. The levels of proficiency vary and are not a key factor to be enrolled in the activity. Each partnership usually lasts from 8 to 15 sessions, depending on the learning scenario. All participants signed a consent form – developed within the exigencies of each university – for video recording oral sessions[3] which are stored[4].

DOTI contains data from 2012 to 2015, in a total of over 650 hours of conversation (Portuguese and English – Italian and English). Some data have been transcribed. Among other communicative data so far described during conferences and in literature following the IS model, DOTI is peculiar since it is compiled by synchronous multimodal interactions during which different modes are employed for communication (text, gestures, oral, images, etc.). Thus, DOTI data represent a complex environment.

Teletandem interactions are part of different learning scenarios which, in both institutions, are shaped in macro and microtasks (objectives and description). UNESP and Unisalento share the macrotasks' aim which is preparing students to participate actively in (computer mediated) oral interactions with a proficient speaker and be aware of all the linguistic and cultural strategies that such a

---

3. So far we have been using Evaer, a capture Skype video and audio data to record (see www.evaer.com).
4. In Brazil, a detailed description of storage process can be found in Aranha, Luvizari-Murad and Moreno (2015).

practice involves. In the Brazilian and Italian universities, such an objective is reached via different microtask sequences carried out during mediation sessions and computer mediated oral sessions.

These mentioned features are useful guidelines for defining metadata.

3. Discussion

Some metadata will be presented: first of all, those concerning teletandem as IS and secondly, those related to the learning scenario.

DOTI will be described according to the data type it contains:

- interactions are dyadic; teletandem involves just 2 participants;
- the environment is synchronous (as opposed to non-synchronous such as blogs);
- the time frame is one session (usually from 50 to 60 minutes);
- the communication modality is via VoIP technology;
- communication modes are different such as oral, written via text chat as well as gestures and emoticons.

Specifically, concerning each time frame (i.e. session), the option is given to choose among languages used for communication (e.g. English, Italian) and the number of online sessions (e.g. S1, S2, S3).

Regarding participants, data can be interrogated according to student's course at the university (e.g. UNESP), gender, and language level (broadly assessed based on performance during teletandem sessions).

In relation to the discourse type, DOTI will be described using free discussion, topic discussion, and task completion (e.g. information/opinion gap).

Metadata for LS are typology of tasks (alternate monolingual interaction or intercomprehension), integrated and non-integrated teletandem modalities (Aranha & Cavalari, 2014), descriptions (aims, materials), teachers' roles, and macrotask and microtask sequences.

DOTI will allow researchers within teletandem contexts to be more coherent in generating, collecting and annotating procedures and thus, will save them time to analyse such multi-faceted, multi-tasking environments more deeply and thoroughly.

Although all the participants have signed consent forms[5] and are enrolled in one of the courses or universities that participate in the Teletandem Network (Leone & Telles, 2016), there are still ethical issues concerned with identification in the future. Hence, we are now considering if the degree of anonymization can be decided on the basis of what participants opt for (i.e. blurring or not their faces).

Besides, a wide range of data is generated every year due to the increasing number of students that participate in the telecollaborative practice. This poses a question of keeping the databank open for including ongoing sessions.

4. Conclusion

For developing criteria of a DOTI, two important concepts have been relevant: interaction space and learning scenario. The former framework places DOTI in a broader field which includes research in corpora compiled by other computer mediated communication such as Facebook or Twitter. Defined metadata will allow us to cross data with other colleagues who are working in the field and there will be guidelines for sharing data collection principles among other colleagues from the teletandem network.

---

5. The items of the terms vary from institution to institution and an agreement of common ones is still in progress.

DOTI is compiled in an open access corpus perspective. We strongly believe that it will be useful to (applied) linguists, professors, and computer experts who want to develop software based on CMC for language learning.

References

Aranha, S., & Cavalari, S. (2014). A trajetória do projeto Teletandem Brasil: da modalidade institucional não-integrada à institucional integrada. *The ESPecialist, 35*(2), 70-88.

Aranha, S., Luvizari-Murad, L., & Moreno, A. (2015). A criação de um banco de dados para pesquisas sobre aprendizagem via teletandem institucional integrado (TTDII). *(Com) Textos Linguísticos, 9*(12), 274-293.

Brammerts, H. (1996). Tandem language learning via the internet and the International E-Mail tandem network. In D. Little & H. Brammerts (Eds), *A guide to language learning in tandem via the Internet*. Dublin: CLCS.

Chanier, T., Poudat, C., Sagot, B., Antoniadis, G., Wigham, C. R., Hriba, L., Longhi, J., & Seddah, J. (2014). The CoMeRe corpus for French: structuring and annotating heterogeneous CMC genres. *Journal for Language Technology and Computational Linguistics, 2*(29), 1-30.

Foucher, A.-L. (2010). *Didactique des langues-cultures et Tice : scénarios, tâches, interactions*. Université Blaise Pascal - Clermont-Ferrand II.

Leone, P., & Telles, J. (2016). The teletandem network. In T. Lewis & R. O'Dowd (Eds), *Online intercultural exchange: policy, pedagogy, practice* (pp. 243-248). London: Routledge.

Mangenot, F. (2008). La question du scénario de communication dans les interactions pédagogiques en ligne. *Jocair (Journées Communication et Apprentissage Instrumentés en Réseau*, 13-26.

Vassallo, M., &Telles, J. (2006). Foreign language learning in-tandem: teletandem as an alternative proposal in CALLT. *The ESPecialist, 27*(2), 189-212.

Author index

Abruquah, Emmanuel x, 7, 105
Akiyama, Yuka xi, 13, 277
Appel, Christine xi, 13, 305
Aranha, Solange xi, 14, 327

Batardière, Marie-Thérèse xi, 14, 313
Blin, Françoise xi, 13, 297

Capobianco, Stephen xii, 12, 261
Castro, Paloma xii, 6, 77
Ceo-DiFrancesco, Diane xii, 6, 59

De Martino, Sandro xiii, 10, 211
Derivry-Plard, Martine xii, 6, 77
Deutscher, Jelena xii, 11, 233
Dey-Plissonneau, Aparajita xiii, 13, 297
Dosa, Ildiko xiii, 7, 105
Duda, Grażyna xiii, 7, 105

Fernández, Susana S. xiii, 12, 239

Gazeley-Eke, Zoe xiv, 13, 283
Gijsen, Linda xiv, 8, 163
Giralt, Marta xiv, 10, 195

Hagley, Eric xiv, 11, 225
Harel, Efrat xiv, 9, 179
Helm, Francesca xv, 14, 313
Hoffstaedter, Petra xv, 13, 291
Hoshii, Makiko xv, 8, 147

Jager, Sake viii, 1

Jauregi, Kristi xv, 9, 185
Jeanneau, Catherine xv, 10, 195
Johnson, Erica xvi, 7, 97

Kano, Mikio xvi, 7, 121
Kinginger, Celeste xvi, 3, 19
Kohn, Kurt xvi, 13, 291
Kurek, Malgorzata viii, 1

Leinster, Hannah xvi, 13, 283
Leone, Paola xvi, 14, 327
Líppez-De Castro, Sebastian xvii, 12, 261
Little, David xvii, 4, 45
Loizidou, Dora xvii, 8, 155
Loranc-Paszylk, Barbara xvii, 7, 131

Malerba, Maria Luisa xvii, 13, 305
Mangenot, François xviii, 8, 155
Marczak, Mariusz xviii, 12, 245
Mason, Jonathan xviii, 12, 267
Melchor-Couto, Sabela xviii, 9, 185
Mesh, Linda Joy xviii, 12, 253
Millner, Sophie xix, 11, 217
Mora, Oscar xix, 6, 59
Müller-Hartmann, Andreas xix, 3, 31

Nicolaou, Anna xix, 7, 113
Nissen, Elke xix, 10, 201

Okazaki, Hiroyuki xx, 7, 121
O'Rourke, Breffni viii, xxv, 1
Orsini-Jones, Marina xx, 13, 283

Author index

Pack, Dwayne xx, 7, 121

Renner, Julia xx, 14, 321
Rojas-Primus, Constanza xx, 6, 69
Romero Alfaro, Elena xx, 9, 171
Rubaii, Nadia xxi, 12, 261

Sauro, Shannon xxi, 6, 83
Schumacher, Nicole xxi, 8, 147
Schwab, Götz xxi, 9, 179
Serna Collazos, Andrea xxi, 6, 59
Sevilla-Pavón, Ana xxii, 7, 113
Shimizu, Yoshihiko xxii, 7, 121

Valcke, Jennifer xxii, 9, 171
Van der Heijden, Casper xiv, 11, 217
Van der Velden, Bart xxii, 11, 217
Vidal, Julie xxii, 8, 139

Waldman, Tina xxiii, 9, 179
Whyte, Shona xxiii, 8, 163
Wigham, Ciara R. xxiii, 8, 139

Yamamura, Hiroto xxiii, 7, 121
Yang, Se Jeong xxiii, 6, 89

www.ingramcontent.com/pod-product-compliance
Lightning Source LLC
Chambersburg PA
CBHW021830220426
43663CB00005B/193